All
Through the
House

Conceived, edited and published
under the direction of:

Ralph Mosley   Chairman of the Board
Thomas Milam   President and Publisher
Betty Ann Jones   Vice President of Marketing
Ron Hartman   Vice President of Operations
Debbie Seigenthaler   Executive Editor

All Through the House

Editor: Mary Jane Blount
Managing Editor: Robin Crouch
Creative Director: Philip Sankey
Essayist: John Bridges
Art Director: Steve Newman
Project Leader: Mary Cummings
Crafts Editor: Kathleen English
Associate Editors: Georgia Brazil, Jane Hinshaw,
Linda Jones, Mary Wilson
Test Kitchen: Charlene Sproles
Illustrator: Barbara Ball
Contributing Editor: Fran Morley
Typographers: Pam Newsome, Jessie Anglin, Sara Anglin
Production: John Moulton
Manufacturing Assistant: George McAllister

Manufactured in the United States of America.
First Printing, 1993

Contents

A Season for Beginning
Introduction

The McElvees could have afforded their own Christmas tree—they did not need to steal ours. "The McElvees are people who ought to know better," my grandfather would say, stalking back and forth across my parents' living room and squeaking his rubber-tipped cane against the floor. "Furvis McElvee has children to raise."

Every year, my grandfather would find the tire tracks on the Saturday after Thanksgiving. And every year, he would grumble, "Don't tell me it's not Furvis McElvee," as he stabbed at the dry Alabama mud with his cane. "Nobody else has a truck as big as that!" Every Sunday after that, until sometime in April, when we passed the McElvees in the churchyard, we would not speak to them.

My grandfather raised his cedar trees for his own children—which meant, directly, my Uncle Jesse and my mother and, by extension, my brother and me. "If other people want cedar trees, they can grow them for their own children," he would say while my father loaded our tree into the station wagon. "If people get started stealing 'em, there won't be a tree left anywhere in my woods."

One Friday afternoon before Christmas, waiting in line for the school bus, I turned and saw Bonnie McElvee. Our eyes met, and I looked down at the ground. "You're not talking to us again, aren't you?" she said. I looked into her eyes again and told her it was because of the Christmas tree. On the bus, lots of seats were empty, but Bonnie squeezed herself into a nearly full place, way on the back row.

The next morning, my mother said we were going to my grandfather's because there was something he wanted us to see. We stopped on the road alongside the cedar thicket, but, even from the station wagon, we could see something glinting in the sun. My grandfather motioned to us with his walking stick, and we ran toward him through the dry blond grass.

The trunks of the cedar trees had been strung with tinfoil garlands. Here and there, but never more than four or five feet from the ground, a crayon-colored star had been stuck to a tree trunk with an open safety pin.

My grandfather only lived through two more Christmases, but he did not look for the tire tracks again. Instead, he had a gate built in the barbed wire alongside the cedar thicket. On Saturday mornings, toward the end of November, he would walk down to make sure it was open. He would not close it until the crayon-colored stars appeared.

A Season for Sharing
Food Gifts

Every year, my mother apologized for the orange cake. No matter how hard she tried, she never could make it rise. Every year, it lay there on its second-string cake plate, leaden and thick and unworthy as an offering to any visiting out-of-town relative. In a season of triumph, everything about it filled my mother with shame.

"I don't think I'm ever going to try this orange cake again," she would say as it came out of the oven, once again a flat, rubbery rectangle that refused even to brown. Standing in the kitchen door, surrounded by platters full of shimmering, perfect divinity, trays piled high with silken, pecan-crunchy fudge, and Lane cakes with their bourbon-rich fillings, I would feel a sinking dip of Christmastide terror.

I could not speak up in defense of the orange cake. It was, in that kitchen at that one unexplainable moment, the one thing I painfully and unquestioningly adored.

I loved it from the first moment the crinkly-skinned oranges came home in their red-string net bag. They seemed like treasures, out-of-place and mysterious, there in those gray winter days.

When my mother grated the oranges, the air, already heavy with cinnamon and ginger and nutmeg, would grow suddenly fresh with the first burst of the oranges' sweet, exotic perfume. Minutes after the cake had gone into the oven, its smell filled the whole house with warmness and sunshine and summer, curious and magic and strange.

Every year, however, the cake itself would flop. "I guess you've got your own private orange cake again," my mother would sigh, giving a little shrug and wiping her hands on her apron. Without another word, our eyes would meet, and we would both smile.

Years later, even after I was full-grown, my mother still made her orange cake. Every year, when I got home for Christmas, I knew I could find it waiting on a side counter, shamefaced and inexcusable and covered with foil.

By that time, my parents were going to bed early, but late at night, long after the Christmas tree lights had been unplugged, I would steal downstairs, sneaking past my parents' bedroom door and into the kitchen. There, standing in the quiet, I would finish my mother's orange cake. Slice by slice, I would finish every bite.

Merry giving is easy with our delectable Cheery Cranberry-Chocolate Chip Bread with Cocoa Drizzle Glaze, Holiday Chocolate Fruitcake, and Jingle Bell Chocolate Pretzels, pages 23, 31 and 41.

Cheery Christmas Cookies

MELT-IN-YOUR-MOUTH DROPS

1 cup butter, softened
1/2 cup confectioners'
   sugar
1 1/2 cups all-purpose flour
Red and green candied
   cherries

❖ Preheat oven to 325 degrees.
❖ Cream butter and confectioners' sugar in mixer bowl for 2 minutes. Add flour. Beat for 5 minutes.
❖ Drop by teaspoonfuls onto foil-lined cookie sheet. Top with candied cherries.
❖ Bake for 12 to 15 minutes or until very light brown. Cool on cookie sheet for 2 minutes; remove to wire rack to cool completely.
❖ Do not substitute margarine for butter.
❖ Yield: 2 1/2 dozen.

AMBROSIA BARS

1 1/2 cups all-purpose flour
1/3 cup confectioners'
   sugar
3/4 cup butter or
   margarine, chilled
2 cups packed light
   brown sugar
4 eggs, beaten
1 cup finely chopped
   pecans
1 cup flaked coconut
1/4 cup all-purpose flour
1/2 teaspoon baking
   powder
2 cups confectioners'
   sugar
3 tablespoons bottled
   lemon juice
2 tablespoons butter or
   margarine, softened
36 pecan halves

❖ Preheat oven to 350 degrees.
❖ Mix 1 1/2 cups flour and 1/3 cup confectioners' sugar in medium bowl. Cut in 3/4 cup butter until crumbly. Press over bottom of lightly greased 9-by-13-inch baking pan.
❖ Bake for 15 minutes.
❖ Combine brown sugar, eggs, chopped pecans, coconut, 1/4 cup flour and baking powder in large bowl; mix well. Spread over baked layer.
❖ Bake for 20 to 25 minutes longer or until set. Cool on wire rack.
❖ Combine 2 cups confectioners' sugar, lemon juice and 2 tablespoons butter in bowl; mix until smooth. Spread over cooled layer.
❖ Chill in refrigerator. Cut into bars. Top each with pecan half. Store, covered, in refrigerator.
❖ Yield: 3 dozen.

RIDDLE-IN-THE-MIDDLE COOKIES

1/2 cup sugar
1/2 cup packed light
   brown sugar
1/2 cup butter or
   margarine, softened
1/4 cup peanut butter
1 egg, beaten
1 teaspoon vanilla extract
1 1/2 cups all-purpose flour
1/2 cup baking cocoa
1/2 teaspoon baking soda
3/4 cup peanut butter
3/4 cup confectioners'
   sugar

❖ Preheat oven to 350 degrees.
❖ Cream first 4 ingredients in mixer bowl until light and fluffy. Beat in egg and vanilla.
❖ Add mixture of flour, baking cocoa and baking soda; mix well.
❖ Blend 3/4 cup peanut butter and confectioners' sugar in small bowl. Shape into small balls.
❖ Shape about 1 tablespoon flour mixture around each peanut butter ball with floured hands, enclosing completely. Arrange 2 inches apart on greased cookie sheet. Flatten with bottom of glass.
❖ Bake for 8 to 10 minutes or until brown. Remove to wire rack to cool.
❖ Yield: 2 dozen.

APPLE BUTTER BARS

2 cups packed light
   brown sugar
2 1/2 cups all-purpose
   flour
1 1/2 cups butter or
   margarine
2 1/2 cups oats
1 1/2 cups apple butter

❖ Preheat oven to 350 degrees.
❖ Combine brown sugar and flour in bowl; mix well.
❖ Cut in butter until crumbly. Add oats; mix lightly.
❖ Press half the oat mixture into greased 10-by-15-inch baking pan.
❖ Spread apple butter to within 1/2 inch of edge. Press remaining crumbs on top.
❖ Bake for 45 mintues or until brown.
❖ Cool on wire rack. Cut into bars.
❖ Yield: 3 dozen.

"CARAMEL APPLE" COOKIES

2/3 cup butter or margarine, softened	1/4 teaspoon salt
3/4 cup confectioners' sugar	30 light caramels
1 tablespoon frozen apple juice concentrate	2 tablespoons frozen apple juice concentrate
1 1/2 cups all-purpose flour	2 tablespoons water
	3/4 cup finely chopped walnuts

❖ Preheat oven to 350 degrees.
❖ Cream butter, confectioners' sugar and 1 tablespoon apple juice concentrate in large mixer bowl until light and fluffy. Add flour and salt; mix well.
❖ Shape into 3/4-inch balls; place 1 inch apart on ungreased cookie sheet.
❖ Bake for 12 to 17 minutes or until edges are light brown. Insert flat wooden pick into center of each cookie. Remove to wire rack to cool.
❖ Combine caramels, 2 tablespoons apple juice concentrate and water in heavy 1-quart saucepan.
❖ Cook over low heat until smooth, stirring constantly. Spoon over each cookie, letting excess drip off.
❖ Coat bottom of each cookie with walnuts. Let stand on waxed paper until set.
❖ Yield: 6 dozen.

TRIPLE CHOCOLATE COFFEE BROWNIES

1 egg, beaten	3/4 cup milk chocolate chips
1 (21-ounce) package fudge brownie mix	1/2 cup semisweet chocolate chips
1/4 cup corn oil	1/2 cup chopped walnuts or pecans
1/4 cup strong coffee	
1/4 cup water	
3/4 cup white baking chips	

❖ Preheat oven to 350 degrees.
❖ Combine egg, brownie mix, oil, coffee and water in bowl; mix well. Add remaining ingredients; mix well.
❖ Spread in greased 9-by-13-inch baking pan.
❖ Bake for 30 minutes. Cool on wire rack. Cut into squares.
❖ Yield: 2 dozen.

BROWNIE BITES

1 (15-ounce) package brownie mix	1 egg
1/3 cup hot water	48 miniature peanut butter cups or caramel cups
1/4 cup vegetable oil	

❖ Preheat oven to 350 degrees.
❖ Combine brownie mix, water, oil and egg in mixer bowl; mix well.

❖ Fill paper-lined miniature muffin cups 1/2 full. Press 1 peanut butter cup into batter in each cup.
❖ Bake for 15 to 20 minutes or until brownies are set. Remove to wire rack to cool.
❖ Yield: 4 dozen.

BUTTERSCOTCH THINS

1/2 cup butter or margarine	1 egg
1 cup butterscotch chips	1 1/3 cups all-purpose flour
2/3 cup packed light brown sugar	3/4 teaspoon baking soda
	3/4 teaspoon vanilla extract
	1/3 cup chopped pecans

❖ Preheat oven to 300 degrees.
❖ Combine butter and butterscotch chips in double boiler. Melt over hot water; mix well. Cool slightly. Beat in brown sugar and egg.
❖ Sift in flour and baking soda; mix well. Add vanilla and pecans.
❖ Chill until mixture can be easily handled. Shape into roll; wrap in waxed paper. Chill overnight.
❖ Cut into very thin slices; place on ungreased cookie sheet.
❖ Bake for 10 to 12 minutes or until golden brown. Remove to wire rack to cool.
❖ Yield: 5 1/2 dozen.

CHERRY CHIP COOKIES

1/4 cup butter or margarine, softened	2 cups confectioners' sugar
8 ounces cream cheese, softened	2 tablespoons butter or margarine, softened
1 egg, beaten	2 tablespoons (about) maraschino cherry juice
1/4 teaspoon vanilla extract	
1 (2-layer) package cherry chip cake mix	

❖ Preheat oven to 375 degrees.
❖ Cream 1/4 cup butter and cream cheese in mixer bowl until light and fluffy. Stir in egg and vanilla. Add cake mix gradually, stirring to blend.
❖ Chill until dough is firm. Drop by teaspoonfuls onto ungreased cookie sheet.
❖ Bake for 8 to 10 minutes or until light brown. Cool completely on cookie sheet.
❖ Frost with mixture of confectioners' sugar, 2 tablespoons butter and cherry juice.
❖ May substitute white cake mix for cherry chip cake mix if desired.
❖ Yield: 5 dozen.

CHEERY CHOCOLATE TEDDY BEAR COOKIES

1 2/3 cups Reese's peanut
   butter chips
1 cup Hershey's
   semisweet chocolate
   chips
2 tablespoons shortening

1 (20-ounce) package
  chocolate sandwich
  cookies
1 (10-ounce) package
  teddy bear-shaped
  graham snack crackers

❖ Combine chips and shortening in glass bowl.
❖ Microwave on High for 1 1/2 to 2 minutes or until chips are melted; stir until smooth.
❖ Dip 1 cookie at a time into chocolate mixture with fork, tapping off excess gently.
❖ Place on waxed paper-lined tray. Top each with cracker. Chill for 30 minutes or until set.
❖ Store in airtight container in cool dry place.
❖ Do not substitute butter, margarine or oil for shortening in this recipe.
❖ Yield: 4 dozen.

CHEWY CHOCOLATE COOKIES

1 1/4 cups butter or
   margarine, softened
2 cups sugar
2 eggs
2 teaspoons vanilla
   extract

2 cups all-purpose flour
3/4 cup Hershey's baking
  cocoa
1 teaspoon baking soda
1/2 teaspoon salt
1 cup chopped pecans

❖ Preheat oven to 350 degrees.
❖ Cream butter and sugar in mixer bowl until very light and fluffy. Beat in eggs and vanilla.
❖ Beat in mixture of next 4 ingredients gradually. Stir in pecans.
❖ Drop by rounded teaspoonfuls onto ungreased cookie sheet.
❖ Bake for 8 to 9 minutes or until puffed and light brown. Cool on cookie sheet for 1 minute or until set. Remove to wire rack to cool completely. Cookies will flatten as they cool.
❖ May add 1 2/3 cups Reese's peanut butter chips to batter before baking.
❖ Yield: 4 1/2 dozen.

CHIPPY CHOCOLATE CHIP COOKIES

3/4 cup shortening
1 cup packed light brown
   sugar
1 cup sugar
2 eggs, beaten
1 teaspoon vanilla extract
2 cups all-purpose flour

1/2 teaspoon salt
1 teaspoon baking soda
2 cups crushed potato
  chips
1 cup semisweet
  chocolate chips

❖ Preheat oven to 350 degrees.
❖ Cream shortening, brown sugar and sugar in mixer bowl until light and fluffy.

❖ Add eggs and vanilla; beat well. Stir in flour, salt and baking soda. Add potato chips and chocolate chips; stir gently. Drop by teaspoonfuls onto ungreased cookie sheet.
❖ Bake for 7 minutes. Cool on cookie sheet for 1 minute; remove to wire rack to cool completely.
❖ Yield: 7 dozen.

CHOCOLATE-MARSHMALLOW SQUARES

8 graham crackers
1/2 cup butter or
   margarine
1/2 cup semisweet
   chocolate chips

1/2 cup butterscotch chips
1 egg, beaten
1 cup confectioners' sugar
2 cups miniature
  marshmallows

❖ Line 8-by-8-inch dish with graham crackers. Melt butter in saucepan over medium heat. Add chips. Cook until melted, stirring constantly. Remove from heat.
❖ Stir in egg and confectioners' sugar. Cool slightly. Stir in marshmallows. Pour into dish.
❖ Chill until serving time. Cut into squares.
❖ Yield: 1 1/2 dozen.

DOUBLE CHOCOLATE CRUMBLE BARS

1/2 cup butter or
   margarine
3/4 cup sugar
2 eggs
1 teaspoon vanilla extract
3/4 cup all-purpose flour
2 tablespoons baking
   cocoa
1/4 teaspoon salt

1/4 teaspoon baking
  powder
1/2 cup chopped pecans
2 cups miniature
  marshmallows
1 cup chocolate chips
1 cup peanut butter
1 1/2 cups crisp rice cereal

❖ Preheat oven to 350 degrees.
❖ Cream butter and sugar in mixer bowl until light and fluffy. Beat in eggs and vanilla.
❖ Mix flour, baking cocoa, salt, baking powder and pecans in bowl. Stir into creamed mixture. Spread in greased 9-by-13-inch baking pan.
❖ Bake for 15 to 20 minutes.
❖ Sprinkle evenly with marshmallows. Bake for 3 minutes longer. Cool on wire rack.
❖ Melt chocolate chips and peanut butter in saucepan over low heat, stirring constantly. Stir in cereal. Spread over cooled layers. Chill until firm. Cut into bars. Store in refrigerator.
❖ Yield: 4 dozen.

Chewy Chocolate Cookies, Chocolate Macaroons, Peanut Butter Cut-Out Cookies, Chocolate Shortbread with Cocoa Glaze, and Mocha Hot Chocolate Mix, pages 12, 16, 18, 19, and 38

WHITE CHOCOLATE CHUNK COOKIES

1/2 cup unsalted butter or margarine, softened	1/3 cup baking cocoa
1/2 cup packed dark brown sugar	1 egg
1/2 cup sugar	1/2 teaspoon baking soda
1 teaspoon vanilla extract	1 cup all-purpose flour
1/2 teaspoon salt	2 cups chopped white chocolate

❖ Preheat oven to 325 degrees.
❖ Combine butter, brown sugar, sugar, vanilla and salt in large bowl. Beat with spoon until light and fluffy.
❖ Add baking cocoa, egg and baking soda; beat well. Stir in flour and white chocolate.
❖ Chill, covered, for 4 hours to overnight.
❖ Shape by 2 tablespoonfuls into balls. Place several inches apart on greased cookie sheet, allowing only 6 per cookie sheet.
❖ Bake for 12 to 14 minutes or until top is cracked. Cool on cookie sheet for 2 minutes. Remove to wire rack to cool completely.
❖ Yield: 2 dozen.

HOLIDAY CITRUS LOGS

1 (12-ounce) package vanilla wafers, crushed	1 tablespoon light corn syrup
8 ounces candied cherries, chopped	2 tablespoons orange liqueur
1 3/4 cups chopped dates	Light corn syrup, heated
1 cup chopped pecans or almonds	Toasted finely chopped pecans or sliced almonds
1/4 cup bottled lemon juice	

❖ Combine cookie crumbs, cherries, dates, 1 cup pecans, lemon juice, 1 tablespoon corn syrup and liqueur in large bowl; mix well.
❖ Shape mixture into two 10-inch rolls. Brush with additional corn syrup; roll in toasted pecans.
❖ Chill, wrapped, for 3 to 4 days to blend flavors.
❖ Cut into 1/4-inch slices to serve.
❖ Yield: 6 1/2 dozen.

DISAPPEARING MARSHMALLOW SQUARES

1 cup butterscotch chips	2 eggs
1/2 cup butter or margarine	1 teaspoon vanilla extract
1 1/2 cups all-purpose flour	1/2 teaspoon salt
2/3 cup packed light brown sugar	2 cups miniature marshmallows
2 teaspoons baking powder	2 cups semisweet chocolate chips
	1/2 cup chopped pecans

❖ Preheat oven to 350 degrees.
❖ Melt butterscotch chips with butter in saucepan over medium heat, stirring constantly to mix well. Cool to lukewarm.
❖ Add flour, brown sugar, baking powder, eggs, vanilla and salt; mix well. Fold in marshmallows, chocolate chips and pecans. Spread in greased 9-by-13-inch baking pan.
❖ Bake for 20 to 25 minutes or until brownies test done; do not overbake. Cool on wire rack. Cut into squares.
❖ Yield: 2 dozen.

RASPBERRY KISSES

3 egg whites, at room temperature	3 1/2 tablespoons raspberry gelatin
1 teaspoon vinegar	1 cup semisweet chocolate chips
1/8 teaspoon salt	
3/4 cup sugar	

❖ Preheat oven to 250 degrees.
❖ Beat egg whites with vinegar and salt in mixer bowl until stiff. Add mixture of sugar and gelatin gradually, beating well after each addition and until very stiff. Fold in chocolate chips.
❖ Drop batter by teaspoonfuls onto parchment-lined cookie sheet.
❖ Bake for 25 minutes. Turn off oven. Let stand in closed oven for 20 minutes; do not open oven door.
❖ Yield: 3 dozen.

LEMON BLOSSOM COOKIES

2 cups butter or margarine, softened	1/4 cup bottled lemon juice
1 1/2 cups confectioners' sugar	4 cups all-purpose flour
	Flaked coconut
	Fruit preserves

❖ Preheat oven to 350 degrees.
❖ Cream butter and confectioners' sugar in large mixer bowl until light and fluffy.
❖ Add lemon juice; mix well. Add flour gradually, mixing well after each addition. Chill for 2 hours.
❖ Shape into 1-inch balls. Roll in coconut. Place 1 inch apart on greased cookie sheet. Make indentation in center of each cookie. Fill with preserves.
❖ Bake for 14 to 16 minutes or until light brown. Remove to wire rack to cool. Store, covered, at room temperature.
❖ Yield: 6 dozen.

Cheery Chocolate Teddy Bear Cookies, Jolly Peanut Butter Gingerbread Cookies, Merry Chocolate Nut Clusters, and Chocolate Popcorn Balls, pages 12, 18, 26, and 41

SLICE AND BAKE LEMON COOKIES

1/2 cup butter or
  margarine, softened
1/2 cup shortening
1/2 cup sugar
1/2 cup packed light
  brown sugar
1 egg

2 1/4 cups all-purpose flour
1/4 teaspoon baking soda
3 tablespoons bottled
  lemon juice
1 egg white, beaten
Sliced almonds

❖ Cream butter, shortening, sugar and brown
sugar in large mixer bowl until light and fluffy.
Beat in egg.
❖ Mix flour and baking soda together. Add to
creamed mixture with lemon juice, mixing well.
❖ Chill for 2 hours. Shape into two 10-inch rolls;
wrap well. Freeze until firm.
❖ Preheat oven to 350 degrees.
❖ Cut rolls into 1/4-inch slices; place 1 inch apart
on ungreased cookie sheet. Brush with egg white;
top with almonds.
❖ Bake for 10 to 12 minutes or until light brown.
Remove to wire rack to cool.
❖ Yield: 5 dozen.

CHOCOLATE MACAROONS

24 red candied cherries
5 1/3 cups flaked coconut
1/2 cup Hershey's baking
  cocoa

1 (14-ounce) can
  sweetened condensed
  milk
2 teaspoons vanilla extract

❖ Preheat oven to 350 degrees.
❖ Cut candied cherries into halves.
❖ Mix coconut and baking cocoa in large bowl.
Stir in condensed milk and vanilla.
❖ Drop by rounded teaspoonfuls onto greased
cookie sheet. Press 1 cherry half into each cookie.
❖ Bake for 8 to 10 minutes or until almost set.
Remove immediately from cookie sheet to wire
rack to cool.
❖ Store, loosely covered, at room temperature.
❖ Yield: 4 dozen.

*Search the house for original gift-wrap ideas.
Use broken-bead necklaces, ribbon remnants,
drapery cord or gold-sprayed dried flowers
and leaves.*

STRAWBERRY ANGEL MACAROONS

1 (15-ounce) package one-step angel food cake mix	2 teaspoons vanilla extract
	2 cups unsweetened flaked coconut
1/2 cup strawberry soda	1/2 cup chopped walnuts

❖ Preheat oven to 350 degrees.
❖ Combine cake mix, strawberry soda and vanilla in large mixer bowl. Beat at low speed for 30 seconds. Beat at medium speed for 1 minute or until very stiff, scraping sides of bowl frequently.
❖ Fold in coconut and walnuts. Drop by teaspoonfuls 2 inches apart onto foil-lined cookie sheet.
❖ Bake for 10 to 12 minutes. Remove to wire rack to cool. Store in airtight container.
❖ Yield: 5 dozen.

MOUNDS BARS

1 cup butter or margarine, softened	1 cup sweetened condensed milk
1 cup all-purpose flour	1/2 cup butter or margarine, softened
1 1/4 cups sugar	1/4 cup baking cocoa
3 eggs	6 tablespoons milk
3 tablespoons baking cocoa	1 (1-pound) package confectioners' sugar
1/2 teaspoon salt	Vanilla extract to taste
2 1/2 cups flaked coconut	

❖ Preheat oven to 350 degrees.
❖ Combine 1 cup butter, flour, sugar, eggs, 3 tablespoons baking cocoa and salt in bowl; mix well. Spread in greased 10-by-15-inch baking pan.
❖ Bake for 20 minutes.
❖ Spread mixture of coconut and condensed milk on hot layer. Bake for 12 minutes longer. Cool on wire rack.
❖ Combine 1/2 cup butter, 1/4 cup baking cocoa, milk, confectioners' sugar and vanilla in mixer bowl; mix until smooth.
❖ Spread over cooled layers. Cut into bars.
❖ Yield: 2 dozen.

NUTMEG COOKIES

1/2 cup butter or margarine, softened	Grated rind of 1 orange
1/2 cup sugar	2 1/2 cups flour
6 tablespoons whipping cream	2 teaspoons baking powder
	1 1/2 teaspoons nutmeg

❖ Cream butter and sugar in mixer bowl until light and fluffy. Add cream and orange rind; mix well.
❖ Add mixture of flour, baking powder and nutmeg; mix well.

❖ Shape into 2 1/2-inch roll. Chill, wrapped in foil, for 3 to 4 hours.
❖ Preheat oven to 375 degrees.
❖ Cut roll into thin slices; cut holes near edge with doughnut hole cutter. Place on greased cookie sheet; prick with fork.
❖ Bake for 7 to 10 minutes. Cool on wire rack.
❖ Yield: 5 dozen.

VERMONT OATMEAL COOKIES

1 1/2 cups butter or margarine, softened	2 teaspoons vanilla extract
	6 cups oats
1 3/4 cups maple syrup	2 cups all-purpose flour
1 cup sugar	2 teaspoons baking soda
2 eggs	1 teaspoon salt

❖ Preheat oven to 350 degrees.
❖ Combine butter, syrup, sugar, eggs and vanilla in mixer bowl; beat until smooth. Stir in oats.
❖ Add mixture of flour, baking soda and salt; mix well. Drop by teaspoonfuls onto greased cookie sheet. Bake for 9 minutes or until golden brown. Remove to wire rack to cool.
❖ Yield: 9 dozen.

O'HENRY BARS

2/3 cup butter or margarine, softened	1/2 cup light corn syrup
	4 cups oats
1 cup packed light brown sugar	1 cup semisweet chocolate chips
1 tablespoon vanilla extract	2/3 cup peanut butter

❖ Preheat oven to 350 degrees.
❖ Cream butter and brown sugar in mixer bowl until light and fluffy. Add vanilla, corn syrup and oats; mix well. Spread in greased 9-by-13-inch baking pan. Bake for 15 minutes. Cool.
❖ Melt chocolate chips with peanut butter in heavy saucepan over low heat, stirring to mix well. Spread over cooled layer; cool. Cut into bars.
❖ Yield: 3 dozen.

EASY PECAN BARS

1/2 cup melted butter or margarine	1 tablespoon vanilla extract
2 1/4 cups packed dark brown sugar	1 1/2 cups baking mix
	2 cups chopped pecans
2 eggs, beaten	1 cup flaked coconut

❖ Combine first 6 ingredients in bowl; mix well.
❖ Pour into 8-by-11-inch glass baking dish.
❖ Microwave on High for 8 to 10 minutes, turning 3 times. Top with coconut. Let stand until firm.
❖ Yield: 3 dozen

Ambrosia Bars, Holiday Citrus Logs, and Slice and Bake Lemon Cookies, pages 10, 14, and 16

JOLLY PEANUT BUTTER GINGERBREAD COOKIES

1²/₃ cups Reese's peanut butter chips	2 eggs
³/₄ cup butter or margarine, softened	5 cups all-purpose flour
	1 teaspoon baking soda
1 cup packed light brown sugar	¹/₂ teaspoon cinnamon
	¹/₄ teaspoon ginger
1 cup dark corn syrup	¹/₄ teaspoon salt

❖ Place peanut butter chips in small glass bowl.
❖ Microwave on High for 1 to 2 minutes or until chips are melted when stirred.
❖ Mix with butter in mixer bowl. Beat in brown sugar, corn syrup and eggs until smooth.
❖ Mix flour, baking soda, cinnamon, ginger and salt together. Add half the mixture to peanut butter mixture; beat until smooth. Stir in remaining flour mixture with wooden spoon.
❖ Divide into 3 portions; wrap in plastic wrap. Chill for 1 hour or until firm enough to roll.
❖ Preheat oven to 325 degrees.
❖ Roll dough 1 portion at a time ¹/₈ inch thick on lightly floured surface. Cut into desired shapes; place on ungreased cookie sheet.
❖ Bake for 10 to 12 minutes or until light brown. Cool on cookie sheet for several minutes. Remove to wire rack to cool completely. Frost and decorate as desired.
❖ Yield: 6 dozen.

PEANUT BUTTER CUT-OUT COOKIES

¹/₂ cup butter or margarine	1¹/₃ cups all-purpose flour
	³/₄ teaspoon baking soda
1 cup Reese's peanut butter chips	¹/₂ cup finely chopped pecans
²/₃ cup packed light brown sugar	²/₃ cup Reese's peanut butter chips
1 egg	1 tablespoon shortening
³/₄ teaspoon vanilla extract	

❖ Melt butter and 1 cup peanut butter chips in medium saucepan over low heat, stirring to mix well.
❖ Combine with brown sugar, egg and vanilla in large mixer bowl; beat until smooth.
❖ Stir in flour, baking soda and pecans. Chill for 15 to 20 minutes or until firm enough to roll.
❖ Preheat oven to 350 degrees.
❖ Roll dough a small amount at a time to ¹/₄-inch thickness on lightly floured surface or between waxed paper; keep remaining dough in refrigerator. Cut out as desired; place on ungreased cookie sheet.
❖ Bake for 7 to 8 minutes or until almost set; do not overbake. Cool on cookie sheet for 1 minute; remove to wire rack to cool completely.
❖ Combine ²/₃ cup peanut butter chips and 1 tablespoon shortening in small glass bowl.
❖ Microwave on High for 1 minute, stirring after 30 seconds; stir again. Drizzle over cookies. Garnish as desired.
❖ Yield: 3 dozen.

MIRACULOUS PEANUT BUTTER COOKIES

1 (7-ounce) jar
   marshmallow creme
1 cup crunchy peanut
   butter

1/3 cup confectioners'
   sugar

❖ Preheat oven to 350 degrees.
❖ Combine marshmallow creme, peanut butter
and confectioners' sugar in bowl; mix well. Shape
by teaspoonfuls into balls.
❖ Arrange on ungreased cookie sheet, pressing
slightly to flatten.
❖ Bake for 10 minutes. Cool on cookie sheet for 1
minute; remove to wire rack to cool completely.
❖ Yield: 1 dozen.

PIÑA COLADA KRISPIE TREATS

6 cups crisp rice cereal
1 cup (packed) flaked
   coconut
5 tablespoons butter or
   margarine
1 (10-ounce) package
   miniature marshmallows

3/4 teaspoon coconut
   extract
3/4 teaspoon pineapple
   extract
3/4 teaspoon rum extract
1/3 cup finely chopped
   candied pineapple

❖ Combine cereal and coconut in large bowl
sprayed with nonstick cooking spray; toss well.
❖ Melt butter in saucepan. Add marshmallows
and flavorings.
❖ Cook over medium heat until marshmallows
are melted, stirring occasionally.
❖ Add candied pineapple; stir until coated. Add
to cereal mixture, stirring until coated.
❖ Pat mixture into 9-by-13-inch pan sprayed
with nonstick cooking spray. Let stand until firm.
Cut into squares.
❖ Yield: 2 dozen.

RASPBERRY BROWNIES

1/2 cup butter or
   margarine, softened
1 cup sugar
2 ounces unsweetened
   chocolate, melted

2 large eggs
3/4 cup all-purpose flour
1 cup chopped walnuts
1/3 cup raspberry jam

❖ Preheat oven to 350 degrees.
❖ Beat butter at medium speed in mixer bowl
until soft and creamy. Add sugar gradually,
beating constantly. Beat in chocolate and eggs.
Add flour; mix well. Stir in walnuts.
❖ Spoon half the batter into greased and floured
9-by-9-inch baking pan. Spread raspberry jam
over batter; top with remaining batter.

❖ Bake for 28 to 30 minutes or until edges pull
from side of pan.
❖ Let stand until cool. Cut into bars.
❖ Yield: 3 dozen.

CHOCOLATE SHORTBREAD

1 cup butter, softened
1 1/4 cups confectioners'
   sugar
1 1/2 teaspoons vanilla
   extract

1/2 cup Hershey's baking
   cocoa
1 3/4 cups all-purpose flour
Cocoa Glaze

❖ Preheat oven to 300 degrees.
❖ Cream butter, confectioners' sugar and vanilla
in large mixer bowl until smooth. Beat in baking
cocoa and flour gradually, mixing well after
each addition.
❖ Roll or pat dough 1/2 inch thick on lightly
floured surface. Cut into 1 1/2-by-2 1/4-inch
rectangles with sharp knife; place on ungreased
cookie sheet.
❖ Pierce each rectangle several times all the way
through in decorative pattern with fork. Place on
cookie sheet.
❖ Bake for 20 to 25 minutes or just until firm. Cool
slightly on cookie sheet; remove to wire rack to
cool completely.
❖ Drizzle with Cocoa Glaze. Let stand until set.
❖ Do not substitute margarine for butter in
this recipe.
❖ Yield: 3 1/2 dozen.
❖ **Filled Chocolate Shortbread Cookies**: Roll or
pat dough 3/8 inch thick and bake as above. Spread
half the cookies with mixture of 1/4 cup butter, 1/4
cup shortening, 1 cup marshmallow creme, 1 1/4
cups confectioners' sugar and 1 1/2 teaspoons
vanilla extract. Top with remaining cookies.
Drizzle with Cocoa Glaze.
❖ Yield: 20 cookies.

COCOA GLAZE

1 tablespoon butter
1 1/2 tablespoons
   Hershey's baking
   cocoa

2 tablespoons water
3/4 cup confectioners'
   sugar
1/4 teaspoon vanilla extract

❖ Melt butter in small saucepan over low heat.
Stir in cocoa and water.
❖ Cook over low heat until mixture thickens,
stirring constantly; do not boil. Remove from heat.
❖ Blend in confectioners sugar and vanilla.
❖ Yield: 1/2 cup.

Festive Christmas Breads

STRAWNANA BREAD

4 eggs, slightly beaten	1 cup vegetable oil
2 cups sugar	3 cups all-purpose flour
1 1/2 cups mashed strawberries	1 teaspoon baking soda
	1 1/2 teaspoons cinnamon
1 cup mashed banana	1/2 teaspoon salt
1 tablespoon grated orange rind	1/4 teaspoon nutmeg
	1 cup chopped walnuts

❖ Preheat oven to 350 degrees.
❖ Combine eggs, sugar, strawberries, banana, orange rind and oil in mixer bowl. Beat at medium speed for 2 minutes.
❖ Add mixture of flour, baking soda, cinnamon, salt and nutmeg; stir just until moistened. Stir in walnuts. Pour into 2 greased 5-by-9-inch loaf pans.
❖ Bake for 1 hour or until loaves test done. Remove to wire rack to cool.
❖ Yield: 2 loaves.

HEART-SMART BANANA BREAD

2 1/4 cups all-purpose flour	10 tablespoons light corn oil spread
2/3 cup honey-crunch wheat germ	
	1 1/2 cups mashed bananas
1/2 cup oats	1 (6-ounce) can frozen apple juice concentrate, thawed
1/4 cup packed brown sugar	
1 tablespoon baking powder	1/2 cup egg substitute
	1 teaspoon vanilla extract
1/2 teaspoon salt	1/3 cup chopped walnuts
1/4 teaspoon baking soda	

❖ Preheat oven to 350 degrees.
❖ Combine flour, wheat germ, oats, brown sugar, baking powder, salt and baking soda in large bowl. Cut in corn oil spread until crumbly.
❖ Add bananas, apple juice concentrate, egg substitute, vanilla and walnuts; mix just until moistened. Spoon into greased 5-by-9-inch loaf pan.
❖ Bake for 1 hour or until loaf tests done. Cool in pan on wire rack for 10 minutes. Remove to wire rack to cool completely. Serve warm or cool.
❖ Yield: 1 loaf.

CANTALOUPE-PECAN BREAD

1 cup sugar	2 teaspoons baking powder
1/2 cup vegetable oil	
2 eggs	1/2 teaspoon salt
1 1/2 teaspoons vanilla extract	1 teaspoon cinnamon
	1 cantaloupe, peeled, seeded, puréed
1 1/2 cups all-purpose flour	
1/2 teaspoon baking soda	1/2 cup chopped pecans

❖ Preheat oven to 350 degrees.
❖ Beat sugar and oil in mixer bowl until smooth. Add eggs 1 at a time, beating well after each addition. Add vanilla; mix well.
❖ Mix dry ingredients together. Add to batter; mix well. Stir in cantaloupe purée and pecans. Pour into 3 greased and floured 3-by-5-inch miniature loaf pans.
❖ Bake for 35 minutes or until loaves test done. Cool in pans for 10 minutes. Remove to wire racks to cool completely.
❖ Serve spread with soft cream cheese and top with sliced bananas, strawberries or kiwifruit.
❖ Yield: 3 miniature loaves.

ORANGE MARMALADE BREAD

2 1/2 cups all-purpose flour	1/2 cup orange marmalade
1 teaspoon baking soda	1/4 cup white vinegar
1 teaspoon salt	1 cup milk
3/4 cup sugar	2 tablespoons vegetable oil
1 egg, beaten	

❖ Preheat oven to 350 degrees.
❖ Combine flour, baking soda, salt and sugar in large bowl.
❖ Beat egg with marmalade, vinegar, milk and oil in bowl. Add to dry ingredients all at once; stir just until mixed.
❖ Pour into greased 5-by-9-inch loaf pan.
❖ Bake for 1 hour or until loaf tests done. Remove to wire rack to cool.
❖ Yield: 1 loaf.

Hungarian Poppy Seed Loaf, Yogurt Spice Cake, and Austrian Strawberry Tart, pages 22, 34, and 43

NECTARINE-BLUEBERRY BREAD

2/3 cup chopped almonds	1/3 cup butter or
1 tablespoon sugar	margarine, softened
1 cup all-purpose flour	1 teaspoon grated orange
3/4 cup sugar	rind
2 teaspoons baking	2 eggs
powder	1/2 cup all-purpose flour
1/2 teaspoon allspice	2/3 cup coarsely chopped
1/4 teaspoon baking soda	nectarine
1/4 teaspoon salt	1/2 cup blueberries
1/4 cup orange juice	

❖ Preheat oven to 350 degrees.
❖ Mix 1/4 cup almonds with 1 tablespoon sugar in bowl. Set aside.
❖ Combine 1 cup flour, 3/4 cup sugar, baking powder, allspice, baking soda and salt in large mixer bowl.
❖ Add orange juice, butter and orange rind. Beat at low speed until blended. Beat at high speed for 2 minutes.
❖ Add eggs and 1/2 cup flour. Beat at low speed just until mixed. Fold in nectarine, blueberries and remaining almonds.
❖ Pour into greased 4-by-8-inch loaf pan. Bake for 40 to 45 minutes. Sprinkle with mixture of almonds and sugar. Bake for 15 minutes longer or until loaf tests done. Remove to wire rack to cool.
❖ Yield: 1 loaf.

HUNGARIAN POPPY SEED LOAF

1 envelope dry yeast	3/4 cup milk
1/2 cup lukewarm milk	2 tablespoons honey
2 1/2 cups all-purpose flour	2 teaspoons cinnamon
1/4 cup butter or	2 tablespoons butter or
margarine	margarine
1/4 cup sugar	1 tablespoon sugar
1/2 teaspoon salt	1 egg, beaten
1 egg	1 tablespoon water
1/2 cup all-purpose flour	1 cup confectioners' sugar
3/4 cup poppy seed	2 tablespoons milk
3/4 cup raisins	

❖ Dissolve yeast in 1/2 cup lukewarm milk in large bowl. Let stand for 5 minutes.
❖ Add 2 1/2 cups flour, 1/4 cup butter, 1/4 cup sugar, salt and 1 egg; beat until smooth.
❖Add remaining 1/2 cup flour. Knead on floured surface for 10 minutes or until smooth and elastic.
❖ Place in greased bowl, turning to coat surface. Chill in refrigerator overnight.
❖ Mix poppy seed, raisins, 3/4 cup milk, honey, cinnamon, 2 tablespoons butter and 1 tablespoon sugar in small saucepan. Bring mixture to a boil, stirring constantly.

❖ Cook over low heat for 10 minutes or until thickened. Cool to room temperature.
❖ Roll dough into 10-by-14-inch rectangle on lightly floured surface. Spread with poppy seed mixture. Roll as for jelly roll to enclose filling.
❖ Place on greased baking sheet. Slice at 1-inch intervals, cutting to but not through bottom. Pull slices alternately to left and right. Let rise, covered, in warm place for 45 minutes or until doubled in bulk. Brush with mixture of beaten egg and water.
❖ Preheat oven to 350 degrees.
❖ Bake for 30 minutes or until golden brown. Place on wire rack. Drizzle with mixture of confectioners' sugar and 2 tablespoons milk. Sprinkle with additional poppy seed if desired.
❖ Yield: 1 loaf.

RAISIN-PECAN FRUIT BREAD

1/2 cup vegetable oil	1/2 teaspoon salt
1 cup sugar	1/2 teaspoon allspice
2 eggs	1/3 cup orange juice
1 teaspoon vanilla extract	1 cup chopped tart apples
2 cups all-purpose flour	1/2 cup chopped pecans
1 teaspoon baking soda	1/2 cup raisins

❖ Preheat oven to 350 degrees.
❖ Beat oil and sugar in mixer bowl until smooth. Add eggs and vanilla; beat well.
❖ Combine flour, baking soda, salt and allspice in bowl. Add dry ingredients to egg mixture alternately with orange juice, mixing well after each addition. Fold in apples, pecans and raisins.
❖ Spoon into greased and floured 5-by-9-inch loaf pan.
❖ Bake for 55 minutes or until loaf tests done. Remove to wire rack to cool.
❖ Yield: 1 loaf.

PICANTE-SPICE BREAD

2 cups all-purpose flour	1/2 teaspoon allspice
3/4 cup sugar	1 1/2 cups picante sauce
1 teaspoon baking soda	1/2 cup melted butter or
1 teaspoon baking powder	margarine
1/2 teaspoon cumin	2 eggs, beaten
1/2 teaspoon cinnamon	

❖ Preheat oven to 350 degrees.
❖ Combine flour, sugar, baking soda, baking powder and spices in mixer bowl; mix well.
❖ Add picante sauce, butter and eggs; beat well.
❖ Spoon into 3 greased and floured 3-by-5-inch miniature loaf pans.
❖ Bake for 25 minutes or until loaves test done. Remove to wire racks to cool.
❖ Yield: 3 miniature loaves.

CHEERY CRANBERRY-CHOCOLATE CHIP BREAD

1 cup Hershey's semi-
  sweet chocolate
  chips
1 cup fresh or frozen
  cranberries, coarsely
  chopped
1/2 cup broken pecans
2 teaspoons grated orange
  rind
2 cups all-purpose flour

1 cup sugar
1 1/2 teaspoons baking
  powder
1/2 teaspoon baking soda
1/2 teaspoon salt
2 tablespoons shortening
3/4 cup orange juice
1 egg, slightly beaten
Cocoa Drizzle Glaze

❖ Preheat oven to 350 degrees.
❖ Mix chocolate chips, cranberries, pecans and
orange rind in small bowl; set aside.
❖ Combine flour, sugar, baking powder, baking
soda and salt in large bowl. Cut in shortening
with pastry blender until crumbly.
❖ Add orange juice, egg and chocolate chip
mixture; stir just until moistened. Spoon into
3 greased and floured 3-by-5-inch miniature
loaf pans.
❖ Bake for 40 to 45 minutes or until wooden pick
inserted in center comes out clean. Cool in pans
for 15 minutes. Remove to wire rack to cool
completely. Drizzle with Cocoa Drizzle Glaze.
❖ Yield: 3 miniature loaves.

*Homemade bread baked in unique shapes
and gaily wrapped is especially
welcome at the holiday season.*

COCOA DRIZZLE GLAZE

1 tablespoon butter or
  margarine
1 tablespoon Hershey's
  baking cocoa

1 tablespoon water
1/2 cup confectioners'
  sugar
1/2 teaspoon vanilla extract

❖ Place butter in glass dish.
❖ Microwave butter on High for 20 to 30 seconds
or until melted.
❖ Stir in baking cocoa and 1 tablespoon water.
❖ Microwave on High for 15 to 30 seconds or just
until slightly thickened; do not boil.
❖ Remove from microwave. Stir mixture until
very smooth and blended.
❖ Add confectioners' sugar and vanilla; whisk
until smooth.
❖ Whisk in a small amount of additional water
a few drops at a time to make of desired
glaze consistency.
❖ Yield: 1/4 cup.

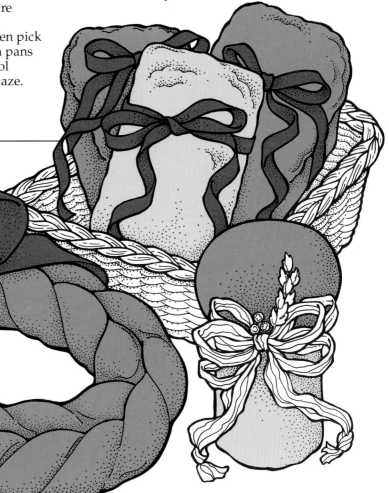

PISTACHIO LUCIA CROWN

1 (16-ounce) package hot
   roll mix
1/2 cup chopped natural
   California pistachios
1/2 cup sugar
1/2 teaspoon cardamom
Saffron to taste (optional)
1 egg
2 tablespoons butter
   or margarine
1 egg, beaten
2 cups sifted
   confectioners' sugar
1 teaspoon vanilla extract
2 tablespoons milk
1/4 cup slivered dried
   apricots
1/4 cup chopped natural
   California pistachios

❖ Combine dry flour mixture and yeast from roll mix with 1/2 cup pistachios, sugar, cardamom and saffron in bowl. Prepare dough with water specified in package directions, butter, 1 egg and flour mixture.
❖ Knead on floured surface for 5 minutes. Divide into 4 equal portions. Roll and pull 3 portions into 20-inch ropes.
❖ Braid ropes on greased baking sheet, shaping into 8- or 9-inch ring; press ends to seal.
❖ Divide remaining portion into halves. Roll and pull into 2 narrow 18-inch ropes. Twist ropes together; place on top of braid, pressing ends to seal.
❖ Brush with beaten egg. Let rise in warm place for 3 hours or until almost doubled in bulk.
❖ Preheat oven to 350 degrees.
❖ Bake crown for 30 to 35 minutes or until bread tests done and is golden brown, covering loosely with foil if necessary to prevent overbrowning. Remove to wire rack to cool.
❖ Blend confectioners' sugar with vanilla and enough milk to make of spreading consistency. Spread over crown. Decorate with apricots and remaining 1/4 cup pistachios.

❖ May add candles to use as centerpiece.
❖ Yield: 1 crown.

CHERRY-PECAN MUFFINS

1 cup packed light brown
   sugar
1 tablespoon (heaping)
   baking powder
2 cups unbleached flour
1 egg

3/4 cup milk
7 tablespoons corn oil
1 cup drained canned tart
   cherries
1/2 cup broken pecans

❖ Preheat oven to 375 degrees.
❖ Combine brown sugar, baking powder and flour in mixer bowl. Add mixture of egg and milk.
❖ Beat at low speed for 3 minutes. Add oil gradually. Stir in cherries and pecans. Spoon into paper-lined muffin cups.
❖ Bake for 26 minutes or until muffins test done.
❖ Yield: 1/2 dozen large or 1 dozen regular muffins.

St. Lucia's Day, December 13, marks the beginning of the Christmas season in Scandinavian countries. The custom is for the oldest daughter to serve her family breakfast in bed, wearing a long white gown and an evergreen wreath on her head with seven lighted candles. It celebrates Lucia, a brave young woman who lit her way in this manner to take food to early Christians who took refuge in caves.

APPLE BUTTER MUFFINS

1³/4 cups all-purpose flour	1 egg, beaten
1/3 cup sugar	3/4 cup milk
2 teaspoons baking powder	1/4 cup vegetable oil
1 teaspoon apple or pumpkin pie spice	1/3 cup apple butter
	1/3 cup chopped pecans
1/4 teaspoon salt	2 tablespoons sugar

❖ Preheat oven to 400 degrees.
❖ Combine flour, sugar, baking powder, apple pie spice and salt in bowl; mix well.
❖ Mix egg, milk and oil in bowl. Add to flour mixture all at once, stirring just until moistened.
❖ Drop by rounded tablespoonfuls into paper-lined muffin cups. Top with generous teaspoonfuls apple butter; fill 3/4 full with remaining batter.
❖ Combine pecans and sugar in bowl; mix well. Sprinkle on top of muffins.
❖ Bake for 20 minutes or until brown.
❖ Yield: 1 dozen.

APRICOT-ORANGE MUFFINS

1/2 cup dried apricots, coarsely chopped	1/2 cup raisins
1 cup orange juice	2 cups all-purpose flour
2 eggs, lightly beaten	1/4 cup sugar
1/4 cup melted butter or margarine	2 teaspoons baking powder
1¹/2 teaspoons vanilla extract	1 teaspoon baking soda
	Pinch of nutmeg

❖ Preheat oven to 350 degrees.
❖ Combine apricots, orange juice, eggs, butter, vanilla and raisins in bowl; mix well.
❖ Add to mixture of flour and remaining ingredients in large bowl; mix just until moistened.
❖ Fill paper-lined muffin cups 3/4 full.
❖ Bake for 20 minutes or until golden brown.
❖ Yield: 1 dozen.

PEACH COFFEE CAKE

2 tablespoons light brown sugar	16 ounces frozen bread dough, thawed
2 tablespoons all-purpose flour	1 (21-ounce) can peach pie filling
2 tablespoons oats	1 cup confectioners' sugar
1/2 teaspoon cinnamon	1 teaspoon vanilla extract
1/4 cup margarine	1 tablespoon milk

❖ Mix first 4 ingredients in bowl. Cut in 2 tablespoons margarine until crumbly; set aside.
❖ Roll dough into 8-by-12-inch rectangle. Place on greased baking sheet. Cut 2-inch strips at 1-inch intervals toward center along the 12-inch sides.
❖ Spoon peach pie filling lengthwise down center of dough. Fold strips alternately across pie filling for a braided effect.
❖ Brush top with 2 tablespoons melted margarine; sprinkle with brown sugar mixture. Let rise in warm area until puffy.
❖ Preheat oven to 350 degrees.
❖ Bake for 30 minutes or until golden brown. Cool.
❖ Drizzle with mixture of remaining ingredients.
❖ Yield: 1 coffee cake.

COCONUT MUFFINS

1¹/2 cups all-purpose flour	2 eggs
1 cup sugar	1 cup plain yogurt
2 teaspoons baking powder	1 cup coconut
	1/3 cup sugar
1/2 teaspoon salt	1 teaspoon cinnamon
1/2 cup vegetable oil	

❖ Preheat oven to 350 degrees.
❖ Combine first 7 ingredients in mixer bowl. Beat for 3 minutes. Fill paper-lined muffin cups 1/2 full.
❖ Sprinkle with mixture of remaining 3 ingredients.
❖ Bake for 20 to 25 minutes or until light brown.
❖ Yield: 1¹/2 dozen.

GINGER MUFFINS

1 cup molasses	1 teaspoon cinnamon
2/3 cup safflower oil	1/2 teaspoon ginger
3/4 cup packed light brown sugar	1/2 teaspoon allspice
	1 teaspoon baking soda
2 eggs, slightly beaten	1 teaspoon baking powder
4 cups all-purpose flour	1 cup buttermilk
1 teaspoon salt	1 cup raisins

❖ Preheat oven to 350 degrees.
❖ Mix first 4 ingredients in bowl. Sift in dry ingredients alternately with buttermilk, stirring well. Stir in raisins. Fill paper-lined muffin cups 3/4 full.
❖ Bake for 15 minutes or until muffins test done.
❖ Yield: 2 dozen.

Heavenly Christmas Candy

BUCKEYES

6 ounces cream cheese, softened
1 (14-ounce) can Eagle® Brand sweetened condensed milk
4 cups peanut butter chips
1 cup finely chopped peanuts
16 ounces Eagle™ Brand chocolate-flavored candy coating

❖ Beat cream cheese in large mixer bowl until fluffy. Beat in condensed milk gradually.
❖ Melt peanut butter chips in heavy saucepan over low heat. Stir into cream cheese mixture. Stir in peanuts.
❖ Chill for 2 to 3 hours. Shape into 1-inch balls.
❖ Melt candy coating in small heavy saucepan over low heat.
❖ Dip candy balls on wooden picks into melted coating, covering 3/4 of each ball. Let stand on waxed paper until firm.
❖ Store in airtight container in refrigerator or at room temperature.
❖ Yield: 5 dozen.

MILK CHOCOLATE BOURBON BALLS

3 cups vanilla wafer crumbs
5 tablespoons bourbon or brandy
2 cups milk chocolate chips
1 (14-ounce) can Eagle® Brand sweetened condensed milk
Finely chopped pecans

❖ Mix cookie crumbs and bourbon in bowl; set aside.
❖ Melt chocolate chips in heavy saucepan over low heat; remove from heat. Stir in condensed milk.
❖ Add cookie crumb mixture; mix well. Let stand at room temperature or in refrigerator for 30 minutes.
❖ Shape into 1-inch balls; roll in pecans. Store in airtight container.
❖ Flavor of candy is enhanced after 24 hours. May store in freezer if desired.
❖ Yield: 5 1/2 dozen.

CHOCOLATE FRUIT BALLS

2 1/2 cups vanilla wafer crumbs
1 (14-ounce) can Eagle® Brand sweetened condensed milk
1 cup finely chopped pecans
1/2 cup chopped candied cherries
8 ounces dates, chopped
2 tablespoons baking cocoa
Confectioners' sugar or baking cocoa
Red and green candied cherries (optional)

❖ Combine cookie crumbs, condensed milk, pecans, 1/2 cup chopped cherries, dates and 2 tablespoons baking cocoa in large bowl; mix well. Chill for 1 hour.
❖ Shape mixture into 1-inch balls. Roll in confectioners' sugar or additional baking cocoa; garnish with additional whole cherries.
❖ Store in airtight container in refrigerator for 24 hours to several weeks to enhance flavor.
❖ Yield: 8 dozen.

MERRY CHOCOLATE NUT CLUSTERS

1 cup Hershey's semi-sweet chocolate chips
1/2 cup Hershey's vanilla milk chips
1 tablespoon shortening
1 (11 1/2-ounce) can lightly salted peanuts

❖ Combine chocolate chips, vanilla milk chips and shortening in small glass bowl.
❖ Microwave on High for 1 to 1 1/2 minutes or until chocolate chips and vanilla milk chips are melted; stir to mix well.
❖ Reserve 1/4 cup peanuts. Stir remaining peanuts into chocolate mixture.
❖ Drop by teaspoonfuls into 1-inch bonbon cups; top each candy with 1 reserved peanut.
❖ Chill, uncovered, for 1 hour or until set. Store in airtight container in cool dry place.
❖ Yield: 3 dozen.

CARAMEL CRACKERS

2 (10-ounce) packages miniature butter crackers	1 cup sugar
	1/2 cup light corn syrup
1 cup chopped pecans	1 teaspoon baking soda
1/2 cup butter or margarine	1 teaspoon vanilla extract

❖ Preheat oven to 250 degrees.
❖ Combine butter crackers and pecans in buttered 9-by-13-inch baking dish.
❖ Bring butter, sugar and corn syrup to a boil in saucepan; remove from heat. Stir in baking soda and vanilla. Add to crackers and peanuts; mix well.
❖ Bake mixture for 45 to 60 minutes, stirring every 15 minutes.
❖ Spread on waxed paper. Let stand until cool. Break into small pieces. Store in airtight container.
❖ Yield: 16 servings.

Buckeyes, Milk Chocolate Bourbon Balls, Creamy Cherry Squares, Fruit Bonbons, Coconut Balls, Mexican Chocolate Fudge, Layered Mint Chocolate Squares, Peanut Butter Logs, and Pecan Critters, pages 26, 28, and 30

CHOCOLATE BRICKLE CARAMELS

1 (14-ounce) package vanilla caramels	2 (6-ounce) packages almond brickle pieces
12 ounces chocolate-flavored candy coating, melted	

❖ Dip caramels into chocolate coating.
❖ Coat with brickle pieces. Place on waxed paper-lined surface. Let stand until firm.
❖ Yield: 4 dozen.

CREAMY CHERRY SQUARES

1½ pounds Eagle™ Brand vanilla-flavored candy coating	⅛ teaspoon salt
	¾ to 1 cup chopped candied cherries
1 (14-ounce) can Eagle® Brand sweetened condensed milk	1½ teaspoons vanilla extract

❖ Melt candy coating with condensed milk and salt in heavy saucepan over low heat, stirring to mix well. Remove from heat. Stir in candied cherries and vanilla.
❖ Spread evenly in foil-lined 8- or 9-inch square dish. Chill for 2 hours or until firm.
❖ Invert onto cutting board; remove foil. Cut into squares. Store in airtight container at room temperature.
❖ Yield: 2¼ pounds.

CHOCOLATE MOUSSE BALLS

16 ounces milk chocolate	⅔ cup crushed vanilla wafers
8 ounces whipped topping	

❖ Melt chocolate in saucepan over low heat, stirring frequently. Cool to room temperature. Beat in whipped topping.
❖ Chill, covered, for 1 hour. Shape into 1-inch balls. Roll in wafer crumbs. Place in paper bonbon cups.
❖ Chill until serving time.
❖ Yield: 5 dozen.

FRUIT BONBONS

1 (14-ounce) can Eagle® Brand sweetened condensed milk	5⅓ cups flaked coconut
	1 cup ground blanched almonds
1 (6-ounce) package fruit-flavored gelatin	1 teaspoon almond extract
	Food coloring (optional)

❖ Combine condensed milk, ⅓ cup gelatin, coconut, almonds, almond extract and enough food coloring to tint as desired in bowl; mix well.
❖ Chill for 1 hour or until firm enough to handle. Shape by ½ tablespoonfuls into balls.
❖ Roll in remaining gelatin on waxed paper, coating well. Place on waxed paper-lined tray. Chill in refrigerator.
❖ Store in airtight container in refrigerator or at room temperature.
❖ Yield: 5 dozen.
❖ **Strawberry Bonbons**: Use strawberry gelatin and shape into strawberries. Pipe green icing onto stem end of each strawberry using star tip to form cap of strawberry.

CHRISTMAS BONBONS

¼ cup melted butter or margarine	1 cup chopped walnuts
	13 maraschino cherries, chopped
⅔ cup peanut butter	
2 cups confectioners' sugar	2 cups semisweet chocolate chips
1 cup flaked coconut	2 tablespoons paraffin

❖ Combine butter, peanut butter, confectioners' sugar, coconut, walnuts and cherries in bowl; mix well. Shape into balls. Chill until firm.
❖ Melt chocolate chips and paraffin in double boiler. Dip candy into melted chocolate mixture, coating completely.
❖ Place on waxed paper. Let stand until set.
❖ Yield: 4 dozen.

COCONUT BALLS

3 cups finely crushed vanilla wafers	¼ cup rum
	1 (14-ounce) can Eagle® Brand sweetened condensed milk
1⅓ cups flaked coconut	
1 cup finely chopped pecans	
	Flaked coconut

❖ Combine cookie crumbs, 1⅓ cups coconut and pecans in large bowl. Add rum and condensed milk; mix well.
❖ Chill for 4 hours. Shape into 1-inch balls. Roll in additional coconut.
❖ Store in airtight container in refrigerator for 24 hours to several weeks to enhance flavor.
❖ Yield: 5 dozen.

MEXICAN CHOCOLATE FUDGE

3 cups semisweet chocolate chips	½ to 1 cup chopped pecans
1 (14-ounce) can Eagle® Brand sweetened condensed milk	1 teaspoon vanilla extract
	1 tablespoon instant coffee
Salt to taste	1 teaspoon cinnamon

❖ Melt chocolate chips with condensed milk and salt in heavy saucepan over low heat; mix well. Remove from heat. Stir in pecans, vanilla, coffee powder and cinnamon.
❖ Spread evenly in waxed paper-lined 8- or 9-inch dish. Chill for 2 hours or until firm.
❖ Invert onto cutting board; remove waxed paper. Cut into squares.
❖ Store, loosely covered, at room temperature.
❖ Yield: 2 pounds.

EASY PEANUT BUTTER AND CHOCOLATE FUDGE

2 cups peanut butter chips
2 tablespoons butter or margarine
1 (14-ounce) can Eagle® Brand sweetened condensed milk

1/2 cup chopped peanuts (optional)
1 cup semisweet chocolate chips
2 tablespoons butter or margarine

❖ Melt peanut butter chips with 2 tablespoons butter and 1 cup condensed milk in heavy saucepan, stirring constantly. Remove from heat. Stir in peanuts. Spread in foil-lined 8-by-8-inch dish.
❖ Melt chocolate chips with 2 tablespoons butter and remaining condensed milk in small heavy saucepan, stirring constantly.
❖ Spread over peanut butter layer. Chill for 2 hours or until firm.
❖ Invert onto cutting board; remove foil. Cut into squares. Store fudge loosely covered at room temperature.
❖ Yield: 2 pounds.

PASTELS

1/3 cup light corn syrup
1/3 cup butter or margarine, softened
1 teaspoon vanilla extract
1/2 teaspoon salt

1 (1-pound) package confectioners' sugar
Red and green food coloring
1 1/2 cups pecan halves

Chocolate Fruit Balls, Easy Peanut Butter and Chocolate Fudge, Ginger and Orange Nut Balls, and Scotchy Turtles, pages 26, 29, and 30

❖ Combine corn syrup, butter, vanilla, salt and confectioners' sugar in bowl; mix well.
❖ Divide into 3 portions. Tint each portion with 2 or 3 drops of food coloring, kneading to mix color.
❖ Shape into 1-inch patties; top with pecan halves.
❖ Yield: 4 dozen.

GINGER AND ORANGE NUT BALLS

1 (16-ounce) package gingersnaps, finely crushed
1 (14-ounce) can Eagle® Brand sweetened condensed milk
1 1/3 cups flaked coconut

1 cup finely chopped pecans
1 cup raisins
1/3 cup orange juice
1 tablespoon grated orange rind
Flaked coconut

❖ Combine cookie crumbs, condensed milk, 1 1/3 cups coconut, pecans, raisins, orange juice and orange rind in large bowl; mix well. Chill mixture for 1 hour or longer.
❖ Shape into 1-inch balls. Roll in additional coconut. Store in airtight container in refrigerator for 24 hours to several weeks to enhance flavor.
❖ Yield: 6 dozen.

LAYERED MINT CHOCOLATE SQUARES

2 cups semisweet
  chocolate chips
1 (14-ounce) can Eagle®
  Brand sweetened
  condensed milk
2 teaspoons vanilla
  extract

6 ounces Eagle™ Brand
  vanilla-flavored candy
  coating
1 tablespoon peppermint
  extract
Green or red food
  coloring (optional)

❖ Melt chocolate chips with 1 cup condensed milk in heavy saucepan over low heat, stirring to mix well. Stir in vanilla.

❖ Spread half the mixture in foil-lined 8- or 9-inch square dish. Chill for 10 minutes or until firm. Reserve remaining chocolate mixture at room temperature.

❖ Melt candy coating with remaining condensed milk in heavy saucepan over low heat; mix well. Stir in peppermint extract and food coloring.

❖ Spread over chilled layer. Chill for 10 minutes or until firm.

❖ Spread reserved chocolate mixture over top. Chill for 2 hours or until firm.

❖ Invert onto cutting board; remove foil. Cut into squares. Store candy, loosely covered, at room temperature.

❖ Yield: 1³/4 pounds.

PEANUT BUTTER LOGS

2 cups peanut butter chips
1 (14-ounce) can Eagle®
  Brand sweetened
  condensed milk

1 cup Campfire®
  miniature
  marshmallows
1 cup chopped peanuts

❖ Melt peanut butter chips with condensed milk in heavy saucepan over low heat, stirring to mix well. Stir in marshmallows until melted.

❖ Cool for 20 minutes. Divide into 2 portions. Chill in refrigerator.

❖ Shape each portion into 12-inch log on 20-inch pieces of waxed paper. Roll in peanuts; press firmly.

❖ Chill, tightly wrapped, for 2 hours or until firm. Remove waxed paper. Cut into 1/4-inch slices. Store, covered, in refrigerator.

❖ Yield: two 12-inch logs.

PECAN CRITTERS

2 cups milk chocolate
  chips
1 cup semisweet
  chocolate chips
1/4 cup butter or margarine
1 (14-ounce) can Eagle®
  Brand sweetened
  condensed milk

1/8 teaspoon salt
2 cups coarsely chopped
  pecans
2 teaspoons vanilla extract
Pecan halves

❖ Melt chocolate chips and butter with condensed milk and salt in heavy saucepan over medium heat, stirring to mix well.

❖ Remove from heat. Stir in chopped pecans and vanilla.

❖ Drop by teaspoonfuls onto waxed paper. Top with pecan halves.

❖ Chill in refrigerator. Store in airtight container.

❖ Yield: 5 dozen.

SCOTCHY TURTLES

1 cup butterscotch chips
1 (14-ounce) can Eagle®
  Brand sweetened
  condensed milk
2 teaspoons white vinegar

4 cups pecan halves
2 cups milk chocolate
  chips
1 teaspoon vanilla extract

❖ Melt butterscotch chips with 1/3 cup condensed milk in small heavy saucepan over low heat; remove from heat. Stir in vinegar.

❖ Drop by 1/2 teaspoonfuls onto waxed paper-lined tray. Arrange 3 pecan halves on each candy.

❖ Melt chocolate chips with remaining condensed milk and vanilla in large heavy saucepan over low heat; mix well. Remove saucepan from heat and place over hot water.

❖ Spoon warm chocolate mixture by generous teaspoonfuls over pecan turtles. Chill for 2 hours or until firm. Store, loosely covered, at room temperature.

❖ Yield: 5 dozen.

SNICKER BARS

2 cups semisweet
  chocolate chips
1/2 cup butterscotch chips
1/2 cup peanut butter
1 cup sugar
1/4 cup butter or
  margarine

1/4 cup milk
1 cup marshmallow creme
1 teaspoon vanilla extract
1/4 cup peanut butter
1¹/2 cups salted peanuts
30 caramels
2 tablespoons water

❖ Melt chocolate chips, butterscotch chips and 1/2 cup peanut butter in saucepan, stirring to mix well. Spread half the mixture in 9-by-13-inch dish. Cool completely.

❖ Combine sugar, butter and milk in saucepan. Cook for 5 minutes, stirring to mix well. Add marshmallow creme, vanilla and 1/4 cup peanut butter; mix well. Spread over chilled layer. Sprinkle with peanuts.

❖ Melt caramels with water in saucepan, stirring to mix well. Spoon evenly over peanuts.

❖ Reheat remaining chocolate mixture to make of spreading consistency if necessary. Spread over top. Let stand until firm. Cut into bars.

❖ Yield: 2 dozen.

Merry Christmas Cakes

CHERRY NECTAR CAKE

1 cup shortening
2 cups sugar
4 eggs
3 cups all-purpose flour
1 tablespoon baking
   powder
1 teaspoon salt
1 cup (scant) milk
1 teaspoon almond extract
1/2 cup chopped pecans
1/2 cup chopped
   maraschino cherries

1/4 cup maraschino cherry
   juice
1/2 cup butter or
   margarine, softened
1/2 cup shortening
1 teaspoon almond extract
1 (1-pound) package
   confectioners' sugar
1/2 cup chopped
   maraschino cherries
1/4 cup chopped pecans

❖ Preheat oven to 350 degrees.
❖ Cream 1 cup shortening and sugar in mixer bowl until light and fluffy. Add eggs 1 at a time, beating well after each addition.
❖ Sift in flour, baking powder and salt; mix well. Beat in milk and 1 teaspoon almond extract. Stir in 1/2 cup pecans, 1/2 cup cherries and cherry juice.
❖ Pour into 4 greased and floured 8-inch cake pans.
❖ Bake for 15 minutes or until layers test done. Cool on wire rack.
❖ Cream butter and 1/2 cup shortening in mixer bowl until light and fluffy. Add 1 teaspoon almond extract and confectioners' sugar; beat until of spreading consistency. Stir in 1/2 cup cherries and 1/4 cup chopped pecans.
❖ Spread frosting between layers and over top and side of cake.
❖ Yield: 12 to 16 servings.

CHOCOLATE-COCONUT-PECAN TORTE

1 (2-layer) package
   chocolate cake mix
1 (14-ounce) can Eagle®
   Brand sweetened
   condensed milk
1/2 cup butter or
   margarine

3 egg yolks, beaten
1 1/3 cups flaked coconut
1 cup chopped pecans
1 teaspoon vanilla extract
2 cups whipped topping
Pecan halves

❖ Preheat oven to 350 degrees.
❖ Prepare cake mix using package directions. Spoon into 3 greased and floured 8- or 9-inch round cake pans.

❖ Bake for 20 minutes or until wooden pick inserted near center comes out clean. Remove to wire rack to cool.
❖ Combine condensed milk, butter and egg yolks in heavy saucepan.
❖ Cook for 10 minutes or until thickened and bubbly, stirring constantly. Stir in coconut, chopped pecans and vanilla. Cool for 10 minutes.
❖ Slice crust from top of each cake layer with sharp knife, leaving 1/2-inch edge. Spread coconut mixture over cut portions of layers.
❖ Stack layers on cake plate. Frost sides with whipped topping; garnish with pecan halves. Chill until serving time.
❖ Yield: 16 servings.

HOLIDAY CHOCOLATE FRUITCAKE

1 1/2 cups coarsely
   chopped red candied
   cherries
1 cup golden raisins
1 cup broken pecans
1/4 cup all-purpose flour
8 ounces cream cheese,
   softened
1/2 cup butter or
   margarine, softened
1 cup sugar

3 eggs
2 cups all-purpose flour
1/4 cup Hershey's baking
   cocoa
1 teaspoon baking powder
1/2 teaspoon salt
1/2 cup orange juice
1 tablespoon brandy or
   2 teaspoons brandy
   extract plus 1 teaspoon
   rum extract

❖ Preheat oven to 300 degrees.
❖ Toss cherries, raisins and pecans with 1/4 cup flour in bowl, coating well; set aside.
❖ Combine cream cheese, butter and sugar in large mixer bowl; beat until smooth. Add eggs 1 at a time, beating well after each addition.
❖ Mix 2 cups flour, baking cocoa, baking powder and salt together. Add to cream cheese mixture alternately with orange juice, mixing well after each addition.
❖ Add fruit mixture and brandy; mix gently. Spoon into greased and floured 10-inch tube pan.
❖ Bake for 1 1/2 hours or until wooden pick inserted near center comes out clean.
❖ Cool in pan for 15 minutes; remove to wire rack to cool completely. Store, covered, in refrigerator. Garnish as desired.
❖ Yield: 16 servings.

Chocolate-Coconut-Pecan Torte, and Black Forest Torte, pages 31 and 34

CARROT FRUITCAKE

3 cups all-purpose flour
2 teaspoons baking
   powder
2 teaspoons baking soda
2 teaspoons cinnamon
1 teaspoon salt
1½ cups vegetable oil
2 cups sugar
4 eggs
3 cups shredded carrots
1 cup chopped candied
   fruit
1 cup chopped dates
1 cup raisins
1½ cups chopped pecans
   or walnuts

❖ Preheat oven to 350 degrees.
❖ Sift flour, baking powder, baking soda, cinnamon and salt together into bowl.
❖ Beat oil and sugar in mixer bowl. Add eggs 1 at a time, beating well after each addition. Add flour mixture gradually, mixing well after each addition.
❖ Stir in carrots, candied fruit, dates, raisins and pecans. Pour into greased 10-inch tube pan.
❖ Bake for 1¼ hours or until top springs back when lightly touched. Cool in pan for 10 minutes. Remove to wire rack to cool completely.
❖ Yield: 16 servings.

PINK GRAPEFRUIT CAKE

3 cups cake flour
3½ teaspoons baking
   powder
¾ teaspoon salt
¼ teaspoon baking soda
1½ cups sugar
1 cup unsalted butter or
   margarine
3 eggs
1 cup pink grapefruit juice
2 cans cream cheese or
   sour cream frosting

❖ Preheat oven to 375 degrees.
❖ Sift cake flour, baking powder, salt and baking soda together.
❖ Cream sugar and butter in mixer bowl until light and fluffy. Add eggs 1 at a time, beating well after each addition.
❖ Add cake flour mixture and grapefruit juice alternately to creamed mixture, beating well at low speed after each addition. Pour into 2 greased and floured 9-inch round cake pans.
❖ Bake for 30 minutes. Cool in pans for 5 minutes. Remove to wire rack to cool completely.
❖ Spread frosting between layers and over top and side of cake.
❖ Yield: 12 servings.

MACAROON CAKE

1 cup butter or margarine, softened	1/4 teaspoon salt
2 cups sugar	1 cup milk
4 eggs	1 teaspoon vanilla extract
3 cups all-purpose flour	1 teaspoon almond extract
1 tablespoon baking powder	2 cups toasted flaked coconut

❖ Preheat oven to 350 degrees.
❖ Cream butter and sugar in mixer bowl until light and fluffy. Add eggs 1 at a time, beating well after each addition.
❖ Mix flour, baking powder and salt together. Add to creamed mixture alternately with milk, beating well after each addition.
❖ Add flavorings and coconut; mix well. Pour into greased and floured tube pan.
❖ Bake for 1 hour. Cool in pan for 10 minutes. Remove to wire rack to cool completely.
❖ Yield: 16 servings.

MANDARIN CAKE

2 (11-ounce) cans mandarin oranges	1 teaspoon salt
2 cups all-purpose flour	1 cup chopped walnuts
2 cups sugar	3/4 cup packed light brown sugar
2 teaspoons vanilla extract	3 tablespoons milk
2 teaspoons baking soda	3 tablespoons butter or margarine
2 eggs	

❖ Preheat oven to 350 degrees.
❖ Combine undrained mandarin oranges, flour, sugar, vanilla, baking soda, eggs, salt and walnuts in mixer bowl; beat until well mixed. Pour into ungreased 9-by-13-inch cake pan.
❖ Bake for 30 to 35 minutes or until cake tests done. Cool in pan. Pierce with fork.
❖ Combine brown sugar, milk and butter in saucepan. Bring to a boil, stirring occasionally. Pour over cake.
❖ Yield: 15 servings.

MARBLE SWIRL CAKE

1 cup butter or margarine, softened	1 1/2 teaspoons baking powder
2 cups sugar	1/4 teaspoon salt
3 1/2 cups all-purpose flour	4 eggs, beaten
1 cup milk	1/4 cup baking cocoa
2 teaspoons vanilla extract	

❖ Preheat oven to 350 degrees.
❖ Cream butter and sugar at high speed in mixer bowl for 4 minutes.
❖ Add flour, milk, vanilla, baking powder, salt and eggs. Beat at low speed until thoroughly mixed. Beat at high speed for 4 minutes longer.
❖ Spoon 2 1/2 cups batter into separate bowl. Whisk in baking cocoa.
❖ Spoon alternate layers of chocolate and vanilla batters into greased 10-inch tube pan. Swirl with knife to marbleize.
❖ Bake for 55 to 60 minutes or until cake tests done. Cool in pan for 10 minutes. Loosen cake from side of pan. Invert onto cake plate.
❖ Yield: 16 servings.

MILKY WAY POUND CAKE

1 (16-ounce) package fun-size Milky Way bars	2 1/2 cups sifted all-purpose flour
1 cup butter or margarine, softened	1/2 teaspoon baking soda
2 cups sugar	1 1/4 cups milk
4 eggs	1 teaspoon vanilla extract
	Milky Way Glaze

❖ Preheat oven to 350 degrees.
❖ Combine 16-ounce package candy bars with 1/2 cup butter in heavy saucepan. Cook over very low heat until melted, stirring constantly; remove from heat.
❖ Cream remaining 1/2 cup butter with sugar in mixer bowl until light and fluffy. Add eggs 1 at a time, beating well after each addition.
❖ Sift flour and baking soda together. Add to creamed mixture alternately with milk, stirring until smooth. Add melted candy bars and 1 teaspoon vanilla, stirring well. Pour into greased and floured bundt pan.
❖ Bake for 1 1/4 hours or until cake tests done. Cool in pan for several minutes. Loosen cake from side of pan. Invert onto cake plate to cool completely.
❖ Spread Milky Way Glaze over top and side of cooled cake.
❖ Yield: 16 servings.

MILKY WAY GLAZE

8 fun-size Milky Way bars	2 cups sifted confectioners' sugar
1/2 cup butter or margarine	1 teaspoon vanilla extract

❖ Melt candy bars and butter in heavy saucepan over low heat. Add confectioners' sugar and 1 teaspoon vanilla. Beat until smooth.
❖ Yield: 1 1/2 cups.

PISTACHIO HARVEST CAKE

1¹/2 cups vegetable oil
2 cups packed brown
  sugar
4 eggs
2 cups grated carrots
1 tablespoon vanilla
  extract
4 cups all-purpose flour
1 tablespoon baking soda
³/4 cup finely chopped
  natural California
  pistachios
4 teaspoons cinnamon
1 teaspoon nutmeg
1 teaspoon ginger

1 teaspoon salt
16 ounces pineapple
  yogurt
1 cup butter or margarine,
  softened
5 cups confectioners'
  sugar
1¹/2 teaspoons grated
  orange rind
3 to 4 tablespoons orange
  juice
¹/4 cup finely chopped
  natural California
  pistachios

❖ Preheat oven to 350 degrees.
❖ Combine oil, brown sugar, eggs, carrots and vanilla in large bowl; mix well.
❖ Mix flour, baking soda, ³/4 cup pistachios, cinnamon, nutmeg, ginger and salt in bowl. Add to carrot mixture alternately with yogurt, mixing well after each addition.
❖ Spoon into greased and floured 14-cup bundt pan or crown ring mold.
❖ Bake for 1¹/4 hours or until wooden pick inserted into cake comes out clean. Cool in pan for 15 minutes. Invert cake onto wire rack to cool completely.
❖ Combine butter, confectioners' sugar and orange rind in mixer bowl. Add enough orange juice to make of spreading consistency, beating until smooth.
❖ Place cake on serving plate. Spread with frosting. Sprinkle remaining ¹/4 cup pistachios over cake.
❖ Yield: 16 servings.

YOGURT SPICE CAKE

2 cups all-purpose flour
1 teaspoon baking powder
¹/4 teaspoon baking soda
1 teaspoon cinnamon
¹/2 teaspoon nutmeg
¹/4 teaspoon salt
¹/2 cup butter or
  margarine, softened
1¹/2 cups sugar
3 eggs
1 cup plain yogurt

¹/2 cup packed light
  brown sugar
1 tablespoon melted
  butter or margarine
¹/2 cup chopped almonds
¹/4 cup sweetened
  shredded coconut
¹/4 cup milk
¹/4 teaspoon vanilla
  extract

❖ Preheat oven to 325 degrees.
❖ Mix flour, baking powder, baking soda, cinnamon, nutmeg and salt together in bowl; set aside.
❖ Cream ¹/2 cup butter with sugar in large mixer bowl until light and fluffy. Add eggs, beating constantly until smooth.
❖ Add flour mixture alternately with yogurt, mixing well after each addition. Spoon into greased and floured 10-inch tube pan.
❖ Bake for 1 hour or until wooden pick inserted in center comes out clean. Cool in pan for 5 minutes. Invert cake onto baking sheet to cool completely.
❖ Combine brown sugar, 1 tablespoon melted butter, almonds, coconut, milk and vanilla in bowl; mix well. Spoon over top of cooled cake.
❖ Preheat broiler.
❖ Broil 3 inches from heat source for 2 minutes or until light brown.
❖ Remove to cake plate.
❖ Yield: 16 servings.

BLACK FOREST TORTE

1 (2-layer) package
  chocolate cake mix
1 cup semisweet
  chocolate chips
1 (14-ounce) can Eagle®
  Brand sweetened
  condensed milk

1 (21-ounce) can cherry
  pie filling, chilled
¹/2 teaspoon almond
  extract

❖ Preheat oven to 350 degrees.
❖ Prepare and bake cake mix using package directions for two 9-inch round cake pans. Remove layers to wire rack to cool.
❖ Combine chocolate chips and condensed milk in heavy saucepan. Cook over medium heat until melted, stirring to mix well. Cook for 10 minutes longer or until thickened, stirring constantly. Cool for 20 minutes.
❖ Pour pie filling into colander. Drain; reserve cherries and ¹/4 cup liquid.
❖ Combine cherries, reserved liquid and almond extract in bowl.
❖ Place 1 cake layer top side up on serving plate. Remove top crust with sharp knife, leaving ¹/2-inch edge.
❖ Spoon half the chocolate mixture over layer; top with cherries. Place remaining cake layer over cherries. Spoon remaining chocolate mixture over top. Chill until serving time. Garnish as desired.
❖ Yield: 16 servings.

Pistachio Harvest Cake, page 34

Favorite Christmas Treats

EASY OVEN APPLE BUTTER

8 cups applesauce
2 cups sugar
1/2 teaspoon ground cloves
1/2 teaspoon cinnamon
1/2 teaspoon allspice

❖ Preheat oven to 275 degrees.
❖ Combine applesauce, sugar, cloves, cinnamon and allspice in baking dish; mix well. Cover loosely with baking parchment.
❖ Bake for 6 to 7 hours or until of desired consistency, stirring occasionally.
❖ Spoon into hot sterilized jars; seal with 2-piece lids. Let stand until cool. Store in refrigerator.
❖ Yield: 4 cups.

BLUEBERRY-RHUBARB JAM

8 cups chopped rhubarb
4 cups sugar
1 large package raspberry gelatin
1 (21-ounce) can blueberry pie filling

❖ Cook rhubarb with sugar in saucepan until tender, stirring frequently; remove from heat.
❖ Stir in gelatin until dissolved. Stir in pie filling.
❖ Spoon into hot sterilized jars; seal with 2-piece lids. Store in refrigerator.
❖ Yield: 8 cups.

STRAWBERRY AND PINK CHAMPAGNE SAUCE

2 cups pink Champagne, sparkling wine or nonalcoholic pink Champagne
4 cups sugar
1 (1³/4-ounce) package dry pectin
4 cups strawberries, cut into halves

❖ Combine Champagne and sugar in large glass bowl. Microwave, covered, on High for 10 minutes. Stir in pectin.
❖ Microwave, uncovered, on High for 5 minutes. Stir in strawberries.
❖ Pour into hot sterilized jars; seal with 2-piece lids. Store in refrigerator.
❖ Serve over ice cream or frozen yogurt.
❖ May substitute thawed no-sugar-added frozen strawberries for fresh strawberries if desired.
❖ Yield: 4 cups.

SPICED TEA HONEY

2 cups water
1 (1³/4-ounce) package dry pectin
1/4 cup spice tea mix
3³/4 cups sugar

❖ Boil water in large glass measuring cup for 3 to 4 minutes. Add pectin, tea mix and sugar.
❖ Microwave, uncovered, on High for 15 minutes.
❖ Pour into hot sterilized jars; seal with 2-piece lids. Store in refrigerator.
❖ Yield: 3 cups.

COCONUT-PECAN SAUCE

1 (14-ounce) can Eagle® Brand sweetened condensed milk
1/4 cup butter or margarine
2 egg yolks, beaten
1/2 cup flaked coconut
1/2 cup chopped pecans
1 teaspoon vanilla extract

❖ Combine condensed milk, butter and egg yolks in heavy saucepan; mix well.
❖ Cook over medium heat for 8 minutes or until thickened, stirring constantly.
❖ Stir in coconut, pecans and vanilla.
❖ Serve warm over ice cream or cake. Store in refrigerator. May reheat over low heat, adding enough water to make of desired consistency.
❖ Yield: 2 cups.

HEAVENLY HOT FUDGE SAUCE

1 cup semisweet chocolate chips or 4 (1-ounce) squares semisweet chocolate
2 tablespoons butter or margarine
1 (14-ounce) can Eagle® Brand sweetened condensed milk
2 tablespoons water
1 teaspoon vanilla extract

❖ Cook first 4 ingredients in heavy saucepan over medium heat until smooth.
❖ Cook for 5 minutes longer or until thickened, stirring constantly. Stir in vanilla.
❖ Serve warm over ice cream or as a sauce for dipping fruit. Store in refrigerator. May reheat over low heat, adding enough water to make of desired consistency.
❖ Yield: 2 cups.

CHRISTMAS PICKLES

2 (16-ounce) jars kosher   3 bay leaves
   dill pickles   3 cinnamon sticks
4 cups sugar   1 tablespoon whole cloves
1 cup white vinegar   1 clove of garlic
1 cup (scant) water

❖ Drain and rinse pickles; cut each pickle into 3 pieces. Return to jars.
❖ Combine sugar, vinegar, water, bay leaves, cinnamon, cloves and garlic in saucepan. Boil for 10 minutes; strain.
❖ Pour over pickles; seal. Chill in refrigerator for 10 to 14 days before serving.
❖ Yield: 2 pints.

Coconut-Pecan Sauce, Heavenly Hot Fudge Sauce, and Homemade Irish Cream, pages 36 and 38

EASY PICKLED BEETS

1¹/₃ cups sugar   3 (16-ounce) cans sliced
1¹/₃ cups cider vinegar   beets, drained
1¹/₃ cups water

❖ Combine sugar, vinegar and water in saucepan. Bring to a boil, stirring occasionally. Add beets.
❖ Bring to a boil; reduce heat. Simmer for 2 to 3 minutes, stirring occasionally. Let stand in saucepan until cool.
❖ Pour into hot sterilized jars; seal with 2-piece lids. Store in refrigerator.
❖ Yield: 3 pints.

CRANBERRY-APPLE CATSUP

2 (16-ounce) cans jellied cranberry sauce
1 (24-ounce) jar applesauce
2 tablespoons red wine vinegar
2 teaspoons pumpkin pie spice
1 teaspoon grated orange rind

❖ Combine cranberry sauce, applesauce, vinegar, pumpkin pie spice and orange rind in large saucepan; mix well.
❖ Cook over medium heat for 15 minutes or until smooth and flavors are blended, whisking occasionally. Cool slightly.
❖ Pour into gift bottles or jars; seal. Store in refrigerator for up to 1 month.
❖ Serve with roast turkey, pork or game.
❖ Yield: 3 cups.

HOT PEPPER MUSTARD

4 cups chopped hot peppers
1½ cups vinegar
1½ cups water
¼ cup salt
3 to 4 cups sugar
1 cup all-purpose flour
1 tablespoon turmeric
1 tablespoon dry mustard
1 (16-ounce) jar prepared mustard

❖ Combine hot peppers, vinegar, water and salt in saucepan. Simmer until peppers are tender.
❖ Mix sugar, flour, turmeric and dry mustard together in bowl. Add prepared mustard; mix well. Add to hot pepper mixture.
❖ Simmer until thickened, stirring frequently. Pour into hot sterilized 1-pint jars, leaving ½ inch headspace; seal with 2-piece lids.
❖ Process in hot water bath for 5 minutes.
❖ Yield: 4 pints.

PINEAPPLE SALSA

1 large pineapple
1 each red, green and yellow bell pepper, chopped
2 hot peppers with seed, chopped
¼ cup (or more) fresh cilantro
¼ cup fresh parsley
1 small onion
3 or 4 green onions with tops
¼ cup safflower oil
2 tablespoons fresh lime juice

❖ Preheat broiler.
❖ Peel pineapple and cut into quarters, discarding core. Place in baking pan.
❖ Broil for several minutes until warm but not brown. Drain and chop pineapple.
❖ Process peppers in food processor just until chopped. Combine with pineapple in large bowl.

❖ Process cilantro, parsley, onion and green onions until chopped. Add to pineapple with oil and lime juice.
❖ Spoon into jars; seal with 2-piece lids.
❖ Store in refrigerator.
❖ Yield: 7 cups.

MOCHA HOT CHOCOLATE MIX

½ cup instant mocha-flavored coffee
½ cup dry nondairy creamer
¼ cup baking cocoa
1⅓ cups confectioners' sugar
¼ cup crushed peppermint candy

❖ Combine all ingredients in blender container.
❖ Process until blended. Store in airtight container.
❖ Add gift tag with instructions to blend 2 tablespoons mix with ¾ cup boiling water for 1 serving.
❖ Yield: 2½ cups mix.

CHRISTMAS COFFEE MIX

1 (2-ounce) jar instant coffee
1 cup sugar
1 teaspoon allspice
1 teaspoon nutmeg
1 teaspoon cinnamon

❖ Combine all ingredients in blender container. Process for 15 seconds or until blended.
❖ Store in airtight container.
❖ Add gift tag with instructions to blend 1 to 2 teaspoons mix with ⅔ cup boiling water for 1 serving.
❖ Yield: 2 cups.

HOMEMADE IRISH CREAM

2 cups Borden® whipping cream or coffee cream
1¼ to 1¾ cups Irish whiskey
2 teaspoons instant coffee granules
1 teaspoon vanilla extract
2 tablespoons chocolate syrup
1 (14-ounce) can Eagle® Brand sweetened condensed milk
½ teaspoon almond extract

❖ Process all ingredients in blender container until smooth.
❖ Chill in airtight container for several hours to enhance flavor. Stir before serving over ice.
❖ Yield: 5 cups.
❖ **Flavored Cream Liqueurs:** Omit whiskey, chocolate syrup, coffee granules and extracts. Add 1¼ cups almond, coffee, orange or mint liqueur to condensed milk and whipping cream.

Party Peanut Crisp, page 40

WHITE CHRISTMAS CRUNCH

1 pound white chocolate	2 cups dry-roasted
3 cups Cherrios	peanuts
3 cups rice Chex cereal	2 cups "M & M's"
3 cups corn Chex cereal	Chocolate Candies
2 cups small pretzel sticks	

❖ Melt white chocolate in double boiler. Pour over mixture of remaining ingredients in bowl; mix to coat well.
❖ Spread on waxed paper. Let stand until cool. Break into small pieces.
❖ May substitute vanilla milk chips and 1 tablespoon paraffin for white chocolate if desired.
❖ Yield: 15 servings.

PUMPKIN PIE NUTS

1 egg white	1 cup sugar
1 teaspoon water	1 tablespoon pumpkin
2 (12-ounce) cans salted	pie spice
mixed nuts	

❖ Preheat oven to 325 degrees.
❖ Beat egg white and water in bowl until foamy. Add mixed nuts; mix well.
❖ Sprinkle sugar and spice over mixed nuts; toss to coat well. Spread in greased foil-lined 10-by-15-inch baking pan.
❖ Bake for 20 minutes or until light brown. Let stand for several minutes.
❖ Remove to waxed paper-lined surface to cool completely. Break into pieces. Store in airtight container.
❖ Yield: 6 cups.

FIVE-SPICE WALNUTS

4 egg whites	1 teaspoon nutmeg
1/2 cup Champagne or	1/2 teaspoon ginger
white grape juice	1/4 teaspoon ground cloves
2 cups sugar	1/4 teaspoon allspice
2 teaspoons salt	8 cups walnut halves
1 teaspoon cinnamon	

❖ Preheat oven to 250 degrees.
❖ Whisk egg whites in large bowl until foamy. Add Champagne, sugar and salt; mix well.
❖ Stir in spices and walnuts. Spread in two 10-by-15-inch baking pans sprayed with nonstick cooking spray.
❖ Bake for 1 hour or until walnuts are dry, stirring occasionally.
❖ Spread on waxed paper-lined wire racks; separate with fork. Let stand until cool.
❖ Store in airtight container.
❖ Yield: 8 cups.

CHINESE OYSTER CRACKER SNACK

1/2 cup vegetable oil	1 teaspoon dillweed
1 (16-ounce) package	1/2 teaspoon garlic powder
oyster crackers	1/4 teaspoon curry powder
1/2 teaspoon Chinese	1/2 envelope ranch salad
5-spice	dressing mix

❖ Combine oil and oyster crackers in large bowl; mix well.
❖ Mix remaining ingredients in paper bag. Add oyster crackers.
❖ Shake bag every 10 minutes for 1 hour. Store in airtight container.
❖ Yield: 6 cups.

CAJUN PARTY MIX

1/2 cup butter or	4 to 8 drops of hot pepper
margarine	sauce
1 tablespoon parsley	3 cups wheat Chex
flakes	cereal
1 teaspoon garlic powder	3 cups rice Chex cereal
1 teaspoon celery salt	3 cups corn Chex cereal
1/2 teaspoon cayenne	1 (3-ounce) can French-
pepper	fried onions

❖ Microwave butter in 3 1/2-quart glass bowl on High for 1 minute or until melted. Stir in parsley flakes, garlic powder, celery salt, cayenne pepper and pepper sauce.
❖ Add cereals gradually, stirring to coat well.
❖ Microwave on High for 3 1/2 to 4 1/2 minutes. Stir in onions. Microwave on High for 1 1/2 minutes.
❖ Spread on paper towel to cool. Store in airtight container.
❖ Yield: 9 cups.

PARTY PEANUT CRISP

1/2 envelope Lipton onion	1 egg
recipe soup mix	1 teaspoon chili powder
3/4 cup all-purpose flour	1 cup spoon-size
3/4 cup melted butter or	shredded wheat
margarine	1/2 cup whole almonds
1/2 cup packed light	1/2 cup unsalted peanuts
brown sugar	1 cup pecans

❖ Preheat oven to 350 degrees.
❖ Beat soup mix, flour, butter, brown sugar, egg and chili powder in mixer bowl until smooth.
❖ Stir in cereal, almonds, peanuts and pecans. Spread in baking pan sprayed with nonstick cooking spray.
❖ Bake for 25 minutes or until golden brown. Cool in pan on wire rack. Break into pieces.
❖ Store in airtight container.
❖ Yield: 1 1/2 pounds.

CHOCOLATE POPCORN BALLS

1 (3½-ounce) bag
   microwave popping corn
   or 10 cups popped
   popcorn
½ cup packed light
   brown sugar
¼ cup light corn syrup

1½ (1-ounce) squares
   Hershey's unsweetened
   baking chocolate
2 tablespoons butter or
   margarine
⅛ teaspoon salt

❖ Prepare microwave popcorn using package
directions. Place in large buttered bowl,
discarding unpopped kernels.
❖ Combine brown sugar, corn syrup, chocolate
and butter in small saucepan.
❖ Cook over medium heat until mixture comes to
a full rolling boil, stirring constantly. Cook for 1
minute longer, stirring constantly. Stir in salt.
❖ Pour over popcorn, stirring to coat evenly.
Shape into 2-inch balls with buttered hands. Place
on tray lined with waxed paper. Let stand until
completely cool.
❖ Place in muffin cups. Serve immediately.
❖ Yield: 1½ dozen.

JINGLE BELL CHOCOLATE PRETZELS

1 cup Hershey's semi-
   sweet chocolate chips
⅔ cup Hershey's vanilla
   milk chips
1 tablespoon shortening
24 (about) salted or
   unsalted 2-by-3-inch
   pretzels

⅓ cup Hershey's vanilla
   milk chips
½ teaspoon
   shortening

❖ Combine first 3 ingredients
in medium glass bowl.
❖ Microwave on High for 1
minute; stir. Microwave for 1 to 2
minutes longer or until chips are melted
and smooth, whisking every 30 seconds.
❖ Dip each pretzel into chocolate
mixture with fork, tapping to
remove excess. Place on tray lined
with waxed paper.
❖ Combine ⅓ cup vanilla milk
chips and ½ teaspoon
shortening in small glass bowl.
❖ Microwave on High for 15 to 30
seconds or until chips are melted and
smooth when stirred with wire whisk.
❖ Drizzle mixture across pretzels using tines
of fork. Chill until coating is set. Store in airtight
container in cool, dry place.
❖ Yield: 2 dozen.

Double the pleasure with two gifts in one—homemade
goodies in delightful reusable containers.

CURRIED SNACK MIX

2 (6-ounce) packages corn chips	1/2 to 1 teaspoon garlic salt
1 quart popped popcorn	1 clove of garlic, crushed
1 (8-ounce) package pretzels	1 teaspoon salt
1 (8-ounce) package puffed corn snack	1 to 1 1/2 teaspoons curry powder
1 cup pecan halves	1/2 cup melted butter or margarine

❖ Preheat oven to 250 degrees.
❖ Place corn chips, popcorn, pretzels, puffed corn snack and pecans in large roasting pan.
❖ Mix garlic salt, garlic, salt, curry powder and melted butter in bowl. Pour over popcorn mixture; toss well.
❖ Bake for 1 hour, stirring occasionally. Store in airtight container.
❖ Yield: 12 cups.

HOLIDAY SNACKERS

1 cup corn oil	1 (16-ounce) package thin wheat crackers
2 teaspoons dillweed	
2 teaspoons lemon pepper	1 (12-ounce) package pretzels
1 envelope ranch salad dressing mix	
1 (16-ounce) package cheese crackers	

❖ Combine oil, seasonings and salad dressing mix in small bowl; mix well.
❖ Pour over mixture of crackers and pretzels in large glass bowl; toss to coat well.
❖ Microwave on High for 5 minutes, stirring after 3 minutes. Cool to room temperature. Store in airtight container.
❖ Yield: 12 cups.

SECONDS-FROM-A-SNACK

16 ounces "M & M's" Plain Chocolate Candies	1 (8-ounce) package pretzel sticks
16 ounces "M & M's" Peanut Chocolate Candies	1 (12-ounce) package Chex cereal
4 ounces sesame sticks	8 ounces white yogurt-covered small pretzels
4 ounces raisins	

❖ Combine candies, sesame sticks, raisins, pretzel sticks, cereal and yogurt-covered pretzels in bowl; mix well.
❖ Spoon into airtight container.
❖ Yield: 13 cups.

CHOCOLATE PIZZAS

2 cups semisweet chocolate chips	1 (6-ounce) jar red maraschino cherries, drained, cut into halves
1 pound white almond bark	
2 cups miniature marshmallows	3 tablespoons chopped green maraschino cherries
2 cups crisp rice cereal	1/3 cup flaked coconut
1 cup peanuts	1 teaspoon vegetable oil

❖ Combine chocolate chips and 14 ounces almond bark in 2-quart glass bowl. Microwave on High for 2 minutes; stir.
❖ Microwave for 1 to 2 minutes longer or until smooth, stirring every 30 seconds. Stir in marshmallows, cereal and peanuts.
❖ Spoon into greased 12-inch pizza pan. Top with cherries; sprinkle with coconut.
❖ Microwave remaining 2 ounces almond bark with oil in 1-cup measure for 1 minute; stir. Microwave for 30 to 60 seconds longer or until melted; drizzle over pizza.
❖ May shape mixture into 6 small circles for individual pizzas.
❖ Yield: 1 large or 6 small pizzas.

PUMPKIN PRALINE CHEESECAKE

1/3 cup butter or margarine, softened	1 teaspoon cinnamon
	1/4 teaspoon ginger
1/3 cup sugar	1/4 teaspoon nutmeg
1 egg	Salt to taste
1 1/4 cups all-purpose flour	1 cup packed light brown sugar
16 ounces cream cheese, softened	
	1/2 cup self-rising flour
3/4 cup sugar	1 cup chopped pecans
1 (16-ounce) can pumpkin	1/4 cup butter or margarine
2 eggs	

❖ Preheat oven to 400 degrees.
❖ Combine first 4 ingredients in bowl; mix well. Press over bottom and halfway up side of 10-inch springform pan.
❖ Bake for 5 minutes. Reduce oven temperature to 350 degrees.
❖ Beat cream cheese and 3/4 cup sugar in large mixer bowl until light and fluffy. Add pumpkin, 2 eggs, cinnamon, ginger, nutmeg and salt; mix well. Spoon into crust.
❖ Mix brown sugar, self-rising flour and pecans in small bowl. Cut in 1/4 cup butter until crumbly. Sprinkle over cheesecake.
❖ Bake for 1 hour. Cool. Chill in refrigerator. Place on serving plate; remove side of pan.
❖ Yield: 12 servings.

Heavenly Light Cheesecake

3/4 cup graham cracker
  crumbs
2 tablespoons melted
  reduced-calorie
  margarine
15 ounces part-skim
  ricotta cheese
1 cup nonfat plain yogurt
1 cup sugar

2 tablespoons all-purpose
  flour
2 tablespoons lemon juice
8 ounces Neufchâtel
  cheese, softened
3/4 cup egg substitute
2 1/2 teaspoons vanilla
  extract

❖ Preheat oven to 325 degrees.
❖ Mix graham cracker crumbs and margarine in bowl. Press over bottom of 9-inch springform pan.
❖ Bake for 5 minutes. Cool to room temperature.
❖ Process ricotta cheese, yogurt, sugar, flour and lemon juice in blender until smooth.
❖ Beat Neufchâtel cheese in mixer bowl until light. Beat in egg substitute and vanilla.
❖ Add ricotta mixture gradually, mixing well. Spoon into crust. Place on baking sheet.
❖ Bake for 1 hour or until center is nearly set. Cool for 15 minutes. Loosen from side of pan with knife.
❖ Cool for 30 minutes longer. Place on serving plate; remove side of pan. Cool completely.
❖ Chill for 4 to 6 hours.
❖ Yield: 12 servings.

Margarita Cheesecake

1 1/4 cups finely crushed
  pretzels
1 tablespoon sugar
1/2 cup melted butter or
  margarine
16 ounces cream cheese,
  softened
1/2 cup sugar
2 envelopes Margarita mix

3 eggs
1 teaspoon grated lime
  rind
1/2 teaspoon vanilla extract
2 cups sour cream
1/4 cup sugar
1 tablespoon lime juice
1/2 teaspoon grated lime
  rind

❖ Preheat oven to 375 degrees.
❖ Mix pretzels, 1 tablespoon sugar and butter in bowl. Press over bottom and part of the way up the side of 9-inch springform pan.
❖ Bake for 6 minutes or until golden brown.
❖ Beat cream cheese in mixer bowl until fluffy. Add 1/2 cup sugar and Margarita mix; beat until light. Beat in eggs 1 at a time.
❖ Stir in 1 teaspoon lime rind and vanilla. Pour into crust.
❖ Bake for 25 to 30 minutes or until center is nearly set. Cool for 30 minutes.
❖ Increase oven temperature to 425 degrees.
❖ Combine sour cream, 1/4 cup sugar, lime juice and 1/2 teaspoon lime rind in bowl; mix well. Spread over cheesecake.

❖ Bake for 10 minutes. Cool on wire rack. Chill cheesecake overnight.
❖ Place on serving plate; remove side of pan. Garnish with lime slices.
❖ May use unsalted pretzels.
❖ Yield: 12 servings.

Austrian Strawberry Tart

1/2 cup sugar
1/2 cup cornstarch
1/2 teaspoon salt
4 cups milk
4 egg yolks, slightly
  beaten

2 teaspoons vanilla extract
Short Pastry Tart Shell
4 cups strawberry halves
1 cup strawberry jelly
1/4 teaspoon nutmeg
1/4 cup chopped pistachios

❖ Combine 1/2 cup sugar, cornstarch and 1/2 teaspoon salt in saucepan. Stir in milk and 4 egg yolks gradually.
❖ Bring to a boil over medium-low heat, stirring constantly. Boil for 1 minute; remove from heat.
❖ Stir in vanilla. Spoon into small bowl; cover surface directly with plastic wrap. Chill for 1 hour.
❖ Spread chilled custard in Short Pastry Tart Shell; arrange strawberry halves on custard.
❖ Melt jelly in small saucepan. Stir in nutmeg. Cook for 2 to 3 minutes or until bubbly.
❖ Spoon jelly mixture over strawberries; sprinkle pistachios around edge. Chill for 1 hour. Remove to serving plate.
❖ Yield: one 9-inch tart.

Short Pastry Tart Shell

1 cup all-purpose flour
1 tablespoon sugar
1/4 teaspoon salt
1/3 cup butter or
  margarine

1 egg yolk
3 tablespoons ice water

❖ Preheat oven to 400 degrees.
❖ Mix flour, 1 tablespoon sugar and 1/4 teaspoon salt in bowl. Cut in butter until crumbly.
❖ Beat 1 egg yolk with ice water in small bowl. Add to flour mixture; mix to form ball.
❖ Roll into 12-inch circle on lightly floured surface; fit into 9-inch tart pan with removable bottom. Pierce bottom and side with fork. Line with waxed paper; fill with dried beans or rice.
❖ Bake for 15 minutes or until light brown. Remove beans and waxed paper. Bake for 5 minutes longer. Cool on wire rack.
❖ Yield: one 9-inch tart shell.

A Season for Giving

Homemade Gifts

I did not like Buckley Waddell. I did not like him because he had a package under the tree. I had watched while my mother wrapped his present, and I said, "Buckley oughta get stuff from his own family."

My mother tore off pieces of red Christmas tape and said, "Buckley's family lives in North Carolina, and they don't have anything. You are ten years old. Seems to me you ought to be old enough to understand that."

All I understood was that Buckley Waddell had lived in our house for three months. All I understood was that, because Buckley took his shower first every morning, when my turn came, the hot water was gone.

My mother made me help her tie the red Christmas ribbon into a bow. I said, "Does this mean Buckley has to give us stuff too?"

Every night Buckley and I did our homework, stretched out beside the Christmas tree. There were already boxes with my name on them. On Christmas morning, I knew, there would be a Ben Hur set and a B.B. gun and a transistor radio. As we studied, however, Buckley stayed close to his gift so that he could watch it, carefully balanced on top of the pile.

On Christmas morning, when we opened our presents, I got my Ben Hur set and my B.B. gun. Buckley, meanwhile, got a pair of brown socks and a clip-on tie. He laid them on his lap and quietly smoothed them with the palm of his hand. Then he said, "I got something for you too."

In a flash of flannel pajamas, he reached behind the sofa and pulled out a box wrapped in Santa paper. My mother opened the package and said, "Buckley, this is lovely, but how . . . ?" She held up a box of chocolate-covered cherries; my father reached out and shook Buckley's hand.

In a rattle of foil and tissue, I shuffled through the piles of wrapping paper and pulled out my one last unopened package. I held it out to Buckley and said, "Hey, look, Buckley, here's something for you."

Buckley took the box from me and unwrapped it carefully, without even tearing the paper. "Gee," he said, "a transistor radio!"

At bedtime, my father said, "Son, your mother and I are very proud of you." Later, when the house was dark, though, Buckley sneaked into my room. All through the night we took turns using the earphone. Together, we played the radio until the batteries were dead.

The heart of Christmas giving comes from the kitchen with Gingerbread Man Basket, Surprise Gift Bags, and Gingerbread Man Spiced Mug Mats, page 73.

Potpourri-Filled Moss Basket

*I*f someone you know appreciates unusual baskets and luscious scents, this is just the gift to make. An inexpensive basket is transformed into an elegant decoration and filled with lavender buds and cedar chips. Drops of oil from time to time will keep the potpourri fragrant, but when it's ready to toss, the basket can go on to hold Christmas cards, fire starter cones, or a new batch of potpourri.

MATERIALS FOR BASKET

1 (10-by-15-inch) basket
Brown fabric dye, if desired
Grapevines, if desired
Hot glue gun
2 bags sheet sphagnum moss
Approximately 75 small pine cones

DIRECTIONS

❖ Antique a light, unfinished basket, if desired, by dipping it in a solution of brown fabric dye. Soak vines in hot water to soften if they are not freshly cut and pliable. Wrap vines around handle of basket and glue, if necessary, on inside of basket. Let dry.
❖ Trim a piece of moss to fit an area of basket. Swirl hot glue on basket and press moss in place. Hot glue edges of moss to secure. Continue process to cover sides and bottom of basket, leaving rim uncovered.
❖ Cover inside of basket with moss from just below rim to approximately 2 inches down sides.
❖ Hot glue pine cones over rim of basket, gluing adjoining cones together occasionally for stability.
❖ Use small pieces of moss to fill in any gaps in cones and to cover any visible glue.

MATERIALS FOR POTPOURRI

4$\frac{1}{2}$ cups cedar chips and shavings
1 cup lavender buds
Lavender and cedar essential oils, if desired
Bay leaves

DIRECTIONS

❖ Mix cedar and lavender together, adding a few drops of essential oils, if desired.

❖ Arrange in basket, making sure some lavender buds are visible on top. Scatter a handful of bay leaves over top.
❖ Add additional oil to refresh scent after it has faded, usually several months to a year later.

Leather-Look Bill Holder

*H*ere's a gift little ones can make for Dad that's both inexpensive and easy. You just recycle old napkin or stationery holders picked up at yard sales and flea markets into attractive bill holders.

MATERIALS

Plastic, metal, or wooden napkin holder or stationery holder
Wide masking tape
Cloth rag
Brown shoe polish

DIRECTIONS

❖ Clean and dry holder.
❖ Tear masking tape into irregular pieces, and apply them randomly over entire holder.
❖ Overlap tape pieces, and add as many layers as needed to cover the design and color of the original holder.
❖ Use rag to apply a heavy coat of shoe polish to holder. Wipe off excess and let dry.

Kindling Bucket

*W*arm the heart of a special man on your list with a stylishly painted bucket filled with kindling and fireplace matches. If you're lucky, you'll be invited to sit by the fireside and enjoy the results.

MATERIALS

Metal bucket, 12-inch diameter at rim
Fleck Stone™ spray paint, Serpentine Marble
6 yards (1$\frac{3}{8}$-inch wide) plaid ribbon
2 long twist ties
3 yards gold metallic twist ribbon
Kindling or fat pine
2 boxes of fireplace matches

MERRY CHRISTMAS HARRY

FROM BOBBY

TO DAD

DIRECTIONS FOR KINDLING BUCKET
(continued from page 46)

- ❖ Follow paint manufacturer's directions to spray paint outside of bucket and handle with Fleck Stone™ paint. Let dry.
- ❖ Cut plaid ribbon in half. Hold 2 pieces together as one, and make a multi-looped bow. Cinch with a twist tie. Make a multi-looped bow with gold ribbon, and gather with a twist tie.
- ❖ Attach gold bow to handle with ends of tie, leaving 1½ inches of twist tie at end. Attach plaid bow over it with ends of tie.
- ❖ Fill with kindling or fat pine and matches.

Lace Jewelry Pouch

If someone you know travels frequently, this frilly little jewelry pouch would be a thoughtful present. It's a perfect size to tuck into a purse for security in transit, and then discreetly slip into a corner of a dresser drawer.

MATERIALS

1 (7-by-12-inch) ecru lace piece
1 (7-by-12-inch) burgundy faille piece
Ecru thread
23 inches (3-inch wide) ecru lace
8½ inches (3/8-inch wide) ecru satin ribbon

DIRECTIONS

- ❖ Position 7-by-12-inch lace piece over faille piece, and stitch with a ½-inch seam allowance, leaving an opening on 1 short end for turning. Trim seam to 1/8 inch, turn, and slip stitch closed.
- ❖ Run a gathering stitch along 1 edge of 3-inch wide lace, and gather to fit short end of fabric-and-lace piece. Machine-stitch lace to fabric-and-lace piece.
- ❖ Fold remaining short end to form 4¼-inch deep pocket. Pin in place. Fold lace-edged top flap over pocket, and mark position where lace begins on pocket. Open top flap and place satin ribbon piece over pocket at marked point, wrapping ends ¼ inch to inside. Topstitch along sides, securing ribbon in seam and stitching to lace edge.

Create heirlooms for those hard-to-buy-for women on your list with Lace Jewelry Pouch, Victorian Cross-Stitch Pillow, Fancy Neckwear, Scissors Keeper Doll, and Bunny Pin, pages 49 and 50.

Victorian Cross-Stitch Pillow

Rich burgundy moiré and delicate lace frame an inspirational cross-stitch design on this plump pillow. This is a present that will convey your affection clearly and dearly.

MATERIALS

1 (11-inch) square of 14-count ecru Aida cloth piece
1 (#24) embroidery needle
DMC® Embroidery Floss = 8m skeins (1 skein each):
#3354 Light Dusty Rose, #3350 Dark Dusty Rose,
#776 Medium Pink, #712 Cream, #3051 Dark Green,
#535 Ash Gray
2 (14½-inch square) burgundy moiré fabric pieces
28 inches (3/8-inch wide) ecru lace
1⅓ yards (2-inch wide) ecru lace
1 (12-inch) pillow form
See Patterns

DIRECTIONS

- ❖ Mark center of cross-stitch fabric both ways with long running stitch using needle and thread.
- ❖ Work cross-stitch according to chart and color key, beginning at intersection of arrows on chart to ensure proper placement of design on fabric.
- ❖ Each square on chart represents 1 fabric thread. Use 3 strands of floss for cross-stitch, 2 strands for border backstitch, and 1 strand for scroll outline, lettering, and Bible reference backstitch.
- ❖ Press finished work, and trim to a 7-inch square.
- ❖ Position stitchery in center of 1 moiré fabric piece. Position small ecru lace over edge of stitchery and machine-satin-stitch lace to stitchery and pillow front. Position wide lace 1 inch from edge of pillow front, mitering corners. Stitch to fabric along inner edge.
- ❖ Sew 2 moiré fabric pieces together with right sides facing with a ¼-inch seam allowance, leaving 12 inches in 1 side open. Turn.
- ❖ Insert pillow form, and center behind wide lace border. Check measurements and mark stitching line to enclose pillow. Remove pillow and topstitch front and back together along marked lines, leaving one end open for inserting pillow.
- ❖ Insert pillow, stitch remaining topstitched seam, and slip stitch end of pillow closed.

Fancy Neckwear

Here's a tie any teenage girl would love. Just intercept a man's tie on the way to the charity bin, and dress it up with lace, appliqués, and paint.

MATERIALS

Scrap of crocheted lace
1 man's tie
Fabric glue
Scrap of flower print fabric
Tulip™ Pearl Fabric Paint: Silver
Tulip™ Glitter Fabric Paint: Gold
Gemstone button

DIRECTIONS

❖ Wrap a strip of lace at an angle, approximately 4 inches from bottom of tie, and glue to front and back with fabric glue.
❖ Cut flowers from fabric scrap and position along tie as shown in photograph. Glue flowers in place with fabric glue.
❖ Outline flowers, and paint along details with fabric paint referring to photograph.
❖ Stitch on button for tie tack.
❖ Tie in half Windsor knot.

Scissors Keeper Doll

The tradition of scissors keepers can be traced to quilting bees, where it was necessary to keep your scissors separated from the other quilters'. This doll is also a pin cushion, and it would be a great gift for a needleworker or crafter.

MATERIALS

Small round paintbrush
Acrylic paints: Face Color, Brown, Black, Red
1 (approximately 1/2-inch diameter) 1 1/2-inch long smooth, small stick
Scrap of blue homespun fabric
Polyester stuffing
1 1/8 yards (1/4-inch wide) ecru satin ribbon
Scissors
Hot glue gun
Scrap of lace fabric
1 (3/8-inch diameter) pearl button

DIRECTIONS

❖ Paint stick face color. Let dry. Scrub brown paint over 1 end for hair. Paint black dot eyes and red dot mouth.
❖ Cut a 4 1/2-inch diameter circle from homespun fabric. Run a gathering stitch around edge and gather slightly. Fill with stuffing, insert stick, and cinch closed.
❖ Loop center of satin ribbon through handle of scissors. Hot glue ends to back of doll's head.
❖ Cut lace fabric piece to fit around neck for collar. Fold ends under and position on doll, hiding ends of ribbon. Glue in place.
❖ Sew button to front of collar.

Bunny Pin

This little fellow carries his heart in his hands—literally! Though he's made from the tiniest scraps of fabric, he's big on personality. Stitch him up, add a pin back, and present him to someone deserving.

MATERIALS

Scraps of tan cotton, wool plaid, and white cotton fabric
White thread
Polyester stuffing
1 (#24) embroidery needle
Black embroidery floss
Tan cotton thread
Pin back
Hot glue gun
See Patterns

DIRECTIONS

❖ Fold tan fabric in half.
❖ Transfer bunny pattern to folded tan fabric, and cut out 2 pieces. Transfer heart pattern to wool plaid and white cotton. Cut out.
❖ Sew heart pieces together with right sides facing and raw edges aligned. Cut a small slit in white heart, and turn through opening. Stuff lightly, and slip stitch closed using white thread.
❖ Embroider facial features on 1 bunny piece using black floss as indicated on pattern.
❖ Sew bunny pieces together with right sides facing and raw edges aligned, leaving bottom open for turning. Turn, and stuff lightly, working stuffing into ears and paws. Turn raw ends on bunny's bottom edge to inside.

❖ Position heart on front of bunny, referring to photo. Whipstitch bunny to heart along bunny's bottom edge, closing opening.
❖ Tie tan thread around arms to define paws. Bring arms around heart, referring to photograph, and tack in place.
❖ Glue pin back to back of bunny.

Fragrant Padded Hangers

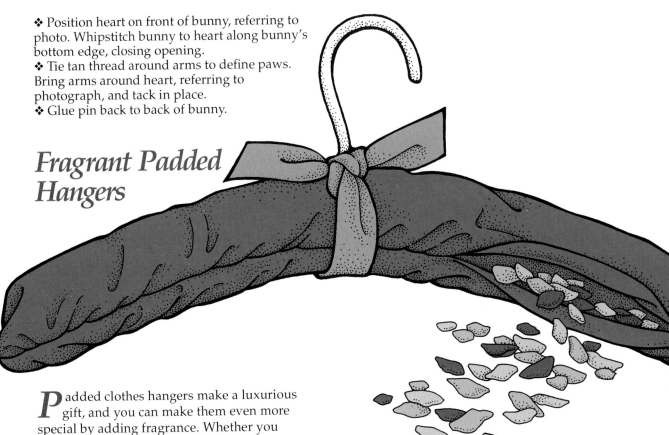

P added clothes hangers make a luxurious gift, and you can make them even more special by adding fragrance. Whether you make the hangers yourself or purchase them, just open the bottom seam, sprinkle in some lavender buds or other delicately-scented potpourri, and reclose the seam. Enclose a small sachet for drawers, and you have a gift perfect for dispelling winter stuffiness and making clothes smell as fresh as summer.

Herbal Moth Swags

L ong before we had high-tech ways to ward off moths, our grandmothers relied on natural materials. Cedar is still popular, but certain herbs also make an effective first line of defense. This moth chaser swag combines those herbs in a subtly beautiful package.

The basis for the swag is artemisia, or wormwood, whose lovely silver foliage dries into feathery strands. Here, 18- to 30-inch long stalks are gathered in a fan shape and tied tightly at the stems with twine. Overlaying them are 8- to 14-inch long stalks of dried garden sage, also fanned and then tied tightly at their stems to the

artemisia. Dried Mexican sage flowers, which hold their violet color, are then placed on top.

Covering the tied stalks is a sachet made from a delicate handkerchief. First the handkerchief is laundered and stiffly starched, then it is gathered with a basting stitch that runs around the fabric at the base of the lace. Fill with lavender flower buds, or make and use some of the potpourri mix featured on page 46.

Finally, the sachet is cinched tight and tied to the swag with pretty ribbon. If you are making it as a gift, you can choose ribbon to coordinate with its intended place of display.

These swags by themselves are probably not enough to protect fine woolens, but adorning a wardrobe or resting atop a cedar chest, moth chaser swags make a fragrant and lovely addition to the arsenal.

Redwork Pine Cone Pillowcases

The time-honored tradition of redwork embroidery finds fresh expression in these pine cone motif pillowcases. Stitch a set for someone special, and you'll have a treasure to be passed down through the family. Or, make a set for yourself to dress up a guest bedroom for the holidays.

MATERIALS

1 pair of white pillowcases
Tracing paper
Embroidery transfer pencil
Straight pins
2 skeins red embroidery floss
1 (#24) embroidery needle
See Patterns

DIRECTIONS

❖ Wash and dry pillowcases.
❖ Lay tracing paper over pattern. Trace firmly over outlines using an embroidery transfer pencil.
❖ Fold 1 pillowcase to find center of hemmed edge. Mark with straight pin. Fold again to locate and mark quarters with pins. Repeat with other pillowcase.
❖ Follow manufacturer's directions to transfer embroidery pencil lines to pillowcases. Repeat design 4 times across hemmed edge, centering it in marked off sections.
❖ Use 3 strands of floss to stitch design. Cone seed ends are worked in satin-stitch. Stem and pine needles are worked in outline stitch.
❖ Press finished embroidery.

Heart Ornament

It's amazing how many uses there are for a simple stuffed heart. Made from scraps left over after decorating a room, it becomes a coordinated accessory. You can hang it from a doorknob, furniture handle, bedpost, or even the Christmas tree. Made in multiples, it is a popular bazaar item. And if you add potpourri to the stuffing, it takes on double duty.

MATERIALS

Scraps of fabric
Polyester stuffing
4 (1/4-inch wide) 14-inch long satin ribbons in colors to match
See Patterns

DIRECTIONS

❖ Transfer pattern to fabric and cut out 2 hearts.
❖ Cut a 3/4-by-8-inch strip from fabric. Fold strip lengthwise, right sides facing, and stitch along long edge with a 1/4-inch seam allowance. Turn.
❖ Place heart pieces together with right sides facing, and place strip between pieces with loop at center and ends even with edges where indicated on pattern. Sew heart together, catching only loop ends in seam and leaving an opening for turning where indicated on pattern.
❖ Turn, stuff firmly, and slip stitch closed.
❖ Holding all ribbons as one, tie into a bow. Tack to top center of heart.

Stenciled Sheet Set

Whether it's a young couple who've recently set up house, a grandmother who needs to refresh her linen supply, or a college student with a small budget and big list, it seems as though there's always somebody who could use pretty sheets. These fit the bill and then some.

MATERIALS

White sheets and pillow cases
Stencils by Zula: 9104 Blueberries
Masking tape
Stenciling paint: Blue, Green, Barn Red
Paper plate or saucer
Stenciling brushes: 3/8 inch to 1/2 inch in diameter, 1 brush for each color
Paper towels

DIRECTIONS

❖ Prewash sheets to remove sizing, and iron.
❖ Refer to photograph for design placement, and follow directions for stenciling on page 61.

Your holiday guests will delight in Herbal Moth Swags, Redwork Pine Cone Pillowcases, Heart Ornament, and Stenciled Sheet Set, pages 51 and 52.

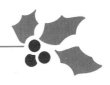

Fashion Flair for the Holidays

Every December the calendar fills with parties, coffees, and open houses. It seems there's always some occasion that calls for a bit of festive sparkle. Considering all the other ways the pocket book can be strained this time of year, a little ingenuity goes a long way in giving your wardrobe a fresh look without cutting another hole in the bottom of the purse. And manufacturers have responded to the call with wonderful new paints, adhesives, and other products. Here we offer some ideas for nighttime glamour that are lovely enough to call for the "one-for-her, one-for-me" rule of gift making. We hope you'll agree.

Sequined Sweatshirt and Spangled Accessories

If you're looking for some glitter for holiday parties, here's a shirt with coordinated accessories that you can throw together even at the last minute. Scribbled paint forms the shirt's tree, and masses of sequins form the flash. Combine the shirt with matching rippled-ribbon and sequin earrings and our sparkling multi-looped hair bow, and you'll sparkle both coming and going.

MATERIALS FOR EARRINGS

16 inches (1-inch wide) black grosgrain ribbon
Matching thread
Stiffy® fabric stiffener
Tulip™ Glitter Fabric Paint: Gold
Multi-colored sequins: 5mm, 8mm, and 12mm
Hot glue gun
Earring posts and backs or clips

DIRECTIONS

❖ Cut ribbon into two 8-inch pieces.

❖ Run a gathering stitch along long edge of 1 piece and gather into circle. Tie off.
❖ Stiffen according to manufacturer's directions, making sure raw ribbon ends are tucked to back and hidden in a fold. Let dry.
❖ Scribble-paint over front of earring, being sure to get paint down into folds of ribbon.
❖ Sprinkle sequins over still-wet paint, and press gently into paint. Let dry.
❖ Glue earring post or clip to earring. Repeat to make remaining earring.

MATERIALS FOR HAIR BOW

25 inches (1¹/2-inch wide) black grosgrain ribbon
Piece of string
Barrette back
Hot glue gun
2¹/4 inches (¹/2-inch wide) gold ribbon
Tulip™ Pearl Fabric Paint: Silver
Multi-colored sequins: 5mm, 8mm, and 12mm

DIRECTIONS

❖ Fold black ribbon into a bow with 4 loops, tie off with string, and trim string ends close to knot. Position barrette back on back of bow, and hot glue in place.
❖ Open barrette back. Wrap gold ribbon around center of bow over string and over barrette back, and glue. Close back.
❖ Place bow on a flat surface with barrette-side down, and fan bow loops and streamers into desired shape.
❖ Scribble-paint continuously over the loops and streamers.
❖ Sprinkle sequins over still-wet paint, and press gently into paint. Let dry.

MATERIALS FOR SHIRT

Dressmaker's chalk
Solid color sweatshirt
Tulip™ Pearl Fabric Paint: Gold, Ruby Red, Jade
Multi-colored sequins: 5mm, 8mm, and 12mm
See Patterns

- ❖ Use dressmaker's chalk to sketch tree pattern on front of shirt.
- ❖ Scribble-paint tree and trunk with gold, red and jade paint colors.
- ❖ Scatter sequins over still-wet paint on tree but not trunk, and press gently into paint. Let dry.
- ❖ Turn inside out, and hand wash in cold water. Lay flat to dry.

Ribbon Bows and Ornament Earrings

*L*ook no further than your wrapping supplies for the makings of these sparkling hair bows. Most card and gift shops carry a wide array of mylar garlands and ribbons, and even discount department stores feature a variety of Christmas motif ribbons. When you stock up at the after-Christmas sales, pick up a little extra to make ribbon bows for gifts and yourself! The ornament earrings are quickly painted wooden disks. You can put together a pair of earrings to match every outfit you have in almost no time!

MATERIALS FOR HAIR BOW

Beading wire
Barrette back
1 yard (1¹/2-inch wide) ribbon
1 yard mylar garland

DIRECTIONS

- ❖ Tie wire onto barrette back through a hole on 1 end.
- ❖ Cut end of ribbon at an angle. Lay garland over ribbon and begin forming loops, securing each loop to barrette back with wire.
- ❖ Cut last end at an angle, and tie off wire in remaining hole on barrette back when loops are desired fullness.

MATERIALS FOR EARRINGS

Medium flat paintbrush
Acrylic paint and paint pens in desired colors
Wooden disks (desired size)
Hot glue
Earring posts and backs or clips

DIRECTIONS

- ❖ Paint both sides of disks a solid color. Let dry.
- ❖ Paint scribbled lines and dots as shown in photograph. Let dry.
- ❖ Glue posts or clips on earrings.

Woven Chinese Box

*C*hinese boxes are great for transporting a whole lot more than egg rolls. That's why they've become available in so many bright colors at craft stores. This simple ribbon-weaving technique takes a good idea one step further by adding a satiny holiday touch.

MATERIALS

Needle nose pliers
Chinese box, red
Cardboard or smooth wood scrap piece
Scrap of graph paper
Craft glue
Metal straightedge
Craft knife
1 yard (3/8-inch wide) green satin ribbon
Transparent tape
16 inches (1/4-inch wide) red, green, and gold ribbon
See Patterns

DIRECTIONS

- ❖ Use needle nose pliers to carefully remove handle from box.
- ❖ Unfold box, and lay face down on cardboard or other surface suitable for cutting.
- ❖ Transfer tree design to graph paper. Cut out, and glue to inside of 1 end of box (not sides where handle attaches).
- ❖ Use straightedge and craft knife to cut along vertical lines on graph paper through box.
- ❖ Cut green ribbon into seven 5-inch-long pieces. Follow pattern, and begin weaving ribbon at top of design. Use 1 ribbon piece for each row. Shaded areas indicate where ribbon should pass under strip. Keep rows pushed together.
- ❖ Trim excess ribbon from ends, pull smoothly across box, and starting at 1 end, secure with transparent tape all along inside of box.
- ❖ Refold box, and reattach handle with pliers.
- ❖ Loop 16 inches ribbon around middle of handles, and tie in a bow.

Fabulous Fabric-Covered Boxes

Cover simple paper shapes with fabric, and you have keepsake containers with style. These bright boxes and envelope are a great way to package gifts small and large.

MATERIALS

Butcher paper for Circular Box
Poster board for Star Box and Envelope
Scraps of cotton fabrics:
  2 (16-inch diameter) circles for Circular Box
  1 (14-by-20-inch) piece for Envelope
  1 (10-by-18-inch) piece for Star Box
Spray mounting adhesive
Clear drying craft glue
Craft knife
Fabric ravel preventer, if desired
Red fabric paint for Star Box
Hole punch
1 yard red cord for Circular Box
See Patterns

DIRECTIONS

❖ Transfer patterns to butcher paper or poster board as directed, and cut out.
❖ Lay fabric on a flat surface. Spray 1 side of paper or poster board with mounting adhesive, and outline edges with craft glue. Lay glue side on fabric, and smooth any wrinkles with your fingers. Let dry.
❖ For Circular Box only, repeat process to cover other side with fabric.
❖ Trim fabric to edges of paper or poster board. Apply ravel preventer to fabric edges, if needed.
❖ For Star Box, outline star with red paint.
❖ For Circular Box, use hole punch to punch holes as indicated on pattern. Thread cord through holes, pulling to cinch top, and shape box as shown in photograph. Tie cord in bow.
❖ Fold Envelope and Star Box as indicated on pattern. Secure bottom of Star Box with craft glue.

Recycled and reusable gift packages make a "green" Christmas with Woven Chinese Box, Laced Gift-Wrap Envelope, Crackle Finish Gift Wrapping Paper, and Fabulous Fabric-Covered Boxes, pages 57 and 59.

Laced Gift-Wrap Envelope

If you are looking for a way to freshen up that yearly gift of money or just want a catchy way to wrap any small present, this quick gift envelope is the way to go. Clear adhesive paper makes the paper sturdy, and satiny laced ribbon gives it polish.

MATERIALS

2 (4-by-12-inch) clear adhesive shelf paper pieces
1 (4-by-12-inch) gift-wrap piece
Hole punch
2 (1/4-inch wide) 18-inch long ribbon pieces
Tapestry or yarn needle

DIRECTIONS

❖ Peel backing off adhesive paper, and carefully apply 1 piece to front and 1 piece to back of gift-wrap. Smooth bubbles.
❖ Fold wrap in thirds and crease. Fold corners of flap to form a point. Cut along fold lines.
❖ Mark points for holes 1/2 inch apart beginning at bottom corner of envelope. Adjust marked points, if necessary, to position holes at corners and point of flap.
❖ Punch holes with hole punch.
❖ Tie end of 1 ribbon piece on inside of bottom right-hand corner. Thread other end through needle and lace front and back together. Continue down side of flap to end at point. Repeat for other side. Tie ribbon ends in bow at point.

Crackle Finish Gift Wrapping Paper

If you have gloss-coated wrapping paper that you'd like to jazz up or if you have some that has gotten crunched in the closet, give it a tinted crackle finish. Just wad up the paper to form a web of cracks over the surface. Flatten paper out, and paint using a diluted paint mixture or fabric dye over the entire surface on the right side. Only the cracks in the paper will take the color. Allow paper to dry flat. Iron paper on the wrong side with a warm iron if you need to flatten it further.

Stenciled Satin Ribbon

*B*eautiful ribbon adds an elegant touch to gift-wrap, handmade garments, and craft projects, but fine ribbon can be very expensive. Here's a way to take plain white satin ribbon and create designer-quality trim. Use it to accent the gift box of your favorite craftsperson—someone who will fully appreciate the ribbon's beauty and versatility.

MATERIALS

3 yards (7/8-inch wide) white satin ribbon
Stencils by Zula: MD34 Hearts and Tulips
Masking tape
Stenciling paint: Dark Rose and Green
Paper plate or saucer
Stenciling brushes: 3/8 inch to 1/2 inch in diameter,
    1 brush for each color
Paper towels

DIRECTIONS

❖ Tape ribbon securely to a rigid surface.
❖ Follow directions for stenciling at right.

Stenciled Child's Sneakers

*P*lain white sneakers take on personality when they're decorated with quick and easy stenciled designs. Here we've used designs with a Native American angle in rose and teal, but other shades will just as easily coordinate with today's wardrobes. Try bright aqua with orange or even red and green for the holidays. Add pony beads in your favorite coordinating colors on the laces, and you'll have a gift any little girl will love.

MATERIALS

Washable fabric marker
White sneakers
Stencils by Zula: MD02 Basket and Border
Masking tape
Stenciling paint: Rose and Teal
Paper plate or saucer
Stenciling brushes: 3/8 inch to 1/2 inch in diameter,
    1 brush for each color
Paper towels
Pony beads to match paint

DIRECTIONS

❖ Use marker to mark positions on top, toe, and heel of shoes for design placement.
❖ Follow directions for stenciling below.
❖ Remove laces. Thread pony beads onto center of laces and relace shoes.

DIRECTIONS FOR STENCILING

❖ Place stencil in position and tape in place with masking tape.
❖ Review paint manufacturer's instructions. Place a small amount of paint on a paper plate or saucer.
❖ Dip tip of brush into paint. Wipe off excess on a paper towel until brush is "dry" and paint is light and smooth in appearance.
❖ Hold brush perpendicular to surface. Start at outside edge of cut-out area and work in a clockwise motion from edge across design area.
❖ Reverse to a counter-clockwise motion and continue building up color to desired shade.
❖ Align Print 2 if using more than 1 print, using register marks as a guide. Change to a clean brush. Stencil Print 2. Continue stenciling until the design is complete.
❖ Clean stencils and brushes gently following paint manufacturer's directions, and allow to air dry before using again.

Lacy Sweatshirt Jackets

*M*other and daughter will look lovely in these coordinated white sweatshirt jackets. While white-on-white is still a popular fashion statement, try other colors, particularly if you're making several of these for family members. Today's favorite color pairs include new-growth greens with cream, berry shades with gold, and rose with teal. Here, the lady's jacket has a large Battenburg lace collar, while the little girl's is embellished with pink satin ribbon roses.

MATERIALS FOR ADULT'S JACKET

1 (16-by-45-inch) Battenburg lace-edged fabric
    piece or table runner
Oversized white sweatshirt
3/4 yard (1/2-inch wide) white double fold bias tape
1/8 yard (36-inch wide) white cotton fabric
1 yard (18-inch wide) iron-on interfacing
5 (6-inch diameter) Battenburg lace doilies
6 (3/4-inch diameter) white buttons
See Patterns

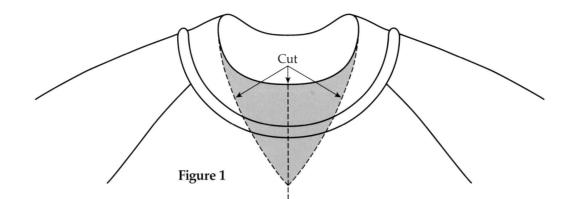

Cut

Figure 1

DIRECTIONS FOR ADULT'S JACKET
(continued from page 61)

❖ Transfer collar patterns to each end of lace piece and cut out.

❖ Cut sweatshirt open along center front. Cut neckline as indicated (Figure 1).

❖ Sew collar back to collar side pieces with right sides facing with a 1/4-inch seam allowance.

❖ Position collar on sweatshirt neckline with wrong side of collar on right side of sweatshirt and raw edges aligned. Open bias tape and pin over collar with right sides facing and raw edge of bias tape aligned with raw edges of collar and sweatshirt. Stitch with a 1/4-inch seam allowance. Refold tape to cover seam, then fold so that folded edge of tape is to inside of jacket. Stitch close to edge. Press collar.

❖ Cut 2 pieces of white fabric 4 inches wide and 1/2 inch longer than sweatshirt opening for placket. Back with interfacing. Zigzag stitch along both long edges.

❖ Cut 1 doily into thirds, and position along 1 placket piece so that outside edge of doily extends halfway across fabric. Zigzag stitch doily pieces to placket piece. This will be side with buttonholes.

❖ Position along sweatshirt opening with raw edges aligned, right sides facing, and ends extending 1/4 inch on top and bottom of jacket. Stitch with a 1/4-inch seam allowance.

❖ Fold placket in half with right sides facing, and stitch ends even with sweatshirt, following curve at neckline. Turn and press.

❖ Repeat to attach other placket.

❖ Position buttons along 1 side of placket, and mark positions on other side. Stitch buttonholes, and sew on buttons.

❖ Transfer pattern for cuffs to edge of remaining lace piece, and cut out.

❖ Cut ribbing cuffs off of sweatshirt sleeves. Open arm seams 6 inches from end.

❖ Turn 1 sleeve inside out. Position lace cuff on sweatshirt with right side of lace facing wrong side of shirt and raw edges aligned.

❖ Stitch together with a 1/4-inch seam allowance. Stitch arm seam back together. Fold cuff to outside of sleeve, and press.

❖ Repeat to attach other lace cuff.

❖ Position a doily just above bottom ribbing on center of each side of sweatshirt front. Position remaining doilies on each side of back just above ribbing. Zigzag stitch to shirt. Cut away sweatshirt material just inside stitching line on wrong side of sweatshirt beneath doilies.

MATERIALS FOR CHILD'S JACKET

White sweatshirt
1/8 yard (36-inch wide) white cotton
1 yard (18-inch wide) white interfacing
6 (1/2-inch diameter) pearl buttons
2 (3-by-6-inch) white Battenburg lace pieces
2 (1/2-inch) pink satin ribbon roses

DIRECTIONS

❖ Cut sweatshirt up center front.

❖ Cut two white cotton pieces 4 inches wide and 1/2 inch longer than sweatshirt opening for placket. Back with interfacing. Zigzag stitch along both long edges of each piece.

❖ Position 1 piece along sweatshirt opening with raw edges aligned, right sides facing, and ends extending 1/4 inch on each end. Stitch with a 1/4-inch seam allowance.

❖ Fold placket in half with right sides facing, and stitch ends even with sweatshirt. Turn and press.

❖ Repeat to attach other side.

❖ Position buttons along 1 side of placket, and mark positions on other side. Stitch buttonholes, and sew on buttons.

❖ Position lace on sweatshirt as shown in photograph. Zigzag stitch to shirt. Cut away sweatshirt material just inside stitching line on wrong side of sweatshirt beneath lace. Sew roses on center top edge of lace.

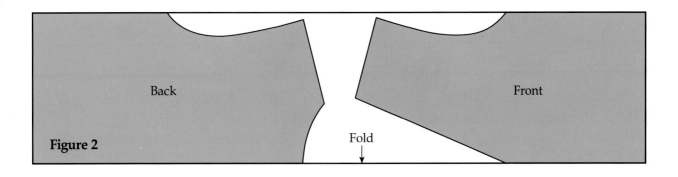

Figure 2 — Back / Front / Fold

Kitchen-Towel Child's Vest

Some of the brightest and sturdiest fabric is used to make kitchen towels, so why not take advantage of this to make a kitchen-towel child's vest? Perfect to combine with leotards, slacks, or even skirts, a towel vest would be just as festive in stripes or a Christmas pattern. (Be sure to hand-match bias tape!) This size-6 vest is not only quick and inexpensive, it's absolutely adorable.

MATERIALS

1 (18¹/₂-by-29-inch) green-and-white checked kitchen towel
Thread to match
1 package (¹/₂-inch wide) double-fold red bias tape
Red thread
Red embroidery floss to match bias tape
1 (#24) embroidery needle
See Patterns

DIRECTIONS

❖ Transfer patterns to towel, and cut out (Figure 2).
❖ Note: All seams are ⁵/₈-inch. All raw edges of towel should be finished to prevent raveling.
❖ Topstitch side seams by overlapping hemmed edges and carefully sewing along edge of each hemmed side of towel.
❖ Follow package instructions to attach bias tape to arm holes.
❖ Sew shoulder seams.
❖ Follow package instructions to attach bias tape to front opening edges and neck.
❖ Refer to photograph for placement of embroidered flowers in white squares of towel. Use a lazy daisy stitch to form flowers.

Christmas Memories Photo Mat

Some grandmother will win the bragging rights contest with this adorable photo mat setting off a child's Christmas picture. It combines stenciling with cross-stitch on perforated paper for a subtle mix of texture and color.

MATERIALS

Pencil
1 (8-by-10-inch) piece 14-count cream perforated paper
Stencil-Ease® Design: CR7 Christmas Tree Border
Stencils by Zula: 9180 Alphabet 2
Masking tape
Stenciling paint: Christmas Red, Green
Paper plate or saucer
Stenciling brushes: ³/₈ inch to ¹/₂ inch in diameter, 1 brush for each color
Paper towels
1 (#24) embroidery needle
Red and gold metallic embroidery floss
Craft knife
See Patterns

DIRECTIONS

❖ Use pencil to lightly transfer window outline to paper. Position tree overlapping upper left hand corner as indicated, and follow directions for stenciling on page 61.
❖ Stencil name, date, and bottom row of trees as indicated.
❖ Work cross-stitch according to chart and color key. Use 3 strands of red floss for cross-stitch and 2 strands of gold floss for stars on trees.
❖ Cut out window with craft knife, carefully cutting around tree in corner.
❖ Frame as desired.

Painted Santa Gift Bag

With hard-to-wrap gifts, it's easiest to use a gift bag. This one is so cute, the recipient will want to use it as a decoration in years to come. And if you need a larger bag, these dimensions and the Santa pattern will enlarge very nicely.

MATERIALS

1 (8³/₄-by-9³/₄-inch) piece of unbleached linen-weave cotton
Pinking shears
Paintbrushes: medium flat, small round
Acrylic paints: Red, Tan, White, Green, Black
Drill with ¹/₈-inch bit
Purchased ³/₄-inch high wooden heart and 1¹/₄-inch high wooden tree
14 inches jute
Craft glue
Toothpick
See Patterns

DIRECTIONS

❖ Cut along one 8³/₄-inch end of fabric with pinking shears.
❖ Fold fabric in half so that pinked ends form top, and stitch side and bottom seams with a ¹/₄-inch seam allowance. Turn.
❖ Transfer Santa pattern to bag 1 inch above bottom seam. Paint in the following order: red coat and hat; tan face, bag, and tree trunk; white beard, cuffs, and coat trim; green gloves and tree, and black eyes, belt, shoes, and arm outline.
❖ Wash brushes thoroughly when switching colors, and allow paint to dry between coats. Paint additional coats for complete coverage if necessary.
❖ Drill holes in top of wooden heart and tree pieces. Twirl ends of jute, and apply tiny bit of glue to hold points.
❖ Put drop of glue in holes of heart and tree with toothpick, and insert ends of jute. Let dry.
❖ Fill bag, and cinch around top with jute.

Simple stitches and splashes of color combine in Kitchen-Towel Child's Vest, Christmas Memories Photo Mat, and Painted Santa Gift Bag, pages 63 and 65.

Scotty Dog Hand Towel

No bones about it! This quick-stitch Scotty dog towel will make a gift both useful and merry. You can stitch several for a set or combine it with other kitchen goodies and food gifts.

MATERIALS

Charles Craft® cranberry Christmas plaid towel
1 (#24) embroidery needle
DMC® Embroidery Floss= 8m skein (1 skein): Black
4 inches (¹/₈-inch wide) green satin ribbon, tied into a bow and thread to match ribbon
See Patterns

DIRECTIONS

❖ Mark center of cross-stitch panel in towel both ways with long running stitch.
❖ Work cross-stitch according to chart, beginning at intersection of arrows on chart to ensure proper placement of design on fabric.
❖ Each square on chart represents 1 fabric thread. Use 2 strands of floss for cross-stitch and 1 strand for backstitch to outline design. Tack bow to neck.

Quilt-Inspired Cross-Stitch Gifts

Quilt motifs provide the theme for the designs decorating these cross-stitched hand towels and Mason jar lids. Present them in groups, along with some home-cooked goodies, and you'll have a gift whole families can enjoy.

MATERIALS FOR JAR LIDS

2 (5-inch square) pieces of 18-count white Aida cloth for holly and basket designs
1 (5-inch square) piece of 18-count ecru Aida cloth for leaf design
1 (#24) embroidery needle
DMC® Embroidery Floss = 8m skeins (1 skein each):
    #321 Red and #699 Green for holly
    #791 Blue and #742 Yellow for basket
    #869 Brown, #920 Rust, and #783 Mustard for leaves
Mason jar lid and ring for each design
Transparent tape
See Patterns

DIRECTIONS FOR JAR LIDS
(continued from page 65)

❖ For holly design, work cross-stitch according to chart, randomly cross-stitching design on white Aida cloth. Each square on chart represents 1 fabric thread. Use 2 strands of floss for cross-stitch and 1 strand for backstitch. Make French knots for holly berries.

❖ For basket design, work cross-stitch according to the chart. Use 1 strand of floss for cross-stitch and backstitch.

❖ For leaf design, work cross-stitch according to chart, randomly cross-stitching design on ecru Aida cloth. Each square on chart represents 1 fabric thread. Use 2 strands of floss for cross-stitch and 1 strand for backstitch.

❖ Center finished design on flat lid of Mason jar, and place ring over lid. Trim excess fabric, and tape design to lid to secure.

MATERIALS FOR PINWHEEL FINGERTIP TOWEL

Evergreen Charles Craft® fingertip towel
1 (#24) embroidery needle
DMC® Embroidery Floss = 8m skeins (1 skein each):
  #321 Red and #550 Purple
See Patterns

DIRECTIONS

❖ Mark center of cross-stitch panel both ways with long running stitch using needle and thread.

❖ Work cross-stitch according to chart and color key, beginning at intersection of arrows on chart to ensure proper placement of design on fabric.

❖ Each square on chart represents 1 fabric thread. Use 2 strands of floss for cross-stitch.

MATERIALS FOR LOG CABIN TERRY TOWEL

Ecru Charles Craft® terry towel
1 (#24) embroidery needle
DMC® Embroidery Floss = 8m skeins (1 skein each):
  #915 Magenta, #742 Yellow, #699 Green, and
  #791 Blue
See Patterns

DIRECTIONS

❖ Mark center of cross-stitch panel both ways with long running stitch using needle and thread.

❖ Work cross-stitch according to chart, beginning at intersection of arrows on chart to ensure proper placement of design on fabric.

❖ Each square on chart represents 1 fabric thread. Use 2 strands of floss for cross-stitch, and turn pattern for each square.

Snowy Woods Cookie Jar

Glass etching transforms this inexpensive glass jar into a snowy scene that is simply beautiful. It's a wonderful way to package your special Christmas goodies for cookie lovers.

MATERIALS

Glass storage jar with 4½-by-5½-inch sides
Clear adhesive shelf paper
Tracing paper
Graphite paper
Fine point permanent marker
Single edge razor blade
Medium flat paintbrush
Armor Etch™ glass etching cream
See Patterns

DIRECTIONS

❖ Cover sides of jar with 3 layers of adhesive paper, smoothing bubbles with each layer.

❖ Trace pattern onto tracing paper. Place graphite paper between jar and pattern, centering trees on opposite corners of jar. Trace over pattern to transfer image. Go over lines on adhesive paper with permanent marker.

❖ Cut through all layers of adhesive paper along pattern lines with razor blade. Remove trees and stripes. Be sure to remove all 3 layers of paper.

❖ Brush a heavy coat of etching cream over tree and line design, being careful not to get etching cream on exposed glass. Brush vertically and horizontally to ensure even coverage.

❖ Leave etching cream on for 3 to 5 minutes. Rinse under running water. Remove remaining adhesive paper.

Kitchen keepsakes make the ideal gift with Scotty Dog Hand Towel, Quilt-Inspired Cross-Stitch Gifts, and Snowy Woods Cookie Jar, pages 65 and 66.

The image we hold of the perfect Christmas usually looks, smells, and tastes a lot like our favorite recollections from childhood. Treasured clothes, decorations, and gifts are remembered long after other memories fade. Here we offer a sweater covered with furry bears that's perfect for picture-taking time. We also have wonderful picture frames to hold those captured moments, and happy ornaments to bring out year after year with a nostalgic smile. If you're a creative person, there can be few more rewarding challenges than creating memories that will shape the celebrations to come in the heart of your child. And that doesn't count how you'll feel in Decembers future.

Polar Bear Christmas Tree Sweater and Earmuffs

Furry white polar bears convert a plain purchased sweater into a holiday garment children will love wearing. Just combine it with the polar bear earmuffs, and you won't get an argument when you bundle your little one against the cold.

MATERIALS FOR EARMUFFS

Scrap of white fur
Embroidery scissors
Black embroidery floss
1 (#24) embroidery needle
Scrap of yellow cotton fabric
4 (5-inch diameter) circles of ecru cotton print
Thread to match fabrics
Craft stick
Washable fabric glue
1 pair of earmuff frames
Polyester stuffing
1 1/8 yards (1 1/2-inch wide) red grosgrain ribbon
See Patterns

DIRECTIONS

❖ Transfer bear pattern to wrong side of fur 1 time. Reverse pattern and transfer to fur 1 time.
❖ Cut out bears with embroidery scissors from the back of fur, keeping blades of scissors close to backing and making small cuts.
❖ Embroider faces of bears as indicated on pattern. For whiskers, stitch through face with black floss leaving a 3/4-inch tail of thread on front of face. Lock stitch on wrong side of fabric, bring floss back to front, and cut 2 pieces of floss into 1/2-inch long whiskers. Repeat to make 4 whiskers on each bear. For eyes, use 2 strands of floss to make French knots.
❖ Transfer ground pattern to yellow fabric and cut out 2. Position 1 yellow fabric piece on 1 ecru circle and machine-satin-stitch in place with yellow thread. Repeat for other circle.
❖ Refer to pattern to position bear on circle. Use craft stick to apply fabric glue to back of each bear. Gently press bears into place, and let dry.
❖ Run a gathering stitch around edge of bear circle. Position circle over outside of 1 side of metal earmuff frame with bear front centered on outside. Gather tightly on inside of frame, and baste gathered edge to inside of earmuff frame.
❖ Place a small amount of stuffing inside earmuff for padding. Turn raw edge of 1 circle piece under to fit over padding and opening on inside of earmuff, and slip stitch in place. Repeat to assemble and attach remaining earmuff.
❖ Cut red ribbon in half, and tie in bows over bear circles on headband.

MATERIALS FOR SWEATER

1 (10-inch) square white fur
Embroidery scissors
Black embroidery floss
1 (#24) embroidery needle
Child's sweater
Craft stick
Washable fabric glue
20 inches (2 1/4-inch wide) red grosgrain ribbon
Red thread
See Patterns

DIRECTIONS FOR SWEATER
(continued from page 68)

❖ Transfer pattern for polar bear to wrong side of fur. Cut with embroidery scissors from the back of fur, keeping blades of scissors close to backing and making small cuts. Repeat to cut out 6 bears.
❖ Embroider faces of bears as indicated on pattern. For whiskers, stitch through face with black floss leaving a 3/4-inch tail of thread on front of face. Lock stitch on wrong side of fabric, bring floss back to front, and cut 2 pieces of floss into 1/2-inch long whiskers. Repeat to make 4 whiskers on each bear. For eyes, use 2 strands of floss to make French knots.
❖ Arrange bears on front of sweater in a tree shape, with 3 on bottom, 2 in middle, and 1 at top. Leave enough room at top of sweater for bow.
❖ Use craft stick to apply fabric glue to back of each bear. Gently press each bear into place, and let dry.
❖ Tie ribbon in a bow, and tack to top of bear tree with matching thread.
❖ Hand wash in cold water, and lay flat to dry.

Fun Frames

*E*veryone loves pictures. Make these colorful craft foam frames for your favorite little tyke's room. Choose just the right photo to display, and watch little eyes go round with delight and fascination. This button frame is a wonderful way to display favorites from your button collection.

MATERIALS FOR FOAM FRAMES

Craft foam:
    yellow and blue for Stars and Moon design
    red, green, and blue for Christmas Tree design
Hole punch
Crafter's cement
2 (3 1/2-by-5-inch) clear acrylic frames
Super glue
See Patterns

DIRECTIONS

❖ Transfer patterns to craft foam, and cut out. Punch holes in red foam to make tree ornaments.
❖ Use crafter's cement to glue designs to frame, referring to photograph for placement. Use super glue to glue ornaments to tree.

MATERIALS FOR BUTTON FRAME

Crafter's cement
Assorted buttons
1 (5-by-7-inch) clear acrylic frame

DIRECTIONS

❖ If you are including a photo with this frame gift, place photo in frame to be sure button design complements photo.
❖ Glue buttons randomly around edge of frame, overlapping as desired. (Note: Cement allows buttons to be moved slightly before it sets.)

Egghead Santa

*W*e always knew he was smart, keeping all of those lists straight, but this egghead version of Santa proves it. It's perfect for small spaces you plan to decorate, and while you have the paints out, you'll want to make extras to give to other good eggs on your list.

MATERIALS

Paintbrushes: small flat, small round, liner
Acrylic paints: Red, Face Color, Black, White, Green
1 (1 3/4-inch diameter) wooden egg
Semigloss water-base varnish
See Patterns

DIRECTIONS

❖ Paint egg with 2 coats of red paint, allowing paint to dry after each coat.
❖ Paint details for face, hair, beard, and holly sprig as indicated on pattern. For overlapping details, allow paint to dry between coats.
❖ Seal with varnish.

Mr. and Mrs. Reindeer

*W*ho can resist this quirky reindeer couple? Mr. Reindeer has a bright red jingle bell body, and Mrs. Reindeer has cinnamon stick legs that she primly crosses when seated. If you are making ornaments to give a child, these should be at the top of your list.

MATERIALS FOR MRS. REINDEER

Scraps of muslin fabric
Thread to match
Polyester stuffing
Black permanent fine point marker
Hot glue gun
1 (1/8-inch diameter) red bead
Red crayon
2 (2-inch long) twigs
Scrap of red Christmas print fabric
4 (2 1/2-inch long) cinnamon sticks
1 (#22) tapestry needle
White heavyweight thread
Scrap of green pindot fabric
See Patterns

DIRECTIONS

❖ Transfer patterns to muslin, and cut out 2 head pieces, 4 ear pieces, and 2 body pieces.
❖ Sew 2 ear pieces together, leaving open where indicated on pattern, and turn. Repeat to make remaining ear.
❖ Refer to photograph to fold top raw edge of ears down 1/8 inch from bottom. Tack in place.
❖ Position ears on 1 head piece where indicated on pattern, with raw edges aligned and ears pointing to inside. Place head pieces together with raw edges aligned, and stitch, leaving an opening at top.
❖ Turn, stuff firmly, and slip stitch closed. Side where ears are cupped will become the face.
❖ Referring to pattern and photograph, make black dot eyes, glue on bead nose, and rouge cheeks and ears with red crayon.
❖ Snip tiny holes in back of head just behind seam line, and insert twig antlers, securing antlers with glue.
❖ Cut a 1-by-1 1/2-inch piece from red Christmas print fabric for bow. Run a 1-inch gathering stitch down middle parallel with short ends, cinch tightly, and tie off. Glue bow to top of head over seam line.
❖ Stitch 2 body pieces together, leaving bottom open as indicated, and turn. Turn bottom edge under 1/4 inch, and run a gathering stitch along edge. Stuff firmly, gather thread tightly, and tie off.
❖ Cut a 3 1/2-by-12-inch piece of red Christmas print fabric for dress. Hem both short sides and 1 long side with a 1/4-inch seam allowance. Run a gathering stitch along remaining long side, and gather to fit around top of body. Overlap back seams, and tack to top of body at the top back of dress.
❖ Gently push a hole through 1 end of a cinnamon stick with needle.

❖ Stitch white thread through stick, stitch through dress and body at top of dress, and run back through cinnamon stick a second time.
❖ Pull stick close to body, and knot thread on outside of stick. Repeat to attach other arm and to attach legs to each side of bottom of body.
❖ Cut a 2 1/4-by-4 1/4-inch piece from green pindot fabric for collar. Fringe edges slightly, and position over top of body with 1 1/2 inches draping over front and 1 3/4 inches, over back. Glue to dress at bottom center of front and back.
❖ Glue head over collar, referring to photograph.
❖ Stitch a 12-inch length of white thread through top back of reindeer, and knot for hanger.

MATERIALS FOR MR. REINDEER

Scraps of muslin fabric
Thread to match
Polyester stuffing
Black permanent fine point marker
Hot glue gun
1 (1/8-inch diameter) red bead
Red crayon
Scrap of blonde mini-curl Curly Hair®
2 (3-inch long) twigs
7 1/2 inches wired artificial greenery
1 (2 1/2-inch diameter) red jingle bell
1/2-by-8-inch plaid fabric scrap
12 inches heavyweight red thread
See Patterns

DIRECTIONS

❖ Transfer patterns to muslin, and cut out 2 head pieces, 2 ear pieces, and 8 leg pieces.
❖ Sew head pieces, leaving an opening on top for turning. Turn, stuff firmly with polyester stuffing, and slip stitch closed.
❖ Sew ear pieces together, leaving an opening in center for turning. Turn and slip stitch closed. Fold each ear piece in half lengthwise, and attach to top of head with a stitch in center, forming a small cup shape.
❖ Referring to pattern and photograph, make black dot eyes, glue on bead nose, and rouge cheeks and ears with red crayon.
❖ Glue hair in front of ears.
❖ Snip 2 tiny holes in back of head below ears, and insert twig antlers, securing with glue.
❖ Make wreath with greenery piece. Position between head and bell as shown in photograph. Glue head to bell through wreath. Tie the fabric strip in a bow, and glue to the wreath below reindeer's chin.
❖ Sew 2 leg pieces together, leaving top open. Turn, stuff firmly, and tie knot in top of leg.

- ❖ Repeat to make other 3 legs.
- ❖ Push knots through openings in bell, and slide down to bottom of slits. Hot glue in place.
- ❖ Loop 12-inch piece of red thread through bell's top loop, and knot for hanger.

Gingerbread Man Basket

Waving gaily from a bountiful basket, our gingerbread man carries the holiday theme to a keepsake decoration. By brushing a light glaze of sealer over him, he's preserved in all his glistening goodness.

MATERIALS

1 (15½-by-15-inch) red plaid fabric piece
20 inches jute
1 (4-by-5-inch) basket with handle
Clear spray varnish
1 (5-inch high) gingerbread man cookie
Hot glue gun
Several sprigs dried white statice
1 (2-inch diameter) grapevine wreath
2 (5-inch long) cinnamon sticks
Spanish moss
2 nuts
2 dried apple slices

DIRECTIONS

- ❖ Rip a ½-inch strip from fabric to form a 15-inch square and a ½-by-15-inch strip.
- ❖ Cut jute into two 10-inch long pieces.
- ❖ Hem square, arrange in basket, and tie with jute as shown in photograph.
- ❖ Spray a coat of varnish on gingerbread man, and let dry.
- ❖ Hot glue bunches of statice to 3 corners of basket as shown in photograph.
- ❖ Tie rag strip around top of wreath, and tie in bow. Trim ends to desired length.
- ❖ Glue wreath to cinnamon sticks so that top of wreath is about 1½ inches from end of sticks.
- ❖ Position gingerbread man, cinnamon sticks, and wreath in back of basket as shown in photograph.
- ❖ Glue gingerbread man and cinnamon sticks to bottom and back of basket.
- ❖ Place a layer of glue on bottom of basket, and fill with Spanish moss to rim.
- ❖ Glue nuts in front of wreath and apple slices in front of gingerbread man.

Surprise Gift Bags

It seems as though there are always lots of little presents to pull together at Christmas—the list keeps growing to include teachers, babysitters, children's friends, neighbors, and co-workers. Unfortunately, time and money can run short. Here are three versions of a simple cloth gift bag that will fit many needs.

The small bag is filled with potpourri and rolled over a twig, becoming a charming sachet. The medium bag is bursting with peppermint candies and rolled over a candy cane. And the large bag contains a dry soup mix. It's rolled over a wooden spoon. If your recipe isn't too precious to divulge, you can also attach a recipe card.

MATERIALS

Pinking shears
Fabric scraps:
(Note: Cut to size with pinking shears.)
   3½-by-12-inch strip for small bag
   4-by-15-inch strip for medium bag
   5-by-18-inch strip for large bag
Twig, candy cane, wooden spoon
Cord, ribbon, or yarn:
   12 inches for small bag
   18 inches for medium and large bags

DIRECTIONS

- ❖ Fold strip in half with right sides facing and short ends together. Stitch side seams with a ¼-inch seam allowance. Turn.
- ❖ Fill bag as desired, ¼ to ⅓ full. Roll top of bag over twig, candy cane or spoon. Tie ribbon around bag, and knot ends to secure.

Gingerbread Man Spiced Mug Mats

Rest a hot mug on this cheerful little fellow, and you'll release the delicious aroma of cloves. That's because these mats have whole cloves tucked between layers of batting. They're a wonderful gift for that person you tell all your secrets to over a cup of coffee or tea.

MATERIALS FOR
GINGERBREAD MAN SPICED MUG MATS

1 (6-inch) square of linen-weave cotton fabric
Paintbrushes: medium flat, small round
Acrylic paints: Brown, Brick Red, Green, White
2 (5-inch) squares of thin quilt batting
1 (6-inch) square of red Christmas print fabric
Whole cloves
See Patterns

DIRECTIONS

❖ Transfer pattern to linen-weave fabric.
❖ Paint gingerbread man with thin coat of brown paint. Paint red berries and green holly leaves. Paint white details and red heart on gingerbread man. Use a clean brush for each color, and allow paint to dry between coats.
❖ Position batting pieces in center of wrong side of both fabric squares.
❖ Place backing piece right side down, and sprinkle cloves over batting. Wrap fabric edges to inside over batting, and pin on fabric side.
❖ Wrap fabric over batting on front piece, and pin to backing piece. Topstitch front and back pieces together 1/4 inch from edges.

Instant Snowman Kit

Help some deserving snow sculptor win the neighborhood snowman competition with this wonderful instant snowman kit. All that's needed to complete the ensemble are the scarf, hat—and snow!

MATERIALS

42 inches (1/8-inch diameter) dowel
Sculpey III™ modeling compound, 1 package each:
   Orange, Black, Tan
Drinking straw
Craft glue
1 (4-by-6-inch) piece white cardstock
Black fine point permanent marker
See Patterns

DIRECTIONS

❖ Cut dowel into ten 3-inch long pieces and two 6-inch long pieces.
❖ Mold all of orange modeling compound into a carrot shape for nose. Flatten large end, and insert a 6-inch dowel into it.

❖ Make eyes and buttons by molding five 1-inch diameter balls from black modeling compound. Flatten into irregularly shaped disks, and insert a 3-inch dowel into each of them.
❖ Make mouth by molding five 3/4-inch diameter balls from black modeling compound. Flatten into irregularly shaped disks, and insert a 3-inch dowel into each of them.
❖ Make corncob pipe by molding a 2-inch diameter ball from tan modeling compound. Roll ball into an oblong shape, and flatten ends to form bowl of pipe. Insert remaining 6-inch dowel into 1 side of bowl. Press end of drinking straw lightly into bowl to make corncob pattern.
❖ Bake modeling compound according to manufacturer's directions.
❖ Glue ends of dowels if needed.
❖ Transfer snowman kit diagram from patterns onto cardstock, and draw over lines with marker.

Kid's Christmas Cards

This coloring card is a perfect way to introduce a child to the pleasure of sending holiday greetings. Copy the pattern on plain white paper (two will fit sideways on an 8½-by-11-inch sheet), set up a table with crayons, markers and scissors, and stand back. Once the coloring is completed, fan-fold the cards and send them off!

Kitty and Puppy Pocket Pals

Adorable little pocket pals go everywhere with their owners. If you know a child who could use the extra company, stitch up some of these little fellows.

MATERIALS

Scraps of white, red print, and blue print cotton fabric
Polyester stuffing
Scrap of blue ribbon
Black fine point permanent marker
Craft glue
Purchased 1/4-inch eyes
See Patterns

SNOWMAN KIT
DIAGRAM

PIPE

EYE
NOSE
MOUTH

BUTTON

HO!
FROM
JAN

DIRECTIONS FOR KITTY AND PUPPY POCKET PALS (continued from page 74)

❖ Transfer body patterns to white fabric and cut out. Stitch body together leaving open where indicated for turning.
❖ Turn, stuff firmly, and slip stitch closed.
❖ Topstitch kitty's legs as indicated on pattern.
❖ Cut a 3½-by-6-inch piece of red print fabric for kitty's dress. Fold in half with right sides facing and short ends together, and stitch back seam with a ½-inch seam allowance. Hem 1 long edge with a ½-inch seam allowance. Cut 1-inch slashes at sides from remaining raw edge for arm holes. Turn raw edge ½ inch to wrong side, and stitch a gathering stitch along it. Slip over kitty, gather neck to fit, and tie off.
❖ Cut a 2⅝-by-4⅛-inch piece of blue print fabric for puppy's pants. Hem both long edges and sew back seam with ½-inch seam allowance. Place on puppy. Cut two 4-inch long pieces of ribbon. Position on puppy for suspenders, crossing in back. Tack to pants. Stitch through pants and body to define legs.
❖ Transfer facial features to kitty and puppy, and draw with permanent marker. Glue on eyes.
❖ Fold puppy's ears to front as indicated on pattern, and tack on inside to secure.

Stars-and-Stripes Denim Jacket and Cap

You'd pay a small fortune for a comparable denim jacket and cap if you bought them off the rack. But a few minutes with an iron and your scrap bag, and you'll have them for little more than their cost.

MATERIALS

Iron-on fabric adhesive
1 (16-inch) square of muslin
16-inch lengths of fabric ribbons in varying widths and coordinating colors and patterns
1 (16-inch) square of dark blue cotton fabric
Scrap of red fabric
Star nailheads
Hot glue gun
Denim jacket
2 yards (¼-inch wide) red satin ribbon
Red baseball cap
See Patterns

DIRECTIONS

❖ Fuse a 16-inch square of fabric adhesive to muslin following manufacturer's directions. Remove backing, and pin to ironing board cover, muslin side down.
❖ Lay 16-inch lengths of ribbon over fusible muslin fabric base, stretching tightly and pinning at ends to ironing board cover to secure. When base is completely covered, place a pressing cloth over ribbon, and fuse ribbon to fabric following manufacturer's directions. Allow to cool.
❖ Turn over, and fuse again from muslin side, pressing hard. Allow to cool completely.
❖ Transfer large star pattern to center of muslin side of fabric. Cut out. Transfer large star pattern to dark blue fabric. Cut out. Stitch ribbon star to blue star with ¼-inch seam allowance, with right sides facing. Clip seam to ⅛ inch.
❖ Make a 4½-inch slit in center of solid blue star, and turn right-side-out through slit.
❖ Transfer largest of smaller star patterns to muslin side of ribbon fabric 1 time and dark blue fabric 1 time. Transfer medium of smaller star patterns to ribbon fabric 2 times and dark blue fabric 2 times. Cut out.
❖ Transfer smallest heart pattern to solid red fabric scrap and to dark blue fabric. Cut out.
❖ Repeat above procedure to back stars with dark blue fabric. Attach star nailheads to stars as desired.
❖ Hot glue small red star to large ribbon star, referring to photograph for placement.
❖ Cut two 6-inch pieces of ribbon, two 10-inch pieces of ribbon, and one 11-inch piece of ribbon for tails of large star. Cut 1 end of each ribbon piece in V.
❖ Position tails on wrong side of star at bottom, with longest piece in center and shortest on outsides referring to photograph for placement. Hot glue in place.
❖ Position large star on back of jacket so that top point is 2 or 3 inches from collar. Position largest and medium of smaller ribbon stars on lower sides of jacket.
❖ Swirl ¼-inch red ribbon loosely throughout design area, weaving it over and under stars. Hot glue ribbon and stars to jacket.
❖ Glue coordinating ribbon around collar and cuffs, slitting for buttonholes on cuffs.
❖ Add star studs as accents near stitching, on hem, and on front pockets. Glue remaining star to center of cap and attach nailheads to each side.
❖ Note: If hot glue doesn't completely attach appliqués and ribbon, a warm iron carefully used on the wrong side of jacket will partially remelt it for resecuring. Jacket should be hand washed in cold water.

Quilted Casserole Carrier

Potluck chefs will appreciate the convenience of this casserole carrier. It attractively and neatly organizes the dish and serving utensil while keeping food warm on the way to dinner.

MATERIALS

3/4 yard (45-inch wide) prequilted floral fabric
3/4 yard (45-inch wide) coordinated cotton backing fabric
Thread to match
1 yard (1-inch wide) ecru grosgrain ribbon
2 (14-inch long) 3/8-inch diameter dowels
Wooden spoon
See Patterns

DIRECTIONS

❖ Cut two 10-by-11-inch pieces from quilted fabric, and two 10-by-11-inch pieces from backing fabric for side flaps. Transfer pattern for rounding corners to 1 short side of all 4 pieces.
❖ Sew 1 quilted piece to 1 backing piece with right sides facing, matching long sides and side with rounded corners. Leave straight side open. Clip curves and turn. Repeat for other 2 pieces.
❖ Cut a 37½-by-15½-inch piece from quilted fabric and from backing fabric. Transfer pattern for ends to both ends of both pieces, and cut out.
❖ Position 1 side flap on center of long side of quilted piece with right sides facing and raw edges aligned. Pin in place. Position other flap on opposite side, overlapping first flap. Place backing fabric over quilted piece with right sides facing and raw edges aligned. Stitch together, leaving an opening for turning beside 1 flap. Turn, and slip stitch closed.
❖ Fold ends of carrier 1 inch to wrong side, and stitch in place. Topstitch 1/8 inch from ends for dowel casings.
❖ Transfer pattern for spoon holder to quilted fabric. Machine-satin-stitch on pattern lines. Cut fabric close to stitching. Position on front of carrier, referring to photograph for placement. Zigzag stitch over satin stitches, leaving end open, to attach.
❖ Cut ribbon in half. Position ribbon pieces on quilted side of flaps as indicated (Figure 3), and topstitch ends to flaps.
❖ Insert dowels in casings and wooden spoon in spoon holder.

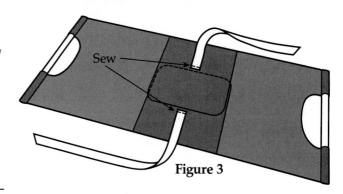

Sew

Figure 3

Stenciled Basket and Bread Board

The gift of homemade bread is always welcome, but you can add extra spice by presenting it in a stenciled basket or on a stenciled bread board. If you know the kitchen colors of the recipient, you can customize the design and create a gift that is both decorative and useful.

MATERIALS FOR BREAD BOARD

Golden Oak Stain
Bread board
Stencils by Zula: 9201 Dogwood
Masking tape
Stenciling paint: White, Green, Light Brown, and Red
Paper plate or saucer
Stenciling brushes: 3/8 inch to 1/2 inch in diameter,
    1 brush for each color
Paper towels

DIRECTIONS

❖ Stain board, and allow to dry thoroughly.
❖ Follow directions for stenciling on page 61.

MATERIALS FOR BASKET

Oblong basket
Stencils by Zula: MD03 Tara
Masking tape
Stenciling paint: White, Rose, and Green
Paper plate or saucer
Stenciling brushes: 3/8 inch to 1/2 inch in diameter,
    1 brush for each color
Paper towels

DIRECTIONS

❖ Follow directions for stenciling on page 61.

A Season for Reminiscing
Memories

My niece Brittany stopped believing in Santa years ago. I know, because I was wearing the red suit.

On the night before Christmas, I sidled silently down the back hall of my brother and sister-in-law's house. The red Santa suit was hanging on a closet door in the guest room. I pulled on my red velvet pants and pulled my red velvet jacket tight around my bed-pillow tummy. Squinting in the pink-shaded light of a guest-bedroom lamp, I pulled the white shiny beard's elastic band snug up under my nose.

"Ho-ho-ho," I said in a hoarse Santa whisper. A white nylon curl began to tickle my left nostril. "Ho-choo!" I sneezed and wiped my nose on my red velvet sleeve.

Through the bedroom door I heard my brother whisper, "Wait for *The Little Drummer Boy* and then hit the hall."

I stepped straight out of the bedroom. "Ho-ho-ho!" I boomed. "Where's that pretty little Brittany who's been so good this whole year?"

Brittany was standing in the middle of the living room in her pink-and-blue footie pajamas. "Ho-ho-ho!" I roared while the stereo thumped pa-rum-pa-pum-pum. Brittany reached up and brushed her straight blond bangs out of her eyes. "Ho-ho-ho!" I thundered.

Brittany burst into uncontrollable tears.

She was not able to open her new dream doll house for days after Christmas. When I called my brother and sister-in-law to see what had happened, they said I should not worry. They said, "This is just all a part of growing up. There is not one thing an uncle can do."

Brittany was halfway through her second year of college before I ever asked her about that Christmas. Walking down her parents' driveway after Christmas Day lunch, I asked her if she remembered that Christmas Eve night, years ago, when she had cried so hard she couldn't open her presents.

I said, "I didn't mean to scare you. I practiced really hard on my ho-ho-ho's."

Brittany reached up and brushed a kiss against my forehead. "It was the chimney," she said. "The real Santa never comes down the bedroom hall." She gripped her arm around my shoulder as we walked back to the house.

That night, standing in my brother and sister-in-law's guest room, I looked at myself in the mirror. The light from the dressing table lamp shone up on my vacation-day whiskers. And even in the half-light, they shone glistening white.

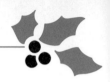

Holiday Calendar

1 December	2 December	3 December	4 December
9	**10**	**11**	**12**
17	**18**	**19**	**20**
25	**26**	**27**	**28**

5 December	6 December	7 December	8 December

13	14	15	16

21	22	23	24

29	30	31	1 January

Family Favorites

Up on the housetop reindeer pause, out jumps good old Santa Claus.
Down through the chimney with lots of toys;
All for the little ones' Christmas joys.
Ho, ho, ho! Who wouldn't go? Ho, ho, ho! Who wouldn't go . . .

Have everyone on your list fill in personal favorites below to help you with gift selection.

	Name	Name	Name	Name
FAVORITES				
Ball Team				
Book Type				
Charity				
Collectible				
Color				
Flower				
Food				
Gadget				
Motif				
Music				
Night Out				
Scent				
Sport				
Store				
Toy				

Christmas Gift Size Chart

Up on the housetop, click, click, click,
Down through the chimney with good Saint Nick.
First comes the stocking of little Nell; oh, dear Santa, fill it well.
Next comes the stocking of little Will; oh, just see what a glorious fill!

Have friends and family fill out the size chart below to be sure your gift is "fitting."

	Name	**Name**	**Name**	**Name**
SIZES				
Bathrobe				
Belt				
Blouse				
Coat				
Dress				
Gloves				
Hat				
Pajamas				
Ring				
Shirt				
Shoes				
Skirt				
Slacks				
Suit				
Sweater				

Christmas Gift Ideas

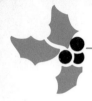

Jolly old Saint Nicholas, lean your ear this way!
Don't you tell a single soul what I'm going to say;
Christmas Eve is coming soon; now you dear old man,
Whisper what you'll bring to me; tell me if you can.

Traditional Carol

INFANTS AND TODDLERS

Basket filled with baby medicines, toiletries
Bath tub baby holder
Bathtime accessories
Birthdate newspaper
Board books
Car shades
Car seat toy attachments
Certificate of deposit
Cotton toys with jingles inside
Diaper service
Engraved sterling
Food mill
High chair harness
Night light
Nursery humidifier
Portable bottle warmer with car lighter attachment
Savings bond
Slippers or mocassins
Toy box
Toy telephone
Tub toys

PRESCHOOLERS

Bed linens featuring favorite character
Board books
Bubble bath
Car seat toy attachments
Cassette player
Child's broom and dustpan
Costume kit
Crayons and paper
Educational cassettes
Flash cards
Flashlight
Hairbrush and comb set
Indoor plant growing kit
Indoor playhouse
Laminated pictures of family
Magazine subscription
Nature books
Oversized, interlocking plastic blocks
Personalized bath set
Purse or wallet
Rocking chair for child's room
Shape sorter
Sneakers
Stepping stool
Sweatsuit
Toy box
Wooden world map puzzle

GRADE SCHOOL CHILDREN

Aquarium and accessories
Baseball card organizer
Baseball card magazine subscription
Battery-powered pencil sharpener
Battery recharger
Belly-pack, stuffed with treats
Bicycle helmet
Blank VHS tapes
Boom box
CDs/audio cassettes
Comic books
Dictionary
Easel
Football
Indoor basketball hoop
Jacket
Knee and elbow protective gear
Microscope
Phone and address book
Piano keyboard
Roller blades
Skateboard
Sled
Small billiard table
Sneakers
Snowboots
Socks
Telephone
Toy box
Umbrella
Video game organizer
Walkie-talkies
Wristwatch

CHILDREN'S STOCKING STUFFERS

Batteries	Fast food gift certificate	Magic set
Bicycle accessory	Fruit	Mini flashlight
Button covers	Gloves	Miniature dollhouse
Candy	Hairbrush and comb set	Miniature toy cars
Combination lock	Hand mirror	Mitten-to-jacket sleeve clip
Comic book	Jacks	attachments
Doll accessory	Jewelry	Movie tickets
Erasable inkpens	Key chain	Small phone and address book

TEENAGERS

Address & phone number	Cordless phone	Phone headset shoulder
book	Desk lamp	attachment
Audio cassette/CD gift	Fast food gift certificate	Small wool blanket in school
certificate	booklet	colors
Caller ID unit	Hairdresser appointment	Sporting event tickets
Car alarm	Locker organizer	Sports highlights/bloopers
Car emergency kit	Money	VHS tape
CD organizer	Movie tickets	Stationery with SASEs
Class ring	Oil change coupon	Thesaurus
Concert tickets	Oversized umbrella	Watch with assorted bands

ADULTS

Babysitting certificate	Firelog carrier	Numbered print by local artist
Ballpoint pen set	Hairstyle certificate	Photograph frames
Caller ID unit	Hand-woven basket filled	Potted flowers in bloom
Camera film	with goodies	Silk longjohns
Canvas attaché case	Housekeeping certificate	Skirt/slacks hangers
Car window defogger	Lighted car visor mirror	Sunday newspaper
CD organizer	Long-handled wooden bath	subscription
Cotton knit boxers	brush	Tanning bed visit
Cotton flannel sheets	Luggage combination locks	Windowsill herb-growing kit
Espresso machine	Lunch for two gift certificate	Wool gloves with leather
Facial and manicure	Massage therapist visit	palms

FAMILIES

Atlas	Family pass to amusement	Personalized bath towels
Beach towels	park or museum	Pet grooming/boarding
Case of microwave popcorn	Fire extinguisher	certificate
Cheese assortment	Flatware	Pizzas delivered
Coat rack	Fruit	Plants
Collection of Christmas music	Full-length mirror	Plastic sleds
Dictionary	Futon	Silly drinking glasses
Doorbell for back door	Games	Smoke alarm
Doormat	Kitchen-sized television	Stacking pillows
Empty photo album	Message center	Telephone
Encyclopedias	Oversized rolodex	VCR programmer

Our Yuletide Photographs

Welcome here, welcome here,
All be alive and be of good cheer.
I've got a pie all baked complete;
Pudding too, that's very sweet.
Chestnuts are roasting; join us here
While we dance and make good cheer.

Traditional Shaker Poem

Photo Space

Year-Round Christmas Shopping

Somehow, not only for Christmas, but all the long year through,
The joy that you give others is the joy that comes back to you;
And the more you spend in blessing the poor and lonely and sad,
The more of your heart's possessing, returns to make you glad.

John Greenleaf Whittier

Name	Gift	Storage Place

Our Yuletide Photographs

Everywhere, everywhere, Christmas tonight!
Christmas in lands of the fir tree and pine,
Christmas in lands of the palm tree and vine,
Christmas where snow peaks stand solemn and white,
Christmas where cornfields lie sunny and bright,
Everywhere, everywhere, Christmas tonight.

Phillips Brooks

Photo Space

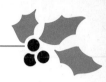

Our Christmas Card

God bless the master of this house, likewise the mistress too;
And all the little children that round the table go.
Love and joy come to you, and to you glad Christmas too,
And God bless you, and send you a Happy New Year,
And God send you a Happy New Year.

Traditional English Carol

Christmas Card Space

Christmas Eve

On Christmas Eve the bells were rung;
The damsel donned her kirtle sheen;
The hall was dressed with holly green;
Forth to the wood did merry men go,
To gather in the mistletoe.

Sir Walter Scott

Gathering Place

Family and
Friends
Attending

Our Menu

Traditions

Moments
to Remember

Special Gifts

Christmas Day

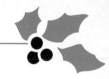

It is a good thing to observe Christmas Day.
The mere marking of times and seasons,
When men agree to stop work and make merry
Together, is a wise and wholesome custom.

Henry Van Dyke

Gathering Place

Family and
Friends
Attending

Our Menu

Traditions

Moments
to Remember

Special Gifts

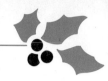

Our Yuletide Photographs

*A*fter dinner, eaten, let it be confessed, with more haste and less accompaniment of talk than usual, the parlor doors were opened, and there stood the Christmas tree in a glow of light, its wonderful branches laden with all manner of strange fruits not to be found in the botanies.

Hamilton Wright Mabie

Photo Space

Yes, Virginia, There Is a Santa Claus

*from **The New York Sun,** September 21, 1897*

We take pleasure in answering at once and thus prominently the communication below, expressing at the same time our great gratification that its faithful author is numbered among the friends of *The Sun*:

Dear Editor:
*I am 8 years old. Some of my little friends say there is no Santa Claus. Papa says, "If you see it in **The Sun**, it's so." Please tell me the truth, is there a Santa Claus?*
Virginia O'Hanlon, 115 West 95th Street

Virginia, your little friends are wrong. They have been affected by the skepticism of a skeptical age. They do not believe except they see. They think that nothing can be which is not comprehensible by their little minds. All minds, Virginia, whether they be men's or children's, are little. In this great universe of ours, man is a mere insect, an ant, in his intellect, as compared with the boundless world about him, as measured by the intelligence capable of grasping the whole truth and knowledge.

Yes, Virginia, there is a Santa Claus. He exists as certainly as love and generosity and devotion exist; and you know that they abound and give to your life its highest beauty and joy. Alas! how dreary would be the world if there were no Santa Claus! It would be as dreary as if there were no Virginias. There would be no childlike faith then, no poetry, no romance to make tolerable this existence. We should have no enjoyment, except in sense and sight. The eternal light with which childhood fills the world would be extinguished.

Not believe in Santa Claus! You might as well not believe in fairies! You might get your papa to hire men to watch in all the chimneys on Christmas Eve to catch Santa Claus, but even if they did not see Santa Claus coming down, what would that prove? Nobody sees Santa Claus, but that is no sign that there is no Santa Claus. The most real things in the world are those that neither children nor men can see. Did you ever see fairies dancing on the lawn? Of course not, but that's no proof that they are not there. Nobody can conceive or imagine all the wonders there are unseen and unseeable in the world.

You tear apart the baby's rattle and see what makes the noise inside; but there is a veil covering the unseen world which not the strongest man, nor even the united strength of all the strongest men that ever lived, could tear apart. Only faith, fancy, poetry, love, romance can push aside that curtain and view and picture the supernal beauty and glory beyond. Is it all real? Ah, Virginia, in all this world there is nothing else real and abiding.

No Santa Claus! Thank God he lives, and he lives forever. A thousand years from now, nay, ten thousand years from now, he will continue to make glad the heart of childhood.

Francis P. Church

Christmas Traditions

The happiest moments of my life have been the few which
I have passed at home in the bosom of my family.
Thomas Jefferson

Our childhood memories of home brim with the thoughts of Christmases past . . . untangling the big colored lights to hang on the evergreen in the yard, Dad's sawing off the too-long trunk of the Christmas tree on the back porch, Mother's patiently draping the tinsel strand by strand. Each year, traditional scenes blend with those of years' past, creating a living tapestry of images and feelings that grows in each of us. Each home has its special traditions, and gathered here are a suggested few to add to your own Christmas tapestry of memories.

Love Thy Neighbor

Every year during early December, volunteer a simple service to a shut-in neighbor. Be specific about what you want to do to help— bring in the newspaper or mail every day for a week, shovel a path to the mailbox every Saturday, or help address Christmas cards.

Ornaments-to-Treasure Christmas Party

From the craft store, purchase an ample supply of ornament-making supplies—the more variety, the better. Set up work stations in the kitchen and dining room, stock the buffet with appetizers and punch, then invite your friends, family, or neighbors in for an ornament-making party. Have an undecorated tree strung with lights nearby, and let your guests trim as they will. Be sure to have them sign and date their ornaments to distinguish each years' handiwork as the traditional gathering is held again and again.

The Lights of Christmas

Light a traditional Advent wreath, one candle in the evening four weeks before Christmas, two the following, and so on, until the center candle is lit to commemorate Christ's birth. (Use four communion cup candle holders and fruit—see page 129—with a large candle in the center and surrounded with greenery.)

Santa Sends the Little Ones to Bed

When Dad is hanging the lights around the front of the house, have him use a couple of eye-hooks to run a string up the side of the house in an unnoticeable corner. Attach jingle bells to the end of the string, and affix them near the little ones' bedroom window. Attach the other end of the string somewhere near the back door, too high to be seen by a small child. Then, on Christmas Eve, when excitement runs high and little eyes just don't seem to want to close, have a knowing older child or visitor pull the string a few times. The thought that the sleigh could be flying above the neighborhood will motivate even the most exited children to ask to be tucked in posthaste.

Gifts for the Neighborhood

Whether you live in an apartment or a farmhouse, admiring your neighbors' holiday decorations is a big part of Christmas. Share this appreciation with your neighbors by taking photographs of their decorated doorways during the weeks before Christmas. Frame them with holiday-colored construction paper, label and date each one, then glue thin magnets to the backs. Place each on a tin of holiday cookies and give to the appropriate neighbor. These patiently personalized, but simple and quick-to-make gifts, will be treasured for years to come and could easily become part of a holiday tradition in your neighborhood.

Add-a-Year Stocking

For a Christmas stocking that becomes more special each year, purchase or make a simple stocking of red flannel, wool, or heavy velvet. Then choose one trim piece of lace, ruffle, ribbon, or braid to stitch around the top of the stocking. Each year, add another row. Be creative—wide plaid ribbon one year, thin gold braid the next. Stocking getting full? Tie small jingle bells on ribbons and let the ribbons hang from the top of the stocking. With a new addition every year, this is one Christmas stocking that will "grow" with the child!

For the Birds

If you feed the birds in your yard, it's important to do it all winter long as they come to depend on your generosity. But why not make a special treat for them for Christmas? Gather or purchase large pine cones and stuff them with a mixture of peanut butter and bird seed. Tie a long red ribbon to each pine cone and tie the filled pine cones in the trees and bushes of your back yard. Different birds feed at different levels, so vary the height that you place the pine cones, and your entire yard will be decorated with bright and happy birds.

Recycled Greetings

Instead of throwing away the pretty Christmas cards you receive this year, let the children (supervised, of course) cut out the pictures from the front of the cards to make them over into new cards for next year. Pick a medium-weight paper in a neutral color, and cut and fold it to the right size. Then let your child hand-print a greeting inside and paste one of the cut-out pictures on the front. This is a great activity for a dreary January day that brings a little of the joy of Christmas back into your life.

Easy-to-do Christmas Gift Thank-Yous

Teenagers and grade-schoolers have such busy schedules during the holidays that writing those necessary thank-you notes is often postponed for too long. Since you usually know in advance who will be giving gifts to your children or grandchildren, you can help with this important task. As a special present to these children and teens, use a typewriter to address a box of thank-you note envelopes, and affix a stamp to each one. Place the envelopes back in the note box, and present it with the rest of your gifts. Then, during a slow part of New Year's Day, have them sit at the coffee table and write their notes while the gifts are still out and accessible. This New Year's Day tradition of appropriate manners and timely responses will be greatly admired and appreciated by gift-giving family members and friends.

Bringing Christmas Joy to the Elderly

If your child or grandchild has a Christmas play or pageant at school or church, then you have a ready-made performance to take to or videotape for a nearby retirement community. So many elderly people live far from their immediate family members. While the days closest to Christmas are usually busy for them, early and mid-December are often lonely and uneventful. They miss the hub-bub of preparation and the blossoming excitement of the children—just an hour or two of your time will provide them with both. Round up a few mothers with mini-vans who are willing to help in this venture for an hour after dress rehearsal. (Skip the stage parts, and simply sing the songs in costume.) Ask non-attending mothers to pick up their children at the original rehearsal site. Even a fifteen or twenty minute visit will help instill respect and responsibility in the youngsters, as well as create a touching and memorable holiday moment for the elderly.

The Twelve Months of Christmas

I have always thought of Christmastime, when it has come round, as a good time; a kind, forgiving, charitable, pleasant time; the only time I know of in the long calendar of the year when men and women seem by one consent to open their shut-up hearts freely, and to think of people below them as if they really were fellow passengers, and not another race of creatures bound on other journeys. And therefore, though it has never put a scrap of gold or silver in my pocket, I believe that it has done me good, and will do me good, and I say, God bless it!

Charles Dickens

December

Mid-month shortcuts will save you extra effort when the big day approaches. Each evening during the second and third week of December, prepare a dish or appetizer, wrap it well, label it, and place it in the freezer for your use later when time will run short.

It's one week before Christmas. Spend an hour in the guest room, checking cleanliness and stocking the tables with potpourri (see page 46), magazines, notepads, stamps, and pens. Just before the guests arrive, place a bowl of fresh fruit, an electric teapot, assorted teas, and china in their room.

Christmas Day at last! If there is an abundance of presents, keep a gift-and-giver list as the presents are opened to prevent confusion later. It's nice to let each family member open one single gift and focus the attention of the whole family on that single person and gift. This will help to develop the joy that extends beyond personally giving and receiving, encompassing an appreciation and delight in the joy of others. Play low-key instrumental carols in the background to help contribute to this loving, sharing tradition.

Organize your ornaments and decorations as you take them down. Discard items you haven't used in several years, or label and store them to be sent to Goodwill in November of next year.

January

Happy New Year! On New Year's Day, during half-time or just in between family events, have the children sit down with their pre-addressed and stamped thank-you notes while the thoughts about their gifts are still fresh. This could even be a lunch-time event—serve them sandwiches as they write.

Back on the diet track. Keep gym clothes in the car and go in to work an hour early every Tuesday and Thursday. Work out during lunch hour, then have a homemade salad after co-workers have already eaten. This every-other-workday workout and rotation low-fat lunch will help you shed pounds!

Update your copy of **All Through the House.** Place your Christmas mementos and information on the appropriate pages.

Linen and white sales are this month.

February

Watch for plant and seed catalogs to arrive. Your garden can provide hundreds of gift and craft ideas. Plan to plant items that can be dried or preserved and later used as gifts, such as herb vinegars, dried flower crafts, or pickled vegetables. See page 66 for an etched glass jar to use for dried herb and veggie gifts!

Revive your Christmas spirit. Select a craft or decorating project from this book to help pass the time during the cold wintry days.

Winter clothing sales start. Watch for incoming spring fashions in the stores—their appearance means price reductions on winter apparel. Remember to buy children's sizes planning for a year's growth. (Record your purchases and their storage areas on page 89.)

March

It's time to start your seedlings indoors. Most gardening and hardware stores now feature inexpensive, indoor mini-greenhouses just for starting seedlings. Be sure to use a good soil mixture, and once the seedlings are up, fertilize them every week.

Start budgeting for a food dehydrator. These small, inexpensive appliances can be used in summer to preserve herbs, flowers, and vegetables to use later in creating homemade Christmas gifts.

In some areas of the country, you can begin preparing the soil for spring planting.

Begin a long-term craft project. One good example is the Redwork Pine Cone Pillowcases and the Stenciled Sheet Set on page 52.

April

It's springtime! If you have an outdoor cold frame to protect young plants at night, indoor seedlings may now be placed inside it. Be sure to open the cold frame door or window during sunny days, and close it before sundown.

Start organizing for a June yard sale. There is no easier way than a yard sale to raise a few hundred dollars for your Christmas shopping. Set aside an area of the guest room and arrange empty boxes so that they may be filled without interfering with one another. Tackle one closet at a time, and begin labeling and boxing items according to prices. Encourage children and other family members to thin out their own stockpiles.

Watch after-Easter sales for craft accessories which could just as easily be used for Christmas.

May

Now is the time to plan your holiday vacation. Traveling is heavy during the holiday season and contacting your travel agent now can prevent last-minute mix-ups and difficulty in obtaining reservations.

Plant your summer herbs and flowers in early May. Keep in mind the blossom colors which you will need dried for Christmas crafts—gold, yellow, red, mauve, and greens. Plant enough herbs so that you can dry them for foodstuffs as well as potpourris and sachets.

Review your progress on the yard sale and schedule this month's weekends accordingly. Pick up packages of small adhesive-backed labels and have lots of markers on hand. Send toddlers to a friend's house, and invite as many helpers as you can enlist. Start in the garage or main storage area. First create a space for yard sale materials—you could even move the car to the driveway for a few days. Put a price tag on anything you have not used in a year or more. Don't throw broken items away unless they're irreparable—just put a *very* low price tag on them! Keep everything neat and stacked until time for the yard sale.

June

Contact your local nursery for information about fertilizing your shrubbery. The extra attention now will make your greenery clippings much more attractive at Christmastime.

Update the Christmas Gift Size Chart on page 85.

Have the yard sale. Watch extended weather forecasts to plan the date, and put a small ad in the newspaper if you are in an off-the-beaten-track location. Have children make signs the weekend before. Completely free your time on the day before your sale, and farm out the children too young to help. String clotheslines from tree-to-tree for hanging clothes, etc., and set up temporary tables with crates, sawhorses, removable doors, or plywood. Use picnic benches as tables. Spread out your wares the night before if weather permits. Be willing to negotiate—remember, you don't want to put any of this stuff back where it was!

July

It is halfway to Christmas!

Double-check scheduling on your long-term craft projects. Keep in mind that school starts in just a month or so and the evenings will be much shorter. Complete as much of your handiwork as possible to prevent a last-minute rush this fall and winter.

Shop festivals and craft fairs for unique and inexpensive gift ideas. Don't forget teachers, bosses, and secretaries! (Record purchases and storage areas on page 89.)

Start dehydrating veggies, herbs, and flowers for use later.

August

Watch for fall fashions to arrive in department stores. Availability and selection is at its best. Record your purchases and their storage areas on page 89.

It's vacation time. If you make it to the beach—or if you have a friend who does—remember to gather shells for a Christmas wreath. (See page 119.)

Share the summer's bounty at Christmas! Harvest delicious goodies from your garden or take a trip to the local farmer's market. Try our Blueberry-Rhubarb Jam on page 36, Easy Pickled Beets on page 37, or tangy Hot Pepper Mustard on page 38.

Have children and grandchildren prepare their wish lists now.

September

Lay-away toys and other items which will be in short supply as the holiday season draws near. Order catalog items now to allow plenty of delivery time. (Record purchases and storage areas on page 89.)

Look at unfinished craft and decorating projects. Are your goals realistic or should you move to easier, less time-consuming projects?

Update your Christmas card list.

October

Select the planting site for your live tree. Dig the hole now before the ground freezes. Shovel the remaining dirt into a wheelbarrow—store it in the garage for easy handling later.

Make holiday appointments with hairdressers and photographers. Record these dates on your Holiday Calendar on pages 82–83.

November

It's time! Update your Holiday Calendar. Christmas is almost here—your gift lists and craft projects should be near completion, and your shopping should be progressing.

Christmas card preparation should begin in early November. Sprinkle a little potpourri in each envelope, or dot the outside of each with a Christmas-scented essential oil. (See below and page 46 for potpourri ideas.)

Test your smoke alarm.

Test camera and camcorder and have them serviced if necessary. Pick up extra film and batteries.

Ship gifts if possible on the Monday after Thanksgiving. Pack them with paper scented with essential oils, such as cinnamon and clove, or sprinkle the packing paper with potpourri and fresh greenery.

December

Invite your friends over one Saturday morning before the stores open for a Christmas potpourri party. Serve coffee and pastry, and ask each guest to bring a specific potpourri ingredient in an oversized, reusable container. (Cinnamon sticks, hemlock cones, pine needles, citrus peels, and spices.) Combine all the ingredients and then divide the potpourri.

Create a shopping day for you and your friends. Find three or more teenagers who need to earn Christmas money. Have them keep a "shopping day care" in your playroom while you and your friends shop. Send out invitations including information that each parent should be responsible for their hours and pay the sitters.

A Season for Trimming
Decorating

The Holy Family arrived in a tube from Chicago. Without asking anybody, my father had ordered them in early October from an ad in the Sunday paper.

Walking into the kitchen, on a Wednesday evening before church, my mother dropped the tube on my father's still empty plate. "Now just where do you think we are going to put a nativity scene?" she said.

My father said, "I thought we could put them in the side yard, down next to the road. I thought we could build us a little shed."

"I hope you know this is entirely your project," said my mother, who weeks ago had already lugged boxes of electrified candles and tinsel and tree lights in from the garage. "Just put a sign up saying that, from now until the day after Christmas, you and the boys own that whole side of the yard."

That Saturday afternoon, my brother and I watched my father roll the Holy Family out on a piece of plywood. When my father unrolled the last edge of the last sheet of paper, my brother put down his glue brush and said, "Wow!"

Drifting upside down in the uppermost corner was a twelve-inch-tall, ivory-skinned angel with gold-covered wings.

Every night that week, while the Holy Family's final coat of varnish dried in the garage, my brother and I helped our father carry planks and fence posts to the side yard. My brother handed Dad nails while he built a rough wood wall with a roof jutting shakily out from it. While I scattered hay around the baby Jesus, my father set a flood lamp in place behind the manger.

Then using only one nail and tapping very, very lightly, he carefully tacked the golden-winged angel in place.

"Wow!" my brother said.

It was Friday night and a car was coming down the road. "Quick, plug the light in," my father said, and my brother rushed past him, into the garage. In an instant, the house and the yard were plunged into blackness.

Over the quiet, we heard the door of the sleeping porch creak open. "Somebody's in for trouble now," my brother said as he and I and my father turned to face the house.

Through the porch door, however, we saw nothing but the flickering light of a candle. My mother had placed it on the edge of the piano. When the engines of the cars hushed to stillness, we could hear what she was playing. My mother was playing *Silent Night*.

A touch of wildlife creates a natural appeal with Wooden Moose and Embellished Pillar Candles, pages 104 and 131.

Wooden Moose

Reindeer aren't the only antlered creatures that make good holiday decorations. This moose ornament and a free-standing herd are the answer to decorating prayers—they're easy, inexpensive, and wonderful!

MATERIALS FOR MOOSE ORNAMENT

Tracing paper
Graphite or carbon paper
Scrap of 1/4-inch plywood or balsa wood
Band saw or jigsaw
Drill with 3/8-inch drill bit
Sandpaper
Black paint pen
8 inches thin jute
See Patterns

DIRECTIONS

❖ Transfer pattern onto tracing paper. Place graphite paper between tracing paper and plywood, and trace over pattern to transfer image.
❖ Cut along outline with band saw or jigsaw. Drill a hole where indicated on pattern.
❖ Sand all surfaces and edges.
❖ Paint eye as indicated on pattern.
❖ Insert jute through hole, and knot for hanger.

MATERIALS FOR FREE-STANDING MOOSE HERD

Tracing paper
Graphite or carbon paper
1 (9-by-9-by-3/4-inch) pine piece
Band saw or jigsaw
Sandpaper
Black paint pen
See Patterns

DIRECTIONS

❖ Transfer pattern onto tracing paper. Place graphite paper between pattern and wood. Trace over pattern to transfer image.
❖ Cut along outline with band saw or jigsaw.
❖ Sand all surfaces and edges.
❖ Paint eye as indicated on pattern.

Gingerbread Kids Tree Skirt and Stocking

Smiling gingerbread boys and girls encircle this bright Christmas-plaid tree skirt and stocking set. Simple embroidery provides their happy features, and washable fabrics make them suitable for years of service. On the stocking, use gingerbread girls for the young ladies of the house and gingerbread boys for the little men.

MATERIALS FOR TREE SKIRT

2 1/2 yards (45-inch wide) prewashed plaid flannel or cotton fabric
Water-soluble marker
1 yard washable tan felt
1 1/2 yards (3/8-inch wide) green rickrack
Straight pins
1 (#24) embroidery needle
DMC® Embroidery Floss = 8m skeins:
  8 skeins #699 Green, 1 skein Black
Thread to match fabric
2 hooks and eyes
See Patterns

DIRECTIONS

❖ Cut two 44-inch squares from cotton fabric. Fold 1 square in half and in half again to make a 22-inch square.
❖ Measure 3 inches from center folded corner, and mark. Measure 22 inches from center folded corner, and mark. Draw 2 arcs (Figure 4).
❖ Cut along both arc lines, and open skirt.
❖ Mark and cut a straight line from center circle to edge for skirt opening.

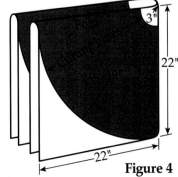

Figure 4

❖ Repeat with second 44-inch square piece to make skirt lining.
❖ Transfer pattern for gingerbread figures to tan felt, and cut out 17 boys and 17 girls.
❖ Cut 17 (3-inch long) pieces of rickrack. Position on gingerbread girls as shown on pattern, and tack ends to back of figures. (Continued on page 107.)

DIRECTIONS FOR TREE SKIRT
(continued from page 104)

❖ Position gingerbread figures 1½ inches from outer edge of skirt, alternating girls and boys. Pin in place.

❖ Blanket stitch around edges of figures with 2 strands of green floss to attach to skirt.

❖ Make French knots for eyes and running stitches for mouths with 2 strands of black floss as indicated on pattern.

❖ Place skirt top and lining together with right sides facing and stitch leaving a ½-inch seam allowance, leaving an opening on a straight side for turning.

❖ Clip curves, turn, and press. Slip stitch closed.

❖ Stitch hooks and eyes to skirt opening.

MATERIALS FOR STOCKING

1 yard (45-inch wide) plaid flannel or cotton fabric
Thread to match fabric
Scrap of washable tan felt
6 inches (³/8-inch wide) green rickrack for girls
DMC® Embroidery Floss = 8m skeins (1 skein each):
  #699 Green, Black
1 (#24) embroidery needle
See Patterns

DIRECTIONS

❖ Transfer stocking pattern to fabric 2 times. Reverse pattern, and transfer to fabric 2 times. Cut out 4 pieces.

❖ Cut a 1½-by-4-inch strip from fabric for hanger. Fold long sides of strip ¼ inch to wrong side and press. Fold strip in half lengthwise and press. Topstitch along open long edge.

❖ Transfer gingerbread pattern to felt 2 times, and cut out. Cut two 3-inch long pieces of rickrack if using girl figures. Position rickrack on gingerbread girls as shown on pattern, and tack ends to back of figures.

❖ Position gingerbread figures on front of stocking, 1½ inches from top edge, and pin figures in place.

❖ Blanket stitch around edges of figures with 2 strands of green floss to attach to stocking.

❖ Make French knots for eyes and running stitches for mouths with 2 strands of black floss as indicated on pattern.

Make spirits bright with a Gingerbread Kids Tree Skirt and Stocking, Patchwork Ball Ornament, Bandana Pillow Cover, Starfish Santa and Snowman, and Painted Wooden Soldiers, pages 104, 107, and 108.

❖ Align raw edges with right sides facing. Stitch stocking front to stocking back along sides and foot. Turn right-side out.

❖ Repeat with remaining 2 pieces to make lining, leaving a 3-inch opening on back straight side. Do not turn lining.

❖ Fold loop for hanger in half, and pin to outside of stocking at back seam with raw edges aligned and loop pointed down.

❖ Slip stocking into lining so that right sides are facing and top raw edges are aligned. Stitch together along top edge.

❖ Clip curves, and turn through opening. Slip stitch lining opening closed, and fold lining inside stocking. Press.

Patchwork Ball Ornament

These fluffy patchwork balls look as though they'd take a fair amount of time to stitch, right? Wrong. They're really foam balls with bits of fabric tucked into grooves. You'll be able to turn out dozens of ornaments in no time, having loads of spares for bazaars, ornament swaps, or just admirers.

MATERIALS

Scraps of Christmas fabric
1 (3-inch diameter) craft foam ball
Butter knife or metal nail file
16 inches (¹/8-inch wide) red satin ribbon
Hot glue gun

DIRECTIONS

❖ Cut fabric scraps into odd shapes between 2 to 3 inches in size.

❖ Place 1 fabric scrap on ball, and push along edges with knife or file to create groove and conceal scrap edges.

❖ Fit another fabric piece next to first, and secure in existing groove. Work remaining edges into ball, making new grooves. Continue adding fabric pieces, trimming edges of fabric when necessary, until ball is covered.

❖ Cut a 5-inch long piece of ribbon. Loop, tuck ends into a groove in the ball, and secure with glue for hanger. Tie remaining ribbon in a bow, and glue over hanger's ends.

Bandana Pillow Cover

*L*ooking for a quick way to add seasonal color to your home decor? Stitch up a few of these bright bandana pillow covers, and you can quickly transform your throw pillows into holiday accents. And once the season is over, just wash off any eggnog spills, and store them away for future Christmases.

MATERIALS

9 1/3 yards (1-inch wide) green grosgrain ribbon
2 (22-inch square) bandanas
Washable marker
Thread to match

DIRECTIONS

❖ Cut ribbon into eight 42-inch long pieces.
❖ Measure 7 inches in from all 4 edges of 1 bandana, and mark central square for ribbon placement.
❖ Center ribbon pieces along marked lines on the right side of bandana, leaving 10 inches on each end for ties. Pin in place.
❖ Stitch along both edges of ribbon from 1 crisscrossed point to the next until all sides of square are stitched.
❖ Repeat for second bandana.
❖ Place pillow between bandanas, and tie ribbons in bows to secure.

Starfish Santa and Snowman

*T*his jolly Santa and snowman with outstretched arms began as starfish swimming the seas. A quick makeover with paint and scraps turns the little starfish into ornaments to treasure.

MATERIALS FOR STARFISH SANTA

Medium flat paintbrush
Acrylic paints: Red, Black, White, Face Color, Gold
Starfish
Hot glue gun
7 inches jute

DIRECTIONS

❖ Paint all but outer tips of both front and back of starfish red.
❖ Paint black boots and white fur cuffs on front and back of leg tips.
❖ Paint appropriately colored hands and white cuffs on front and back of arm tips.
❖ Paint white top to cap on front and back of remaining tip.
❖ Paint white brim of cap and white beard on front, referring to photograph.
❖ Paint face and black dot eyes and black belt with gold buckle, referring to photograph.
❖ Glue looped jute to back of Santa ornament for hanger.

MATERIALS FOR STARFISH SNOWMAN

Medium flat paintbrush
Acrylic paints: White, Black, Orange
Starfish
Hot glue gun
Purchased black hat, 1/2-inch to 3/4-inch diameter
7 inches jute
Scraps of plaid fabric

DIRECTIONS

❖ Paint both sides of starfish white.
❖ Paint black dot eyes and buttons and orange carrot nose, referring to photograph.
❖ Glue hat to top of head.
❖ Glue looped jute to back of snowman ornament for hanger.
❖ Cut a 1/4-by-7-inch piece from plaid fabric.
❖ Wrap around snowman's neck for scarf, and glue in place.

Painted Wooden Soldiers

*I*f you are handy with a paintbrush, you can whip in shape this company of wooden soldiers in no time. Children will enjoy them as toys, but these colorful warriors make an enchanting window display. If you like, you can even attach eye screws to them and hang them on the tree! They're delightful as both decorations and toys, adding military polish to arrangements and dreams of battlefield glory to little hearts.

MATERIALS

Tracing paper
Carbon or graphite paper
1 (6-inch long) piece of 1¹/₈-inch diameter wooden
    dowel
Transparent tape
Paintbrushes: medium flat, liner
Acrylic paint: Black, White, Red, Blue, Yellow, Rose,
    Brown, Face Color
Semigloss water-base varnish
Eye screw, if desired
See Patterns

DIRECTIONS

❖ Transfer pattern onto tracing paper. Cut out
along outline. Cut graphite paper the same size as
the pattern. Lay the graphite paper beneath
pattern, and wrap both around dowel. Tape in
place. Trace over pattern lines to transfer pattern
details to the dowel. Remove the pattern and
graphite paper.
❖ Paint soldiers as indicated on pattern. If
painting several soldiers, you may want to vary
facial expressions slightly. Let paint dry.
❖ Apply a coat of semigloss varnish and let dry.
❖ Insert an eye screw in the top of each soldier, if
desired, for hanger.

Where the Treetops Glisten

During the holidays, homes take on a different light with glowing candles and sparkling strings of lights. This year, turn up the magic in your home with the golden accessories shown here and on the following pages. The lustrous ribbons and fabrics will catch and reflect light in unexpected ways, creating the kind of drama that best suits Christmas.

Glittering Gold Wreath

Nothing catches light the way gold does. This wreath takes full advantage of that fact, combining golden decorations with yards of glimmering ribbon and garland. Okay, this much ribbon can be expensive, but if you shopped last year's after-Christmas sales and tucked some ribbon away, this wreath is a wonderful way to put it to good use.

MATERIALS

Hot glue gun
Purchased 9-inch high gold tree
Purchased small packages, horns, and glass balls
1 (14-inch) grapevine wreath
5 yards gold wire and mylar star garland
5 yards (1 1/2-inch wide) gold ribbon
Floral wire

DIRECTIONS

❖ Glue tree, packages, horns, and glass balls to bottom of the wreath, referring to photograph for placement. Cut 1 yard of star garland, and loop through the arrangement.
❖ Make a large multi-looped bow with gold ribbon leaving 14-inch streamers, and gather bow in center with floral wire. Make same size loops with remaining star garland, and arrange within ribbon bow, securing with floral wire. Attach to top of wreath with wire. Twist excess wire in back into circle for hanger.
❖ Ripple bow streamers down sides of wreath, catching along wreath with glue to hold shape. Trim ends and tuck into arrangement at bottom.

Gold Lamé Cornucopia Ornament

Display berries, presents, candies, or other wonderful things on your tree by making and filling up glittering cornucopia ornaments. They are an excellent way to use scraps left over from our gold lamé tree skirt, or you can use other fabric scraps to obtain a totally different effect—one that's just right for you.

MATERIALS

Poster board
Scrap of red felt
Scrap of prequilted gold lamé fabric
Thread to match
Hot glue gun
24 inches (1-inch wide) red ribbon with gold wire edges
16 inches gold cord
9 inches (1/4-inch wide) red satin ribbon

DIRECTIONS

❖ Draw a 10-inch diameter circle on poster board. Cut out circle. Fold circle into quarters, and cut apart at folds.
❖ Place 1 poster board piece on red felt as a pattern, and cut out.
❖ Add 1/4-inch seam allowance to 1 poster board piece. Place on gold lamé fabric as a pattern, and cut out.
❖ Fold gold lamé piece in half with right sides facing and raw edges aligned, and sew long edge with a 1/4-inch seam allowance. Turn.
❖ Form 1 poster board piece into a cone shape, and hot glue together along long edge.
❖ Insert poster board cone into gold lamé cone, pull fabric taut, and glue gold lamé to poster board along top edge.
❖ Place felt piece inside cone, glue felt together along overlapping long edge, and glue to cone around top. Trim felt extending beyond the top of the ornament.
❖ Make 1/4-inch pleats in 1-inch wired ribbon, checking to be sure it will fit around top of ornament. Machine-stitch 1/4 inch from edge of pleated ribbon. Glue ribbon around top edge of cone, turning under final edge and gluing over beginning edge.
❖ Tie ends of gold cord in knots, glue over ribbon stitching line, and tie in bow.
❖ Glue ends of red satin ribbon inside ornament for hanger.

Gather natural materials like magnolia leaves, pine cones, and sweet gum balls. Spray with gold paint and arrange in vases, cups or bowls to spread glitz all through the house.

Gold Lamé Tree Skirt and Stocking

*T*ree lights will glisten from this lustrous gold lamé tree skirt and stocking. The skirt's seams are hidden on the sides so they don't detract from the elegant ribbon appliqué work, and the construction is designed to allow you to make the skirt, stocking, and several ornaments from only three yards of fabric. The wire-edge ribbon updates ribbon rosettes and loose bows. Matching rosette ornaments (see page 114) are made just like the stocking's rosette, but with narrower ribbon.

MATERIALS FOR TREE SKIRT

3 yards (45-inch wide) prequilted gold lamé fabric
Water-soluble marker
Thread to match
3/4 yard (45-inch wide) unquilted gold lamé fabric
Straight pins
12 yards (1 1/2-inch wide) striped wire-edge ribbon
Metallic thread to match outer edges of ribbon
6 (1/2-inch diameter) decorative gold buttons

DIRECTIONS

❖ Measure and mark two 29-inch radius semicircles on prequilted fabric (Figure 5). Measure and mark two 3 1/2-inch radius semicircles on center of flat edges (Figure 5). Cut out skirt halves, reserving remaining fabric for stocking and ornaments.
❖ Stitch skirt halves together with right sides facing leaving a 1/2-inch seam allowance.
❖ Cut opening for skirt in middle of 1 panel (Figure 5). This will be back of skirt.

Figure 5   Cut here for back opening once two sides are stitched together.

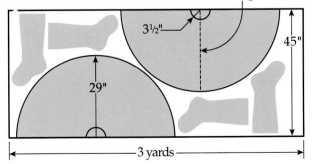

29"   3 1/2"   45"

3 yards

❖ Cut and sew together enough 2-inch wide bias strips from unquilted gold lamé to make 8 yards of binding. Fold binding in half lengthwise, wrong sides facing.
❖ Pin binding around right side of skirt with raw edges aligned, mitering corners. Stitch leaving a 1/4-inch seam allowance.
❖ Fold binding to back of skirt, pin to secure, and stitch top of skirt.
❖ Fold skirt in half, and mark halfway point with a straight pin. Fold again and mark quarters. Continue folding and marking until 16 points are marked with pins. These are position points for ribbon bows and swags.
❖ Cut 14 pieces of ribbon 30 inches long.
❖ Position first swag with center of dip 2 inches above center front mark. Ends of swag will align 6 1/2 inches above pins to each side of center front mark. Pleat ribbon as shown to form contour of swag. Pin in place.
❖ Turn under ribbon ends 1/4 inch. Continue to position swags around skirt. For swag that breaches skirt opening, cut ribbon in 2 pieces, and turn ends under to align with binding seam.
❖ Machine-topstitch swags along both edges of ribbon just inside wire using coordinating metallic thread.
❖ Loop a piece of ribbon into a bow, twisting wire at center to cinch. Do not tie. Pin over swag intersections. Sew a button to center of bow to secure to skirt.
❖ Whipstitch top and sides of bow loops to skirt to secure. Cut ends of streamers in V's. Leave remaining parts of bow free and shape wire to achieve desired effect.
❖ Repeat to attach and arrange remaining bows to mark all but rear 2 intersections.

MATERIALS FOR STOCKING

1/2 yard (45-inch wide) prequilted gold lamé fabric
Note: If making tree skirt, stocking can be made from remaining fabric (Figure 5).
Thread to match
2 yards (1-inch wide) striped wire-edge ribbon
Straight pins
Metallic thread to match outer edges of wire-edge ribbon
2/3 yard (1/4-inch wide) red satin ribbon
26 inches (1 1/2-inch wide) striped wire-edge ribbon
1 (3/4-inch diameter) decorative gold button
7 inches (5/8-inch wide) gold ribbon
See Patterns

❖ Transfer stocking pattern to fabric, reverse, and transfer again. Cut out 2 stockings.

❖ Sew from top of stocking to top of heel with right sides facing. Open stocking and press flat.

❖ Begin at left-hand side, and position top edge of 1-inch wide ribbon approximately 8½ inches from top raw edge of stocking. Pleat ribbon as shown in photograph to create a swag that peaks approximately 6½ inches from stocking top and 1½ inches from seam. Pin ribbon in place. Continue pleating, dipping, and pinning swag around back of stocking, ending even with beginning point 8½ inches from top.

❖ Machine-topstitch both edges of the ribbon inside wire using metallic thread.

❖ Repeat pleating to position red ribbon approximately 1 inch above striped. Attach by hand along both edges with running stitch and matching thread. Fold top edge of stocking ¼ inch to wrong side, and machine-stitch.

❖ Refold stocking with right sides facing, and stitch remaining foot and front seam. Do not turn.

❖ Fold top 3 inches of stocking over outside, and slip stitch to stocking. Turn.

❖ Fold 1½-inch wide ribbon in eight 1½-inch accordion pleats, leaving a 1-inch tail on each end. Tack through pleats at 1 bottom corner (Figure 6).

❖ Fan into rosette by lifting and turning 1 pleat at a time. Align tails and stitch across them ¼ inch from tacked point. Trim edges to ⅛ inch and fold ribbon other direction. Stitch ¼ inch from top seam to make a French seam.

❖ Cut one 8-inch and two 7-inch pieces of 1-inch wide ribbon. Tack to high point of swag on stocking front. Position button in center of rosette, and stitch both to stocking over streamers. Trim streamer ends in V's.

❖ Fold gold ribbon in half, and tack to inside back of stocking for hanger.

❖ Make rosette ornaments with same technique, but use 1-inch wide wire-edge ribbon. Tack streamers to the back, loop 8 inches of a coordinating ribbon in half, and tack to back for hanger.

Figure 6 Tack One Corner

Festivity glimmers from Gold Lamé Cornucopia Ornament, Gold Lamé Tree Skirt and Stocking, Stocking Ornament, and Potpourri Heart Ornament, pages 111, 113, 115, and 116.

Stocking Ornament

Little stocking ornaments in glowing red faille fabric open up so many possibilities. First, they're beautiful just hanging on the tree, but they also could hold candies for grandbabies, clues to find hidden presents, loving notes passed between members of the family during the days leading up to Christmas, and even money! Hang them on bedroom doors, hutch shelves, and windows. And that's just a start. If you have a tradition in your family that could make use of a lovely little container, stitch a few of these ornaments—and then make extras to just hang on the tree.

MATERIALS

1 (8½-inch square) red faille fabric piece
Red thread
22 inches (1½-inch wide) striped wire-edge ribbon
16 inches (¼-inch wide) gold metallic ribbon
Hot glue gun
1 (¼-inch diameter) gold jingle bell
6 inches gold cord
See Patterns

DIRECTIONS

❖ Transfer pattern to red faille fabric 2 times, and cut out. Stitch stocking together on side and bottom edges using red thread. Do not turn.

❖ Turn top edge ¼ inch to outside, and stitch. Turn top edge another 1⅛ inches to inside, and slip stitch to stocking. Turn stocking right side out.

❖ Make ¼-inch pleats in wire-edge ribbon, checking to be sure it will fit around top of ornament. Machine-stitch ¼ inch from edge of pleated ribbon.

❖ Pin stitched ribbon ½ inch from top of stocking beginning and ending at back seam. Turn ribbon end under ¼ inch, and overlap beginning end of ribbon. Baste ribbon to stocking along machine stitching line.

❖ Cut a piece of ¼-inch gold ribbon to fit around pleated ribbon over stitching line. Hot glue in place. Tie remaining gold ribbon in a bow, knot ends, and glue on gold ribbon on stocking front. Tack jingle bell to knot of bow.

❖ Loop gold cord, and glue inside stocking at back seam for hanger.

Moss-Covered Cones and Spheres

Simple geometric shapes take on earthy beauty when they're covered with sheet sphagnum moss and embellished with glittering trims. Here we've arranged them on a mantel, but they would also make striking centerpieces, topiary trees, and ornaments. And for added nighttime drama, you could twirl tiny white lights around them or surround them with candles.

MATERIALS

Craft foam cones and spheres in desired sizes
Craft glue
Sheet sphagnum moss
Floral pins
Clear nylon thread
Vines
Metallic ribbons and cord
Straight pins

DIRECTIONS

❖ Cover foam shape with a heavy coat of glue.
❖ Press pieces of moss over surface until foam is completely covered. Secure with pins and thread. Let dry.
❖ Soak vines in water to soften if they are not freshly cut and pliable.
❖ Swirl vines, ribbons, and cord over moss-covered shapes as desired, securing with floral pins or straight pins.

Potpourri Heart Ornament

Scatter several of these heart-shaped ornaments on your tree, and fragrance will cascade from the branches. Framed in the center of each is a potpourri-filled net heart. These also make nice gift-toppers—just loop the hanger with ribbon and tie to the top of a gift box. Another decorating idea: Hang Potpourri Heart Ornaments from different lengths of ribbon attached to the top of a window. In the sun, the richly toned potpourri flowers add a spattering of bright color in the midst of the glowing red fabric.

MATERIALS

Scraps of red faille fabric
10 inches (3/8-inch wide) red braid
Hot glue gun
Scraps of small-mesh bridal net
Potpourri with pretty flowers
5 inches (3/8-inch wide) red grosgrain ribbon
See Patterns

DIRECTIONS

❖ Transfer large heart pattern to faille 2 times and cut out. Transfer window opening from pattern to 1 heart. Stay-stitch a seam just outside window area to prevent fraying, and cut out window.
❖ Stitch faille hearts together with right sides facing. Trim seam to 1/8 inch, and turn through window opening.
❖ Position braid around window so that it covers stitching line and raw edge of fabric. Begin gluing braid at top center point of heart. Trim and fold under final end of braid; secure with glue.
❖ Transfer small heart pattern to net 2 times and cut out. Sew together, leaving a 2-inch opening.
❖ Arrange potpourri flowers on bottom of net, and fill net heart with potpourri. Stitch opening closed.
❖ Fill faille heart with a 1/4-inch layer of potpourri. Insert net heart carefully so that flowers show through window, and glue to faille heart under braid.
❖ Loop grosgrain ribbon, and glue to top center back of heart for hanger.

Potpourri Wax Ornaments

Honey sweet beeswax, married to potpourri and essential oils, is irresistible when fashioned into star and ball ornaments. Find inexpensive beeswax through a local beekeeper. You will need to heat, then strain all but the purest (and most expensive) wax through old pantyhose to filter debris, and use leftover beeswax candles and remelt damaged ornaments.

Earthy beauty emanates from a mantel filled with Moss-Covered Cones and Spheres and Potpourri Wax Ornaments, page 116.

MATERIALS FOR PREPARING BEESWAX

Old saucepan
Coffee can
Natural beeswax
Synthetic paraffin, if desired
Pantyhose
Old metal coffee pot

DIRECTIONS

❖ Note: It is extremely important to melt wax only in a double boiler to avoid possibility of overheating and fire.
❖ Fill saucepan with a few inches of water and place coffee can in saucepan for double boiler. Place beeswax in coffee can, and melt over medium heat. Add paraffin to beeswax if desired, but paraffin should not make up more than 25 percent of total solution as it will reduce rich color and scent of beeswax.
❖ Stretch pantyhose over coffee pot as strainer, and pour melted wax through pantyhose.
❖ Place utensils in a plugged sink or large container, and pour boiling water over them for easy cleanup. Add more boiling water as needed to completely cover.
❖ Allow to cool. Wax will rise to top of water and harden, becoming easy to remove.

MATERIALS FOR BALL ORNAMENTS

Prepared beeswax
Aluminum pie pan
Potpourri with pretty flower petals
10-inch piece of heavy wire bent in hook on one end
Essential oils: rose, vanilla, or lavender if desired
Gold cord
Hot glue gun

DIRECTIONS

❖ Pour 1/2-inch layer beeswax in pie pan.
❖ Add 1 cup of potpourri and stir mixture with a metal spoon.
❖ Mold mixture by hand into balls when wax begins to harden and is cool enough to handle.
❖ Insert hooked wire into a ball to use as a handle. Dip ball into melted wax.
❖ Apply pretty flower petals to surface of still-warm ornament, and dip again into wax to seal.
❖ Remove hanger once coatings have set. Repeat above 2 steps with remaining balls. Rub essential oils lightly over warm surface of balls, if desired. Wax will absorb and hold the scent.
❖ Allow ornament to completely cool and harden.

❖ Cut 8 inches of cord per ornament, and hot glue looped cord to ornament for hanger.

MATERIALS FOR STAR ORNAMENTS

Spray cooking oil
Star candy molds, rubber or hard plastic
Prepared beeswax
Potpourri
Essential oils: rose, vanilla, or lavender if desired
Hot glue gun
Gold cord

DIRECTIONS

❖ Spray a light coating of cooking oil in molds, and wipe off excess to leave light film.
❖ Place thick layer of potpourri in bottom of molds. Pour wax over potpourri, shaking molds to be sure wax fills every part. Stop 1/8 inch from top.
❖ Allow wax to cool to white opaque state and place molds in freezer. Remove molds when the ornaments have completely hardened. Cooling should cause ornament to draw away from the sides of molds. Tap the mold sides lightly outside ornaments that haven't pulled away, and lightly tap molds on surface with open side down to help dislodge ornaments.
❖ Remelt broken or failed ornaments and reuse the wax.
❖ Rub essential oils lightly over surface if desired. Wax will absorb and hold the scent.
❖ Cut 8 inches of cord per ornament, and hot glue looped cord to back of ornament for hanger.

Studded Leaf Ornament

Nature often provides the best inspiration for decorations. This ornament is a good example. Fragrant eucalyptus leaves are overlapped and secured with glue and round nailheads, making an ornament that catches light, provides interesting patterns, and gently scents the room.

Stunning window settings can start with a Studded Leaf Ornament, Seashell Wreath, Heavenly Wooden Angel, and Embellished Pillar Candles, pages 118, 120, and 131.

MATERIALS FOR STUDDED LEAF ORNAMENT

Eucalyptus or other flexible preserved leaves
1 (3-inch diameter) craft foam ball
Craft glue
Straight pins
Round nailheads
6 inches (1/4-inch wide) red satin ribbon

DIRECTIONS

❖ Pull leaves gently from stems.
❖ Begin at what will be bottom of ball, dab a small dot of glue on 3 leaves, and form a triangle with points together. Secure with straight pins.
❖ Continue pattern, gluing, overlapping, and pinning leaves around ball until ball is covered.
❖ Let dry for 30 minutes.
❖ Remove pins carefully, beginning at top of ball, and replace with an even distribution of nailheads. (It is not necessary to place a nailhead into every leaf.)
❖ Loop red satin ribbon for hanger, and attach to top of ornament with glue and a straight pin.

Seashell Wreath

Whether you gather seashells when you stroll the shore or seek them out in shops, you'll enjoy this lovely way to display your bounty. A Christmas wreath with a glittering nautical twist adds unusual flair to holiday decor.

MATERIALS

White craft glue
Medium flat paintbrush
2 sand dollars
Acrylic paints: White, Black
6 scallop shells
3 starfish
Brush-on gold liquid glitter
Hot glue gun
1 (14-inch) grapevine wreath
3 1/2 yards (1 1/2-inch wide) gold wire-edge ribbon
Floral wire

DIRECTIONS

❖ Mix a solution of half glue and half water. Paint thick coat on sand dollars to harden. Set aside on nonstick surface to dry.
❖ Paint 4 scallop shells white and 2 black.
❖ Paint starfish white.

❖ Paint dried sand dollars black.
❖ Paint shells with gold liquid glitter when first coat is dry.
❖ Glue 1 starfish in center bottom of wreath. Glue sand dollars to each side of starfish, and glue remaining starfish on top of sand dollars.
❖ Glue scallop shells above starfish, alternating colors as shown in photograph.
❖ Make a multi-looped bow with gold ribbon.
❖ Gather with floral wire, and insert through wreath to attach. Loop excess wire in back of wreath for hanger.

Heavenly Wooden Angel

This angel is simply designed and beautiful, and she comes apart for easy storage! Her body and wings are made of two pieces of wood that are notched to just slip together.

MATERIALS

Tracing paper
Graphite or carbon paper
1 (12-by-17-inch) piece of 1/4-inch balsa or plywood
Band saw or jigsaw
Sandpaper
Drill with 1/8-inch drill bit
1 (1 1/2-inch diameter) wooden ball
Nail
Hot glue gun
Spanish moss
Baby's-breath
8 inches gold cord
See Patterns

DIRECTIONS

❖ Transfer patterns onto tracing paper. Place graphite paper between patterns and wood. Trace over patterns to transfer image.
❖ Cut along outlines with band saw or jigsaw.
❖ Sand all surfaces and edges.
❖ Drill hole in wooden ball and in wood piece as indicated on pattern.
❖ Insert head end of nail into wood ball. Secure with hot glue if necessary.
❖ Glue Spanish moss to ball for hair, referring to photograph for placement.
❖ Tuck baby's-breath in moss.
❖ Loop gold cord, and tie ends in knot. Glue knot to moss for halo.
❖ Insert nail end of head into wooden piece, and slip wooden pieces together.

Deer Crossing Sign

*I*f you warn visitors of squirrel and rabbit crossings in your garden in the summer, shouldn't you warn them where Donder and Blitzen will be coming through in December? This bright sign is just the ticket for alerting foot traffic and raising smiles in the process. And it's a great gift for a gardener if you can bear to part with it.

MATERIALS

Tracing paper
Graphite or carbon paper
1 (19-by-20-inch) 1/4-inch plywood piece
Band saw or jigsaw
1 (1/2-by-3/4-by-19-inch) pressurized wood piece
Sandpaper
White enamel spray paint
Paintbrushes: large flat, medium flat, liner
Red enamel paint
Drill with bit same size as screws
Wood screws
1 yard (11/2-inch wide) indoor/outdoor plaid ribbon
1 (2-inch diameter) red jingle bell
See Patterns

DIRECTIONS

❖ Transfer pattern onto tracing paper. Place graphite paper between pattern and plywood. Trace over pattern to transfer image.
❖ Cut along outline with band saw or jigsaw. Cut 1 end of 19-inch wood piece into a point for stake.
❖ Sand all surfaces and edges.
❖ Spray paint deer with several coats of white paint until surface is smooth and well covered. Let dry. Transfer details from pattern onto tracing paper. Place graphite paper between pattern and wood. Trace over details to transfer image.
❖ Paint details with red enamel paint, using additional coats if needed for good coverage.
❖ Paint stake with 2 coats of red enamel paint. Let dry.
❖ Position stake on back of deer, and drill pilot holes for screws. Screw stake to deer.
❖ Tie ribbon in knot around deer's neck. Thread jingle bell onto ribbon, and tie ribbon in a bow.

Santa's helper watches for Rudolph in a festive Kitchen-Towel Child's Vest, page 63.

Have a Homespun Holiday

Our parents and their parents knew that beautiful decorations didn't mean shopping in expensive boutiques. That's because much of what makes something beautiful is what goes into it. A scrap taken from the loved-out quilt grandma made, the simple needlework done by a child learning the art of stitchery from Mom, buttons saved from years of sewing and mending—these are the richest makings for holiday decorations a heart could hope to have. Add to your wealth this year with some of the decorations we show here.

Mini-Quilt Ornament

At last a new life for the fabric remnants in your sewing basket! Here, we've used wool swatches cut from out-of-date dress suits to make one-of-a-kind miniature quilt ornaments. This ornament would be a good project for a youngster who is just learning to sew. Brightly colored scraps of wool and simple running stitches are all that are needed to make any of the four wonderful ornaments. Mom probably won't be able to resist joining in the fireside stitching to share the magic of passing on skills and creating Christmas memories.

MATERIALS

Scraps of wool or other fabrics
Scraps of quilt batting
16 inches jute
1 (#24) embroidery needle
Black and White embroidery floss
Tan thread
See Patterns

DIRECTIONS

❖ Cut two 3¹/₂-inch squares from fabric and one 3¹/₂-inch square from batting. (Note: We used wool fabric scraps.)

❖ Cut two 1-by-3¹/₂-inch strips and two 1-by-4-inch strips from fabric for binding. Cut jute into two 8-inch-long pieces.
❖ Transfer patterns to fabric scraps, and cut out as indicated on patterns.
❖ Pin appliqué pieces on 1 square fabric piece, referring to photograph for placement. Appliqué to fabric with running stitch and 2 strands of black floss, except for sheep head and legs, which are appliquéd with 2 strands of white floss.
❖ Stack ornament front, batting square, and backing square. Fold two 1-by-3¹/₂-inch strips over opposite sides of ornament for binding, and pin in place. Use 2 strands of white floss and a running stitch using tan thread to sew binding strips to square. Repeat with remaining binding strips on remaining 2 sides.
❖ Tie 1 jute piece into a bow, and tack to center top of ornament. Loop other jute piece, and tack to back of ornament for hanger.

Antiqued Sock Ornament

This ornament provides a great way to recycle those outgrown children's socks. Simply antique the sock, fill it with stuffing, and top with purchased holiday items. A rag homespun bow adds the crowning country touch.

MATERIALS

Folk Art® Antiquing Water-Base Acrylic:
   Down Home Brown
Small child's sock
Polyester stuffing
3 (4-inch long) sprigs of artificial greenery
Hot glue gun
1¹/₂-inch high wooden gingerbread man
Small bunch of preserved berries
1 cinnamon stick
1 (1-by-12-inch) rag-edged homespun piece
3 inches heavy white cotton thread

DIRECTIONS FOR ANTIQUED SOCK ORNAMENT

❖ Mix a bit of paint with warm water. Dunk sock in paint mixture, pat dry, and dry in dryer for 10 minutes. Sock should appear lightly splotched and antiqued.
❖ Fill sock with stuffing to cuff.
❖ Insert greenery so that it sticks out from sock cuff at varying heights, as shown in photograph.
❖ Hot glue gingerbread man, berries, and cinnamon stick in front of greenery in sock.
❖ Tie homespun rag piece in bow, and hot glue to front of sock at cuff.
❖ Stitch string through top back of cuff; knot string for hanger.

Burlap and Ribbon Tree Skirt

*B*urlap's rough, natural texture is great for so many things, and tree skirts are no exception. Nothing could be easier or more frugal than a square of burlap woven with ribbon and fringed all around. It's the perfect complement to a tree filled with homespun, country-style decorations.

MATERIALS

1 yard burlap
Masking tape
Dressmaker's chalk
Thread to match
8 yards (1/4-inch wide) green satin ribbon
1 (#20) tapestry needle

DIRECTIONS

❖ Cut a 36-inch square from burlap. Place a strip of masking tape around outside edges to prevent fraying.
❖ Mark a 6-inch circle in center and a line for skirt opening from center to 1 corner with dressmaker's chalk. Zigzag stitch around circle, and cut out inside stitching line.
❖ Zigzag stitch on either side of line from center to corner, and cut between stitched lines.
❖ Fold over 1/2-inch hems on circle and skirt opening and stitch.
❖ Measure 3 inches from outside edges, and mark for ribbon placement. Repeat 1 inch from first placement line for second ribbon placement line.

❖ Cut ribbon in eight 1-yard long pieces. Thread 1 piece into tapestry needle, and using a running stitch, stitch ribbon along ribbon placement lines at 1 inch intervals. Tie end of ribbon in square knot at corner, and trim to 1 inch. Repeat for remaining ribbon lines.
❖ Remove tape. Fringe bottom 2 inches.

Heart-in-Hands Ornament

*T*he traditional sign of friendship, a heart-in-hands motif makes a welcoming ornament for the Christmas tree. Ours is made from brushed wool felt in pastels, but you could change the effect by using plaid or deep-colored wool suits that are ready for recycling.

MATERIALS

Scraps of pink and cream brushed wool felt
Fabric glue
Heavyweight cotton thread
See Patterns

DIRECTIONS

❖ Transfer patterns to felt, and cut out cream hand and pink heart pieces.
❖ Center heart over hand, and glue in place.
❖ Loop 8 inches of thread through top and knot.

Coverlet Bunny Ornament

*I*t's always a shame to see a beautiful old overshot coverlet in tatters, but here's a way to preserve the good parts and decorate your tree with them. Depending on the condition of your coverlet, you could end up with a hutch-full!

Have a country Christmas with Mini-Quilt Ornament, Antiqued Sock Ornament, Burlap and Ribbon Tree Skirt, Heart-in-Hands Ornament, Coverlet Bunny Ornament, Button Heart Angel, and Quilt Heart Angel Ornament, pages 123, 124, 128, and 129.

MATERIALS FOR COVERLET BUNNY ORNAMENT

Scrap of overshot coverlet
Scrap of tan cotton fabric
Polyester stuffing
18 inches jute
8 inches tan cotton thread
See Patterns

DIRECTIONS

❖ Transfer pattern to coverlet and to tan fabric, and cut out front and back of ornament.
❖ Sew together, right sides facing, leaving an opening for turning.
❖ Turn, stuff firmly, and slip stitch closed.
❖ Tie jute around neck in bow. Stitch thread through top, and knot for hanger.

Quilt-Scrap Sheep

When that old quilt can no longer warm your toes, let it warm your heart. Make it into this country classic—it's a year-round decoration to group with other country-style items in a Christmas setting. And where the fabric is missing, leaving batting exposed—the sheep's wooly effect is especially nice. If you've used up your store of wooden spools, they can still be found at flea markets and garage and estate sales. You can also order them through the resource listed in the photograph index in the back of the book.

MATERIALS

Quilt scraps
Polyester stuffing
2 (1/2-inch diameter) white buttons
1 (1/2-inch diameter) gold jingle bell
18 inches brown yarn
2 yards jute
1 (#20) tapestry needle
2 (2-inch long) wooden spools
See Patterns

A rustic elegance fills the mantel with Quilt-Scrap Sheep, Paper Squirrel Garland, Glitter Stars, "Bringing It Home" Cross-Stitch, and Clever Candlestick Makers, pages 127 through 129.

DIRECTIONS

❖ Transfer sheep pattern to quilt, reverse pattern, and transfer to quilt. Cut out 2 sheep.
❖ Sew together with right sides facing, leaving an opening for turning.
❖ Turn, stuff firmly with polyester stuffing, and slip stitch closed.
❖ Transfer ear pattern to quilt 2 times, and cut out ears.
❖ Zigzag stitch around edge of ears to hold layers together. Position ears on head as indicated on pattern, and attach with a button sewn at top of each ear.
❖ Thread bell on yarn, and tie around sheep's neck, tying yarn in bow at top of head.
❖ Cut jute into four 18-inch long pieces. Thread 1 piece through tapestry needle, and stitch through sheep where indicated for front legs. Thread 1 spool on a piece of jute, and position under body for front legs. Tie ends on each side together in bows to secure spool to sheep. Repeat to attach spool for back legs.

Paper Squirrel Garland

Perky little forest friends munch nuts as their bushy tails form hearts in this paper garland. You may want to enlist little hands to cut out yards of squirrels to circle your tree this year. Even the smallest can help by taping the paper strips together.

MATERIALS

1 sheet white typing paper
Scissors
Brown craft paper
Transparent tape
See Patterns

DIRECTIONS

❖ Trace pattern onto white typing paper. Cut out.
❖ Cut a 6-inch wide strip of brown paper to the desired length.
❖ Fold the brown paper strip in accordion folds using the white paper pattern as a guide. Be sure folds in paper match fold lines on pattern.
❖ Lay pattern on folded paper and trace around the pattern.
❖ Cut out around pattern outlines.
❖ Cut additional strips, taping them together, to form garland of desired length.

Button Heart Angel

*B*ring out the button jar. This sweetheart of an angel is just the place to display some of your collection. She's richly attired with moiré wings and pearl buttons, but after all, she's an angel, perfect in any Christmas setting.

MATERIALS

Scraps of ecru moiré fabric
Scrap of thin quilt batting
Scraps of tan cotton fabric
Ecru thread
Buttons of different sizes
11 inches (1/2-inch wide) ecru scalloped lace
Polyester stuffing
Black paint pen
Red paint pen
Spanish moss
Hot glue gun
Purchased 1/2-inch satin ribbon rose
8 inches gold thread
See Patterns

DIRECTIONS

❖ Transfer wing pattern to ecru fabric 2 times and batting 1 time, and cut out. Transfer heart pattern to tan fabric 2 times, and cut out. Transfer head pattern to tan fabric 2 times, and cut out.
❖ Stack 2 moiré pieces, place batting piece on top, and stitch, leaving an opening for turning. Trim batting from seam, clip curves, and turn. Slip stitch opening closed.
❖ Machine-stitch quilting lines on wings as indicated on pattern.
❖ Sew tan heart pieces together, leaving an opening for turning. Clip curves, turn, and slip stitch closed.
❖ Arrange buttons over front of tan heart, and sew in place.
❖ Slip stitch lace to back edge of heart.
❖ Sew head pieces together, leaving bottom open for turning. Turn, stuff firmly with polyester stuffing, and slip stitch closed.
❖ Dot black eyes and red mouth with paint pens as indicated on pattern. Dab a bit of red paint on your finger, smooth it out, and lightly rouge angel's cheeks.
❖ Twist a bit of Spanish moss into a garland, and glue at an angle onto angel's head. Tack ribbon rose to head. Refer to photograph for placement.

❖ Position head between quilted wings and button heart, referring to photograph for placement, and hot glue angel head to wings and heart to angel.
❖ Thread gold thread onto needle, and stitch through angel's head, knotting ends for hanger.

Glitter Stars

*S*pangle your tree with simple little stars made from glitter stems. These 12-inch long stems may be purchased at most craft stores and are simply wire that is covered with sparkling red tinsel. To make small stars, just bend the wire about every 2 1/4 inches, and twist the ends around each other. To make larger stars, attach 2 stems together, bend about every 4 1/2 inches, and twist the ends.

"Bringing It Home" Cross-Stitch

*B*efore the age of Christmas tree lots, families went into the woods to find the perfect tree for their holiday centerpiece. Those times are recalled in this cross-stitched picture. Maybe it will inspire you to head to the woods to cut your own Christmas tree this year.

MATERIALS

1 (15-by-18-inch) piece 11-count white Aida cloth
1 (#24) embroidery needle
DMC® Embroidery Floss = 8m skeins (1 skein each):
    #828 Pale Blue, #827 Lt. Blue, #813 Blue,
    #825 Dk. Blue, #415 Gray, White, #3348 Pale Green,
    #3347 Green, #895 Dk. Green, #833 Lt. Golden
    Brown, #831 Md. Golden Brown, #829 Golden
    Brown, Black, #725 Golden Yellow, #783 Dk. Golden
    Yellow, #745 Pale Yellow, #612 Beige, #224 Pale Rose,
    #223 Rose, #221 Deep Rose, #498 Wine Red,
    #814 Deep Wine Red, #321 Red
See Patterns

DIRECTIONS

❖ Mark center of the cross-stitch fabric both ways with long running stitch using needle and thread.

❖ Work cross-stitch according to chart and color key, beginning at intersection of arrows on chart to ensure proper placement of design on fabric.
❖ Each square on chart represents 1 fabric thread. Use 3 strands of floss for cross-stitch and 1 strand for back-stitch.
❖ Press finished work.
❖ Frame as desired.

Santa Alarm Stocking

Here's a quick idea to transform a simple stocking into one that will give you and the children loads of giggles. Tie bells to varying lengths of narrow ribbon, and with a few stitches, dangle them from the cuff or top edge of the stocking. Make sure impatient little ones know that those bells are Santa's way of knowing if anyone's peeking.

Clever Candlestick Makers

These simple candle cups allow you to convert all sorts of things into candlesticks. They're communion cups (available at church supply stores) that have been painted and then glued onto the heads of 1½-inch nails. You can stick them in fruit (just make sure the fruit doesn't tend to roll!), use them in foam inserted in floral arrangements, or display them in logs as we have here.

We drilled nail-sized holes into sections of logs of different heights and inserted the candle cups in the logs. If you feel they need to be more carefully secured, you can use a bit of florist's clay on the bottom of the cup. The florist's clay both prevents them from slipping and makes them reusable.

Our candle cups are painted red and green for the holidays and feature ¼-inch wide picot ribbon bows. For a twist, you might try using white or metallic paints. If you paint log sections matching metallic colors, you have a totally different look, suitable for any time of year.

Quilt Heart Angel Ornament

As simple and lovable as an angel from the country should be, this quilt heart ornament is one to cherish. And since the heart is a scrap of an old quilt, all you'll need to put together this angel are scissors and glue.

MATERIALS

Scrap of old quilt
4½ inches (2½-inch wide) scalloped white eyelet lace
1 (2½-inch) wooden clothespin
Hot glue gun
12 inches jute
Spanish moss
2 inches decorative gold wire
See Patterns

DIRECTIONS

❖ Transfer pattern to quilt scrap, and cut out heart. Leave edges unfinished.
❖ Fold end of lace opposite scalloped edge ¼ inch to wrong side and press. Fold 1 short end ¼ inch to wrong side and press. Glue folded short end over raw end to form tube.
❖ Finger-pleat top of tube around head of clothespin, and glue in place to make dress.
❖ Tie jute around neck of dress to back of pin, knot, and knot again near ends for hanger.
❖ Glue Spanish moss to top of head. Form gold wire into circle, and glue to top of head for halo.
❖ Glue angel to heart, making sure jute hanger extends between angel and heart.

Wooden Doorway Bow

*I*f you're tired of wrestling ribbon into hard-to-reach places, spend a little time in the woodworking shop this year and make a bow that will be a cinch to put up and take down for years to come. This wooden bow has very graceful lines to be so big and sturdy. We painted ours red, but you could stain it, stencil it, carve it—use it to display any number of craft skills.

MATERIALS

Tracing paper
Graphite or carbon paper
4 feet (1-by-12) pine shelving piece
Band saw or jigsaw
Router with a rounding-over bit
Sandpaper
Wood glue
C-clamps
Drill with bit same size as screws
Flathead wood screws
Finishing nails
Medium paintbrush
Red enamel paint
Picture hanger
See Patterns

DIRECTIONS

❖ Transfer patterns onto tracing paper. Place graphite paper between patterns and wood. Trace over patterns to transfer image.
❖ Cut along outlines with band saw or jigsaw.
❖ Round top edges of streamer with router. Saw inside edges of 2 smaller bow loop pieces at a 45-degree angle so that they will angle out from knot (Figure 7).
❖ Sand all surfaces and edges.

Figure 7

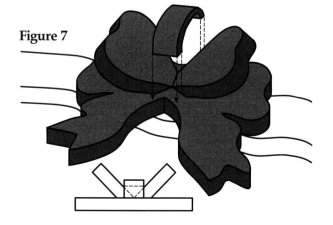

❖ Glue flat bow to center of streamer, and secure with C-clamps. Let dry.
❖ Remove C-clamps and drill holes on back for flathead wood screws. Secure with screws.
❖ Position small bow pieces on bow so that angled points meet. Apply glue to edges, and attach with finishing nails.
❖ Let dry. Nail bow knot over center of bow with finishing nails.
❖ Paint with 2 or 3 coats of red enamel paint, letting paint dry between coats, until bow is evenly covered.
❖ Attach picture hanger to back.

Embellished Pillar Candles

*C*andlelight sets the mood for many Christmas moments. And you can make embellished candles like the designer ones found in expensive boutiques. The trick to preserving the candles' beauty is to first burn them an inch or so and then use votive candles in their recesses.

MATERIALS FOR JEWEL-EMBELLISHED CANDLES

Gemstones with nailhead settings
Metallic nailheads
Pillar candles in desired colors and sizes
Rubber band
Small ruler
Gold wire thread

DIRECTIONS

❖ Determine style of desired arrangement of the nailheads.
❖ For free-form arrangements, simply position nailheads on each candle, and press firmly in place.
❖ For geometric arrangements, indicate positions by placing rubber band around top of each candle and marking vertical measurements on band.
❖ Mark horizontal positions on the ruler.
❖ Place ruler along each candle at marks on rubber band to align nailheads, and use ruler as guide, pressing nailheads firmly into candle.
❖ Make gold wire design by securing 1 end of wire with a nailhead and wrapping wire around candle to get desired effect. Secure at random points with nailheads and secure second end with a nailhead.

MATERIALS FOR NATURE-EMBELLISHED CANDLES

Wire cutters
Floral pins
Dried herbs and flowers, twigs, berries, feathers,
    cinnamon sticks, dried peppers, and excelsior
Pillar candles in desired colors and sizes
Raffia

DIRECTIONS

❖ Cut floral pins so prongs are about ½ inch long.
❖ Clip materials to fit along candle and secure to
candle with floral pins.
❖ Wrap several lengths of raffia around each
candle over pins and knot to secure materials and
conceal pins.
❖ Check to see that any flammable materials are
positioned below or away from candle flame.

Dressed Up Napkin Rings

These sparkling napkin rings are an easy
accent to make for the dinner table. Simple
wooden napkin rings can be unearthed at garage
sales and flea markets. Use a bit of paint and
ribbon, and you have five or so golden rings
adding the perfect festive note.

MATERIALS

Wooden napkin rings
Fine sandpaper
Paper towels
Gold acrylic paint
½-inch wide gold wire-edge ribbon
Hot glue gun
Nailheads, buttons, or other baubles

DIRECTIONS

❖ Rough surface of rings with sandpaper. Wipe
clean of dust with damp paper towel and let dry.
❖ Wipe gold paint lightly over surface with paper
towel, adding coats as needed to get desired effect.
❖ Cut one 8-inch long piece of ribbon for each
ring. Form small bows from each ribbon piece,
and glue onto rings.
❖ Glue nailheads with prongs bent in, buttons, or
other baubles over center of bows.

Marbleized Place Mats

Dress the table for the holidays with elegant
accessories. These place mats add sparkle
and sophistication, but they are really very easy
and inexpensive to make. If you have even basic
painting skills, you can put together a set of mats
in no time. These are painted in warm neutral
tones, but you can change the colors to match
your dining room color scheme. The trick is to
keep all colors close to the same tone so that they
blend well.

MATERIALS

1 (14-by-18-inch) primed artist canvas piece
Pencil
Ruler
Acrylic paints: White, Peach, Gray, Gold, Rose
Paper plates or saucers
Paper towels
Feather
Medium flat paintbrush
Black fine point permanent marker
Semigloss water-base varnish

DIRECTIONS

❖ Draw off a 2½-inch border with pencil and
ruler around all 4 sides of canvas piece.
❖ Place a bit of each paint color in a different
plate or saucer. Use wadded paper towels to dab
paint randomly over central square, mingling
colors to create marble effect. Be careful to dab
and not drag towel through paint. Let dry.
❖ Dilute some gray paint, dip feather in paint,
and twirl as you brush diagonally across marbling
for veins. Repeat with white paint.
❖ Paint border peach. Let dry.
❖ Place some gold paint on a plate. Dip wadded
paper towel into paint, and dab over peach
border. Let dry.
❖ Use ruler and black marker to draw outline
between central square and border.
❖ Finish with a coat of semigloss varnish over
place mat.

*Find upscale table settings or the perfect gifts in
Embellished Pillar Candles, Dressed Up Napkin
Rings, and Marbleized Place Mats, pages 131
and 132.*

A Season for Celebrating

Entertaining

Mrs. Wasley, my third grade music teacher, said, "This year, the Christmas pageant will be a learning experience." Across the classroom, third grade boys and girls groaned in horror. We knew, however, there was no arguing with Mrs. Wasley. Every year, she planned the Christmas pageant for the entire school.

When we gathered in the auditorium, she explained that, in this year's pageant, each class would pretend to be children from a different country. Bonita Mace and I looked at each other and rolled our eyes as Mrs. Wasley said, "My third grade boys and girls will be the boys and girls of Germany. They will learn to sing in German. They will sing *O Tannenbaum*."

Bonita and I looked across the aisle at Margarete. Margarete had actually been born in Germany, but her parents were missionaries who were moving to Africa. When she tried to speak English, the words came out lispy and strange. Bonita and I knew the *tannenbaum* song had to be Margarete's fault.

At recess, Bonita said that, this year, she had really counted on being an angel. It was her year, she said, to sing the pageant solo. We both agreed that we did not want to sing a song in somebody else's language. We did not want to sing about any *tannenbaum*. We did not even know what a *tannenbaum* was.

Because Mrs. Wasley was our very own third grade teacher, however, we did not have any choice. During pageant practice, even though we had no idea what we were singing, we sang *O Tannenbaum* as loudly as we could. Whenever Margarete practiced her solo verse, Bonita stuck out her tongue.

On the night of the Christmas pageant, the third grade boys and girls gathered onstage around a six-foot-tall posterboard Christmas tree. When the curtain rose, we began to hum the *tannenbaum* song and Margarete slowly entered. Wearing a white round-collared choir blouse with a floppy red bow, she carried in her hands a shiny gold star, sewn with golden braid and tinsel that glittered in the stage lights.

When Margarete began her solo verse of *O Tannenbaum*, she sang in a small, gentle voice. When the light danced off the star, it made the posterboard tree sparkle. Bonita and I hummed along quietly and listened. Even though Margarete sang ever so softly, we could understand every word.

Serve a dreamy light finale with Sweet Dream Dessert, page 142.

Dreaming of a Light Christmas

ncle Jeff is on a low-fat diet. Aunt Peggy is cutting back on salt *and* sugar. Is it possible to enjoy the holidays without paying for it later? It is if you join us in *Dreaming of a Light Christmas!* Our appetizer, main course, and dessert recipes are low in fat and calories, yet high in taste and appeal. We've taken some traditional favorites and some exciting new ideas and reduced the fat, sodium, and calories. Surprise! These recipes taste great and are good for you! Use our substitutions and ideas in your own recipes. Here's to good eating and good health!

SPICY APPETIZER MEDLEY

1 cup reduced-calorie mayonnaise
2/3 cup prepared chutney
1 teaspoon curry powder
1/4 teaspoon cayenne pepper
2 cups packed fresh mint leaves
2 cups packed fresh cilantro leaves
2/3 cup cider vinegar
4 jalapeño peppers, seeded
1/4 cup sugar
1 (2-inch) piece of fresh gingerroot, peeled, chopped
1 teaspoon salt
1/2 cup plain nonfat yogurt
3 pounds link turkey sausage
Assorted vegetables such as carrot sticks, broccoli flowerets, cauliflowerets and jicama

❖ Combine mayonnaise, chutney, curry powder and cayenne pepper in bowl; mix well. Chill, covered, until serving time.
❖ Process mint leaves, cilantro leaves, vinegar, jalapeño peppers, sugar, gingerroot and salt in food processor until smooth. Combine with yogurt in bowl. Chill, covered, until serving time.
❖ Grill or cook sausage in skillet until cooked through; drain. Cut into 1-inch pieces.
❖ Arrange sausage pieces in center of serving platter; place wooden pick in each piece. Arrange vegetables around edge of platter.
❖ Serve with curry and cilantro dips.
❖ Yield: 12 servings.

BAKED VEGETABLE AND SEAFOOD WON TONS

1 envelope Lipton vegetable recipe soup mix
15 ounces low-fat ricotta cheese
8 ounces surimi (imitation crab meat), or 1 1/2 cups cooked shrimp, chopped
1/4 teaspoon garlic powder
1/8 teaspoon pepper
40 won ton wrappers
1 tablespoon water
1 tablespoon olive oil or vegetable oil
10 green onion tops

❖ Preheat oven to 350 degrees.
❖ Combine soup mix, ricotta cheese, imitation crab meat, garlic powder and pepper in medium bowl; mix well.
❖ Place 1 tablespoonful mixture in center of each won ton wrapper. Brush edges with water. Bring up corners to enclose filling; press to seal.
❖ Place seam side down on lightly greased baking sheet; brush with oil. (Or spray with nonstick cooking spray to further reduce fat.)
❖ Bake for 25 minutes or until crisp and golden brown, turning once.
❖ Cut each onion top into 4 slivers. Tie 1 sliver around each won ton.
❖ May serve with Spiced Tea Honey (see page 36) and Hot Pepper Mustard (see page 38).
❖ Yield: 40 won tons.

ZUCCHINI AND BLEU CHEESE ROLL-UPS

3 ounces Neufchâtel cheese or light cream cheese, softened
2 ounces bleu cheese, crumbled
1/2 cup finely chopped walnuts
4 small (6-ounce) zucchini

❖ Combine Neufchâtel cheese and bleu cheese in small bowl; mix with fork. Stir in 1/3 cup walnuts.
❖ Cut zucchini into very thin 1-inch wide strips with vegetable peeler or sharp knife. Select 32 strips; reserve remaining zucchini for another use.
❖ Place rounded 1/2 teaspoon cheese mixture onto 1 end of each zucchini strip. Roll zucchini to enclose filling. Dip 1 end into remaining walnuts.
❖ Arrange walnuts side up on serving plate. Chill for 1 hour or until firm.
❖ Yield: 32 roll-ups.

LIGHT ARTICHOKE AND CHEESE DIP

1 cup nonfat cottage
   cheese
2 tablespoons chopped
   chives
2 tablespoons skim milk
Hot pepper sauce to taste
1/4 teaspoon basil
Garlic powder to taste

1/4 teaspoon seasoned salt
3 or 4 canned artichoke
   hearts, drained, finely
   chopped
2 tablespoons grated
   Parmesan cheese
Fresh vegetables

❖ Combine first 7 ingredients in blender or food processor container; process until smooth.
❖ Combine with artichoke hearts and Parmesan cheese in bowl; mix well.
❖ Chill, covered, for 4 hours or longer; mixture will thicken as it chills.
❖ Serve with fresh vegetable dippers.
❖ Yield: 14 servings.

CRANBERRY RELISH APPETIZER

16 to 24 ounces
   Neufchâtel cheese
   or light cream cheese,
   softened
2 cups fresh cranberries
3/4 cup sugar
3/4 teaspoon grated
   orange rind

1/3 cup orange juice
1/2 teaspoon grated
   lemon rind
11/2 tablespoons lemon
   juice
Fresh mint
Strip of lemon peel

❖ Spread Neufchâtel cheese in 8-inch springform pan. Chill, covered, for 8 hours or longer.
❖ Combine cranberries, sugar, orange rind, orange juice, grated lemon rind and lemon juice in saucepan.
❖ Bring cranberry mixture to a boil. Cook for 3 minutes or until cranberries pop.
❖ Cool to room temperature. Chill, covered, for 8 hours or longer.
❖ Place springform pan on serving plate; remove side of pan. Drain cranberry mixture. Spoon over Neufchâtel cheese.
❖ Garnish with mint and strip of lemon peel. Serve with cookies.
❖ May make in plastic wrap-lined bell mold or other Christmas mold and use poster board as a base if preferred.
❖ Yield: 16 to 24 servings.

RED RASPBERRY SOUP

2 (10-ounce) packages
   frozen red raspberries,
   thawed
1/2 cup rosé or cranberry
   juice

1/2 cup light sour cream
1 cup raspberry sherbet
1/2 cup low-fat milk
Lime juice
8 lime slices

❖ Combine first 5 ingredients in blender container; process until smooth.
❖ Strain into small serving bowls. Add several drops of lime juice to each bowl. Garnish each serving with lime slice.
❖ Yield: 8 servings.

HOLIDAY AMBROSIA

1 (20-ounce) can juice-
   pack pineapple
   chunks, drained
1 (11-ounce) can
   mandarin oranges,
   drained
1 banana, sliced

11/2 cups seedless grapes
1 cup miniature
   marshmallows
1/2 cup flaked coconut
1/2 cup chopped almonds
1 cup nonfat vanilla
   yogurt

❖ Combine first 7 ingredients in bowl; mix gently. Fold in yogurt gently. Chill until serving time.
❖ Yield: 8 servings.

PUMPKIN-ORANGE SALAD

1 large package sugar-
   free orange gelatin
11/2 cups boiling water
1 cup canned pumpkin

2 tablespoons apple
   butter
2 tablespoons sugar
1/4 teaspoon ginger

❖ Dissolve gelatin in boiling water in bowl. Stir in pumpkin, apple butter, sugar and ginger.
❖ Spoon into 8x8-inch dish. Chill until partially set, stirring occasionally.
❖ Chill until set. Cut into squares to serve.
❖ May substitute 1 tablespoon light brown sugar for sugar or add 1/2 teaspoon grated orange rind.
❖ Yield: 6 servings.

MARINATED GREEN BEAN AND TOMATO SALAD

3 pounds green beans
Salt to taste
3 tablespoons country-
   style Dijon mustard
1/4 cup sherry wine
   vinegar

2/3 cup olive oil
1/3 cup minced shallots
2 (1-pint) baskets cherry
   tomatoes, cut into
   halves
Pepper to taste

❖ Trim green beans and cut into 2-inch pieces. Combine with water to cover and salt to taste in large saucepan.
❖ Cook for 5 minutes or until tender-crisp. Drain and rinse with cold water. Chill in large bowl.
❖ Combine mustard and vinegar in small bowl. Whisk in olive oil gradually. Stir in shallots.
❖ Add tomatoes and dressing to green beans; toss to mix well. Season with salt and pepper to taste.
❖ Yield: 12 servings.

BEEF TOURNEDOS STUFFED WITH WILD MUSHROOM SAUTÉ

4 (6-ounce) beef tenderloin steaks, 1 inch thick	1 tablespoon fresh oregano or 1 teaspoon dried oregano
2 ounces mixed dried shiitake and porcini mushrooms	1 tablespoon margarine Salt and pepper to taste 1/2 cup Cabernet
1 shallot, finely chopped	2 tablespoons margarine

❖ Trim steaks. Cut horizontal pocket in 1 side of each steak.
❖ Combine mushrooms with water to cover in bowl; weight to hold under water.
❖ Microwave mushrooms on High for 4 minutes or let stand at room temperature for 30 minutes; strain, reserving 1/2 cup liquid. Slice mushrooms, discarding tough stems.
❖ Sauté mushrooms, shallot and oregano in 1 tablespoon margarine in skillet for 2 minutes or until vegetables are tender, stirring occasionally.
❖ Spoon mushroom mixture into pockets in steaks. Place steaks in hot skillet.
❖ Cook over medium heat for 3 minutes on each side or until medium-rare. Remove to warm platter. Season with salt and pepper.
❖ Increase heat to high. Stir wine into pan juices.
❖ Cook for 1 minute, stirring constantly. Stir in reserved mushroom liquid. Cook until reduced to 1/4 cup. Whisk in 2 tablespoons margarine. Serve over steaks.
❖ May substitute 6 ounces fresh wild mushrooms for dried mushrooms, using beef stock for mushroom liquid.
❖ Yield: 4 servings.

BERRY-GLAZED BAKED HAM

1 (4- to 5-pound) cooked boneless ham	4 teaspoons cornstarch 2/3 cup reduced-calorie seedless raspberry jam
1/2 cup dry white wine	
1/4 cup lemon juice	2 tablespoons margarine

❖ Preheat oven to 325 degrees.
❖ Score ham in diamond pattern. Place on rack in shallow roasting pan.
❖ Bake for 1 3/4 hours or to 140 degrees on meat thermometer.
❖ Combine wine, lemon juice and cornstarch in small saucepan. Stir in 1/3 cup jam.
❖ Cook over low heat until bubbly, stirring constantly. Stir in remaining 1/3 cup jam and margarine. Cook until margarine melts, stirring frequently. Brush over ham.
❖ Bake for 10 minutes longer. Place ham on serving plate. Spoon any remaining glaze over ham.
❖ Yield: 12 servings.

DIJON-GINGER CORNISH HENS

4 (1 1/2-pound) Cornish game hens, skinned	1/4 cup olive oil 1/2 teaspoon pepper
1 teaspoon sage	1 cup orange juice
1 teaspoon rosemary	1/4 cup honey
4 cloves of garlic, crushed	1/4 cup red wine vinegar
2 teaspoons minced fresh ginger	3 tablespoons Dijon mustard
1/2 teaspoon pepper	2 teaspoons minced fresh ginger
4 (3-inch) strips orange peel	4 teaspoons grated orange rind
Apricot and Brown Rice Pilaf	

❖ Preheat oven to 375 degrees.
❖ Rinse game hens inside and out and pat dry. Sprinkle cavities with sage, rosemary, garlic, 1 teaspoon ginger and 1/4 teaspoon pepper; place orange peel strips in cavities. Stuff with Apricot and Brown Rice Pilaf.
❖ Place breast side up in shallow roasting pan. Brush with olive oil; sprinkle with remaining 1/4 teaspoon pepper.
❖ Combine orange juice, honey, vinegar, mustard and 1 teaspoon ginger in small saucepan; mix well.
❖ Bring sauce to a boil; reduce heat. Simmer for 5 minutes or until syrupy, stirring frequently.
❖ Roast for 35 to 40 minutes or until hens are tender, basting frequently with sauce.
❖ Yield: 4 servings.

APRICOT AND BROWN RICE PILAF

1 cup shredded carrot	1 cup apple juice
1 tablespoon pine nuts	3/4 cup water
1 tablespoon margarine	6 dried apricot halves, chopped
3/4 cup quick-cooking brown rice	2 tablespoons raisins

❖ Combine carrot, pine nuts and margarine in 1-quart glass dish.
❖ Microwave on High for 2 minutes. Add rice, apple juice and water; mix well.
❖ Microwave, loosely covered, on High for 5 minutes, stirring once. Stir in apricots and raisins.
❖ Microwave, covered, on Medium for 12 minutes or until liquid is absorbed and rice is tender.
❖ May serve immediately or use to stuff Dijon-Ginger Cornish Hens.
❖ Yield: 4 servings.

Baked Vegetable and Seafood Won Tons, page 136

HONEY-BAKED TURKEY BREAST

1 (6-pound) bone-in turkey breast, skinned	2 tablespoons thawed, frozen orange juice concentrate
1/3 cup honey	
1/2 teaspoon allspice	

❖ Preheat oven to 325 degrees.
❖ Rinse turkey and pat dry. Place on rack sprayed with nonstick cooking spray in shallow roasting pan.
❖ Combine honey, allspice and orange juice concentrate in bowl; mix well. Brush over turkey.
❖ Bake, covered with foil, for 1 hour. Bake, uncovered, for 1 hour longer or to 170 degrees on meat thermometer, brushing frequently with honey mixture.
❖ Let stand for 20 minutes before slicing.
❖ Yield: 6 to 8 servings.

PINEAPPLE CARROTS

8 medium carrots, cut into julienne strips	4 teaspoons cornstarch
1 cup orange juice	1/2 teaspoon ginger
1 (16-ounce) can juice-pack pineapple tidbits	

❖ Cook carrots in orange juice in covered saucepan just until tender-crisp, stirring occasionally.
❖ Drain pineapple, reserving juice. Blend reserved juice with cornstarch and ginger in small bowl. Add with pineapple to undrained hot carrots.
❖ Cook over low heat until thickened, stirring occasionally.
❖ Yield: 8 servings.

CAESAR SCALLOPED POTATOES

1 medium onion, chopped	4 cups sliced new potatoes
2 large cloves of garlic, minced	2/3 cup grated Parmesan cheese
3 tablespoons margarine	2 teaspoons Dijon mustard
2 tablespoons all-purpose flour	1 teaspoon low-sodium Worcestershire sauce
2 cups low-fat milk	Pepper to taste

❖ Combine first 3 ingredients in large glass bowl.
❖ Microwave on High for 1 to 2 minutes or until onion is tender. Stir in flour.
❖ Microwave on High for 30 seconds. Whisk in milk until smooth.
❖ Microwave on High for 2 to 4 minutes or until slightly thickened, stirring twice. Stir in potatoes, cheese, mustard, Worcestershire sauce and pepper.
❖ Microwave, covered, on High for 6 to 8 minutes or until potatoes are tender, stirring twice.
❖ Yield: 6 servings.

ARTICHOKE AND SPINACH MINI SOUFFLÉS

1 (10-ounce) package frozen spinach soufflé	Juice of 1 lemon
	1 cup sour cream
2 (16-ounce) cans artichoke bottoms	1 hard-cooked egg, chopped

❖ Preheat oven to 350 degrees.
❖ Thaw spinach. Rinse and drain artichoke; place on baking sheet. Drizzle with lemon juice. Place 1 scoop of spinach on each artichoke.
❖ Bake for 15 to 20 minutes or until spinach is set.
❖ Place a dollop of sour cream on each soufflé. Sprinkle with chopped egg. Place on serving plates.
❖ Yield: 6 servings.

GLAZED SQUASH AND APPLES

2 medium acorn squash	1/4 cup packed light brown sugar
2 apples, cut into wedges	
2/3 cup apple cider or apple juice	1/4 teaspoon apple pie spice
2 tablespoons margarine	1/8 teaspoon salt

❖ Preheat oven to 350 degrees.
❖ Cut squash crosswise into 1-inch rings, discarding seed. Cut rings into halves. Arrange in single layer in 9-by-13-inch baking dish.
❖ Bake, covered, for 40 minutes or just until tender. Arrange apple wedges around squash.
❖ Bring remaining ingredients to a boil in saucepan. Simmer for 3 minutes. Spoon over top.
❖ Bake, uncovered, for 10 minutes or until tender, basting several times.
❖ Yield: 6 servings.

PASTA WITH RED PEPPER SAUCE

4 red bell peppers, chopped	Garlic to taste
	1 tablespoon basil
2 carrots, finely chopped	Salt and pepper to taste
1 tablespoon olive oil	1 (16-ounce) package angel hair pasta, cooked, drained
2 cups canned tomatoes packed in purée	
1/2 pear, chopped	Grated Parmesan cheese

❖ Sauté red peppers and carrots in olive oil in skillet for 4 to 5 minutes or until tender. Stir in tomatoes, pear and seasonings. Simmer for 45 minutes.
❖ Place pasta in large serving dish. Spoon sauce over top. Serve with cheese.
❖ Yield: 6 to 8 side-dish servings.

Beef Tournedos Stuffed with Wild Mushroom Sauté, Caesar Scalloped Potatoes, and Cranberry Cordial, pages 138, 140, and 143

HERBED POPOVERS

1 1/2 cups low-fat milk	3 eggs
1 tablespoon melted margarine	1 tablespoon each minced chives, parsley and thyme
1 1/2 cups all-purpose flour	
1/2 teaspoon salt	

❖ Preheat oven to 450 degrees.
❖ Beat milk with margarine, flour and salt in mixer bowl until smooth.
❖ Add eggs 1 at a time, mixing just until smooth after each addition. Stir in herbs.
❖ Fill greased muffin cups 3/4 full.
❖ Bake for 15 minutes. Reduce oven temperature to 350 degrees. Bake for 20 minutes longer or until golden brown.
❖ Yield: 12 servings.

CHRISTMAS MOUSSE

2 cups thawed frozen unsweetened loose-pack raspberries	1 cup boiling water
	1/2 cup light sour cream
	2 tablespoons lemon juice
1 1/2 cups thawed frozen unsweetened loose-pack strawberries	1 pint strawberry or vanilla frozen yogurt
	Whipped topping
1 large package sugar-free raspberry gelatin	Maraschino cherries

❖ Purée undrained berries in blender until smooth. Strain into large bowl.
❖ Dissolve gelatin in boiling water in bowl.
❖ Combine gelatin, sour cream, lemon juice and frozen yogurt in blender container; process until smooth. Add to berries; mix gently.
❖ Spoon mixture into serving dishes. Chill for 4 to 6 hours or until set. Serve topped with whipped topping and cherries.
❖ Yield: 8 to 10 servings.

RIBBON OF CRANBERRY CHEESECAKE

1 1/2 cups finely crushed vanilla wafers	16 ounces Neufchâtel cheese or light cream cheese, softened
6 tablespoons melted margarine	
1 cup sugar	2 tablespoons all-purpose flour
2 tablespoons cornstarch	
1 1/2 cups fresh or frozen cranberries	2 teaspoons vanilla extract
	3 eggs or 3/4 cup egg substitute
1 cup orange juice	
1 cup low-fat cottage cheese	2 teaspoons finely grated orange rind
	8 ounces low-fat vanilla yogurt
1 cup sugar	

❖ Preheat oven to 375 degrees.
❖ Mix cookie crumbs and margarine in medium bowl. Press over bottom and 1 inch up side of 9-inch springform pan; set aside.
❖ Combine 1 cup sugar and cornstarch in medium saucepan. Stir in cranberries and orange juice.
❖ Cook over medium heat until thickened, stirring constantly. Cook for 2 minutes longer, stirring frequently.
❖ Remove 3/4 cup sauce to blender container; process until smooth. Spoon into bowl. Chill remaining sauce in refrigerator.
❖ Process cottage cheese in blender until smooth. Combine with 1 cup sugar, Neufchâtel cheese, flour and vanilla in large mixer bowl; beat until well mixed. Add eggs 1 at a time, beating at low speed just until mixed. Stir in orange rind.
❖ Spoon half the cottage cheese mixture into prepared springform pan. Drizzle puréed sauce evenly over top. Top with remaining cottage cheese mixture. Place on shallow baking pan.
❖ Bake for 45 to 50 minutes or until center appears nearly set when shaken. Cool on wire rack for 15 minutes. Loosen side of pan. Cool for 30 minutes longer. Place on serving plate; remove side of pan.
❖ Chill for 4 hours or longer. Spread with yogurt. Top with some of the reserved chilled sauce. Serve with remaining chilled sauce.
❖ Yield: 12 servings.

SWEET DREAM DESSERT

1 envelope Knox unflavored gelatin	1/2 cup sugar
	1 teaspoon vanilla extract
1/4 cup cold skim milk	1/2 cup thawed frozen strawberries
1/2 cup skim milk	
1 cup low-fat ricotta cheese	1/4 cup miniature semisweet chocolate chips
1 cup 1% milkfat cottage cheese	
	Pirouette cookies

❖ Sprinkle gelatin over 1/4 cup cold milk in blender container; let stand for 2 minutes.
❖ Bring 1/2 cup milk to a boil in saucepan. Add to blender container; process at low speed for 2 minutes or until gelatin is completely dissolved.
❖ Add ricotta cheese, cottage cheese, sugar and vanilla; process at high speed for 2 minutes or until well blended. Pour equal amounts into 2 bowls.
❖ Purée strawberries in blender; strain if desired. Stir into 1 bowl of pudding.
❖ Chill both bowls of pudding for 3 hours or until set. Whisk until smooth.
❖ Stir chocolate chips into plain pudding. Spoon pudding mixtures side-by-side into 6 dessert bowls.
❖ Serve with pirouette cookies.
❖ Yield: 6 servings.

SPICED PUMPKIN CAKE WITH ORANGE SAUCE

2 eggs
2/3 cup sugar
3/4 cup mashed cooked
    pumpkin
1 teaspoon vanilla extract
3/4 cup all-purpose flour
1 teaspoon baking powder
1 teaspoon cinnamon
1/2 teaspoon ginger
1/4 teaspoon nutmeg
1/4 teaspoon salt

1/8 teaspoon pepper
1/3 cup packed light
    brown sugar
3 tablespoons orange
    liqueur
2 tablespoons cornstarch
11/2 cups orange juice
1 teaspoon lemon juice
1 tablespoon
    confectioners' sugar
Strips of orange peel

❖ Preheat oven to 375 degrees.
❖ Spray 9-inch cake pan with nonstick cooking
spray. Line bottom with waxed paper; spray
waxed paper with nonstick cooking spray.
❖ Beat eggs at high speed in mixer bowl until
foamy. Add sugar 1 tablespoon at a time, beating
for 2 minutes or until thick and lemon-colored. Stir
in pumpkin and vanilla. Stir in mixture of next 7
ingredients. Spoon into prepared cake pan.
❖ Bake for 20 minutes or until cake tests done.
Cool in pan on wire rack for 5 minutes.
❖ Remove to wire rack to cool completely.
❖ Bring brown sugar, liqueur, cornstarch,
orange juice and lemon juice to a boil in heavy
saucepan, stirring constantly. Cook for 1
minute, stirring constantly.
❖ Sift confectioners'
sugar over cake.
Garnish with
strips of orange
peel. Serve with
orange sauce.
❖ Yield: 8 servings.

CRANBERRY CORDIAL

2 (12-ounce) packages cranberries,
    coarsely chopped
3 large bottles of dry white wine
3 cups sugar

❖ Mix cranberries, wine and sugar
in large bowl; cover. Let stand for
22 days, stirring every 3 days.
❖ Strain through cheesecloth 3
times. Pour into decorative
bottles.
❖ Yield: 18 servings.

GUILT-FREE PARTY NOG

1 pint vanilla frozen
    yogurt
2 cups low-fat milk

11/2 to 2 tablespoons rum
    extract
Nutmeg to taste

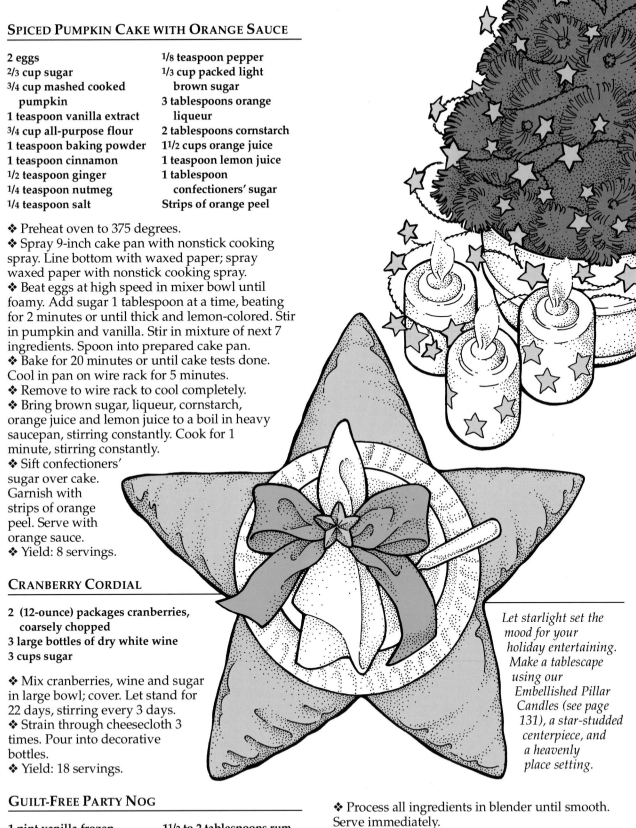

*Let starlight set the
mood for your
holiday entertaining.
Make a tablescape
using our
Embellished Pillar
Candles (see page
131), a star-studded
centerpiece, and
a heavenly
place setting.*

❖ Process all ingredients in blender until smooth.
Serve immediately.
❖ Yield: 8 servings.

Christmas Around the Clock

*T*he holidays are a time for family, friends,
and good food. But so often, everything
gets crammed into one busy afternoon. The cook
spends hours in the kitchen preparing a meal
that is eaten in twenty minutes (then spends
another hour cleaning up)! This year, try
celebrating *Christmas Around the Clock*—a relaxed
version of a traditional holiday feast that spreads
out all your favorite foods throughout the day.
Invite your "morning people" to a breakfast
buffet. Celebrate again with a sumptuous spread
at noontime. And close the day with a variety of
yummy desserts for late evening arrivals.

Menu

Sunrise Sampler

*Spiced Pancakes with
Bananas Foster Topping
Merry Berry Waffles
Mexicali Brunch Casserole
Bacon and Vegetable Bread
Easy Eggs Benedict
Christmas Fruit Compote
Citrus Mimosas*

SPICED PANCAKES

1 cup pancake mix
1 (7-ounce) package bran
  muffin mix
1¼ cups milk
2 eggs, beaten

1½ teaspoons apple pie
  spice
1 teaspoon vanilla extract
Bananas Foster Topping
Vanilla ice cream

❖ Combine first 6 ingredients in bowl; mix well.
Spoon onto heated nonstick griddle.
❖ Bake until light brown on both sides. Serve with
Bananas Foster Topping and ice cream.
❖ Yield: eight 2-pancake servings.

BANANAS FOSTER TOPPING

1 cup pancake syrup
¼ teaspoon cinnamon
½ teaspoon vanilla extract

¼ teaspoon orange extract
2 bananas, sliced

❖ Combine pancake syrup and flavorings in 2-cup
glass measure. Add bananas. Microwave on High
for 1 to 2 minutes or until heated through.
❖ Yield: 2 cups.

MERRY BERRY WAFFLES

1⅔ cups water
⅔ cup sugar
2 tablespoons light corn
  syrup
2 tablespoons cornstarch
1 (3-ounce) package
  raspberry gelatin

1 (8-ounce) package
  frozen raspberries
1 (8-ounce) package
  frozen blueberries
8 frozen waffles,
  toasted

❖ Combine water, sugar, corn syrup and
cornstarch in saucepan; mix well.
❖ Cook over medium heat until thickened, stirring
constantly; remove from heat.
❖ Stir in gelatin until dissolved. Cool slightly.
❖ Fold in raspberries and blueberries. Serve over
hot toasted waffles.
❖ Yield: 8 servings.

MEXICALI BRUNCH CASSEROLE

1½ cups quick-cooking
  grits
6 cups boiling water
1 pound sharp Cheddar
  cheese, shredded
1 pound sausage
3 eggs, beaten

¼ to ½ cup butter or
  margarine, softened
1 (8-ounce) can chopped
  green chilies, drained
Tabasco sauce to taste
2 teaspoons seasoned salt

❖ Preheat oven to 350 degrees.
❖ Cook grits in boiling water in large saucepan
for 5 minutes, stirring frequently. Stir in cheese
until melted.
❖ Brown sausage in skillet, stirring until crumbly;
drain well.
❖ Add sausage, eggs, butter, chilies, Tabasco sauce
and seasoned salt to grits; mix well. Spoon into
greased 9-by-13-inch baking dish.
❖ Bake for 1 hour or until set.
❖ Yield: 8 servings.

BACON AND VEGETABLE BREAD

½ cup melted butter or
  margarine
⅓ cup grated Parmesan
  cheese
3 (10-ounce) cans flaky
  biscuits, cut into
  quarters

1 (12-ounce) package
  turkey bacon, crisp-
  fried, crumbled
½ cup chopped green bell
  pepper
½ cup chopped onion
Green bell pepper strips

❖ Preheat oven to 350 degrees.
❖ Combine butter and cheese in small bowl. Roll
biscuit quarters in cheese mixture.
❖ Arrange ⅓ of the biscuit quarters in bundt pan
sprayed with nonstick cooking spray.
❖ Layer bacon, chopped green pepper, onion
and remaining biscuit quarters ½ at a time in
prepared pan.
❖ Bake for 40 minutes or until golden brown.
❖ Invert onto serving plate lined with green bell
pepper strips. Garnish as desired.
❖ Yield: 20 servings.

Bacon and Vegetable Bread, page 145

EASY EGGS BENEDICT

1/2 cup butter or
  margarine
1/2 cup all-purpose flour
4 cups milk
1 pound cooked ham,
  chopped
1 cup shredded Cheddar
  cheese
8 hard-cooked eggs, cut
  into quarters

1 pound fresh asparagus
  spears, cut into 1-inch
  pieces, cooked
1 tablespoon sherry
  (optional)
Salt and pepper to taste
2 (8-inch pans) baked
  corn bread, cut into
  8 squares

❖ Melt butter in large saucepan. Stir in flour. Add
milk all at once.
❖ Cook until thickened, stirring constantly. Cook
for 1 minute longer. Stir in ham and cheese.
❖ Cook until heated through, stirring constantly.
Stir in eggs, asparagus and wine;
mix gently. Season with salt
and pepper.
❖ Serve over corn bread squares.
❖ Yield: 8 servings.

CHRISTMAS FRUIT COMPOTE

1 (21-ounce) can cherry
  pie filling
1 (21-ounce) can peach
  pie filling
1 (16-ounce) can spiced
  apple rings, drained
1 (16-ounce) can apricot
  halves, drained

1 (16-ounce) can green
  grapes, drained
1 (16-ounce) can plums,
  drained
1/2 cup butter or margarine
Nutmeg and cinnamon
  to taste

❖ Preheat oven to 350 degrees.
❖ Combine pie fillings, apple rings, apricots,
grapes and plums in bowl; mix well.
❖ Spoon into 9-by-13-inch baking dish. Dot with
butter; sprinkle with nutmeg and cinnamon.
❖ Bake for 30 minutes or until bubbly.
❖ Yield: 8 to 12 servings.

CITRUS MIMOSAS

1 cup prepared strawberry daiquiri mix
1 (6-ounce) can frozen orange juice concentrate, thawed
1/3 cup fresh grapefruit juice
3/4 cup water
1/3 cup thawed frozen
  lemonade concentrate
3 tablespoons thawed frozen
  limeade concentrate
Chilled Champagne or soda water
Thin orange slices

❖ Combine first 6 ingredients
  in pitcher; mix well. Chill
  until serving time.
❖ Pour over ice in glasses,
  filling half full. Fill with
  Champagne. Garnish with
  orange slices.
❖ Yield: 8 servings.

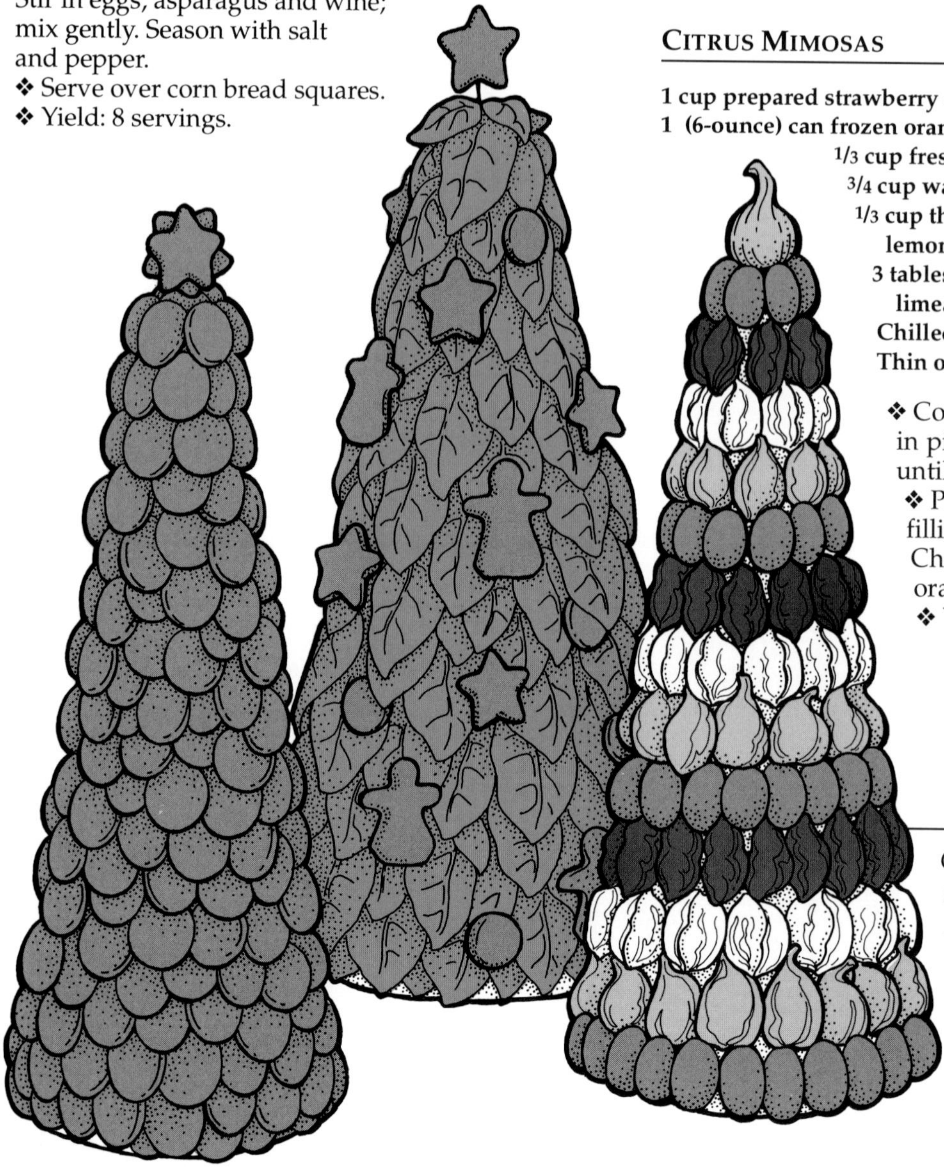

*Christmas topiaries stand
guard over the center of a
festive dining table.
Simply glue candies or
cookies to styrofoam cones.*

Menu

Forenoon Feast

Vegetable and Oyster Stew
Roasted Rack of Pork with
Cranberry and Hazelnut Stuffing
Chestnuts and Sugarplums
Holiday Brussels Sprouts
Festive Florentine Wreath
Holland Rusk Salad
Sesame Seed Rolls
Mulled Fruit Sipper

VEGETABLE AND OYSTER STEW

2 medium potatoes, peeled, chopped	1/4 teaspoon black pepper
1 large onion, chopped	2 medium carrots, thinly sliced
3/4 cup water	1 cup broccoli flowerets
1 teaspoon instant chicken bouillon	1 pint shucked oysters
11/2 teaspoons salt	2 cups milk
1/2 teaspoon cayenne pepper	1 cup light cream
	Butter or margarine

❖ Bring first 7 ingredients to a boil in 3-quart saucepan; reduce heat. Simmer for 12 minutes. Add carrots and broccoli. Simmer, covered, for 10 minutes longer. Add undrained oysters.
❖ Cook over medium heat for 5 minutes or until edges of oysters curl, stirring frequently. Stir in milk and cream.
❖ Cook just until heated through; do not boil. Dot servings with butter.
❖ Yield: 8 servings.

ROASTED RACK OF PORK

1 (4- to 5-pound) loin of pork	Salt and coarsely ground pepper to taste
2 cloves of garlic	Kumquats

❖ Ask butcher to trim excess fat from pork loin, trim rib bones of all extra meat and remove chine bone.
❖ Preheat oven to 350 degrees.
❖ Cut garlic into halves. Rub all surfaces with cut garlic; sprinkle generously with salt and pepper. Place on rack in shallow roasting pan.

❖ Roast for 11/2 to 2 hours or until meat thermometer inserted in center of loin eye registers 170 degrees.
❖ Let stand for 10 minutes. Cut between rib bones to serve. Garnish with kumquats.
❖ Yield: 8 servings.

CRANBERRY AND HAZELNUT STUFFING

8 ounces pork sausage	1 (8-ounce) package herb-seasoned stuffing mix
1/2 cup dried cranberries or raisins	2 cups chopped peeled apples
1/4 cup orange liqueur or orange juice	1 cup cooked wild rice
11/4 cups chopped celery	1/2 cup hazelnuts or slivered almonds
11/4 cups chopped onion	1/2 cup chopped parsley
1/4 cup butter or margarine	3/4 to 1 cup chicken broth
1 teaspoon poultry seasoning	Salt and pepper to taste

❖ Preheat oven to 325 degrees.
❖ Cook sausage in skillet, stirring until crumbly; drain and set aside.
❖ Bring cranberries and orange liqueur to a boil in small saucepan. Remove from heat and set aside.
❖ Sauté celery and onion in butter in skillet until tender but not brown. Stir in poultry seasoning.
❖ Combine sautéed mixture with sausage, cranberry mixture, stuffing mix, apples, rice, hazelnuts and parsley in large bowl; mix well. Add enough chicken broth to moisten, tossing lightly. Season with salt and pepper. Spoon into ungreased 3-quart baking dish.
❖ Bake for 40 to 60 minutes or until stuffing is heated through.
❖ May spoon into bread shell for a unique serving idea.
❖ Yield: 8 servings.

CHESTNUTS AND SUGARPLUMS

3/4 cup canned chestnuts	1 tablespoon butter or margarine
11/2 cups pitted stewed or canned prunes	1 tablespoon sugar
1/2 cup dry white wine or white grape juice	1/4 teaspoon salt

❖ Preheat oven to 350 degrees.
❖ Combine chestnuts and prunes in 8-by-8-inch baking dish.
❖ Combine wine, butter, sugar and salt in bowl; mix well. Pour over prune mixture.
❖ Bake just until heated through, stirring occasionally. Spoon into serving dish. Serve with pork or poultry.
❖ Yield: 8 servings.

HOLIDAY BRUSSELS SPROUTS

2 pints Brussels sprouts	2 large cloves of garlic,
4 cups water	crushed
1 chicken bouillon cube	2 tablespoons butter or
1 bunch green onions, cut	margarine
into 1-inch pieces	1¹/2 (10-ounce) containers
1 cup pearl onions	or 1¹/2 cups crème
1 (1-pint) basket cherry	fraîche
tomatoes	¹/2 teaspoon salt
1 large red bell pepper,	¹/8 teaspoon pepper
thinly sliced	

❖ Trim Brussels sprouts. Cut X in base of each Brussels sprout.
❖ Bring water to a boil with bouillon cube in 3-quart saucepan. Add Brussels sprouts.
❖ Cook, covered, for 9 minutes. Add green onions, pearl onions, cherry tomatoes and bell pepper. Cook for 1 minute longer or until Brussels sprouts are tender-crisp; drain. Place in warm serving bowl; keep warm.
❖ Sauté garlic in butter in saucepan over medium-high heat for 2 minutes. Stir in crème fraîche, salt and pepper.
❖ Bring to a boil, stirring constantly. Simmer for 3 minutes, stirring constantly.
❖ Spoon sauce over Brussels sprouts.
❖ To make homemade crème fraîche, combine 1 tablespoon buttermilk with 1 cup whipping cream. Let stand overnight. Chill in refrigerator.
❖ Yield: 12 servings.

FESTIVE FLORENTINE WREATH

1 (2-ounce) jar sliced	1 (4-ounce) can sliced
pimento	mushrooms
2 (10-ounce) packages	2 tablespoons grated
frozen chopped spinach,	onion
cooked, drained	¹/2 cup shredded Cheddar
8 eggs, beaten	cheese
1 cup small curd cottage	¹/2 teaspoon salt
cheese	¹/8 teaspoon white pepper

❖ Reserve several long strips pimento. Combine remaining undrained pimento with spinach, eggs, cottage cheese, undrained mushrooms, onion, Cheddar cheese, salt and white pepper in bowl; mix well.
❖ Pack into oiled 1¹/2 to 2-quart glass ring mold.
❖ Microwave on High for 13 to 15 minutes. Let stand for 10 minutes.
❖ Unmold onto serving plate. Arrange reserved pimento into bow for garnish. Fill center with cooked vegetables if desired.
❖ Yield: 8 servings.

HOLLAND RUSK SALAD

8 hard-cooked eggs	8 Holland rusks
2 teaspoons grated onion	Leaf lettuce
Pepper to taste	8 tomato slices
Mayonnaise	8 canned artichoke hearts,
8 ounces cream cheese,	rinsed, drained
softened	¹/2 cup red honey French
Anchovy paste to taste	salad dressing
(optional)	Caviar (optional)

❖ Press eggs through sieve or ricer into bowl. Add onion, pepper and enough mayonnaise to make a stiff mixture. Chill in refrigerator.
❖ Combine cream cheese and anchovy paste in small bowl; mix until smooth.
❖ Spread cream cheese mixture on rusks. Arrange on lettuce-lined serving plates. Top each serving with sliced tomato, egg salad and artichoke heart.
❖ Drizzle with salad dressing. Garnish with caviar.
❖ Yield: 8 servings.

SESAME SEED ROLLS

2 cups self-rising flour	1 teaspoon sugar
¹/4 cup mayonnaise	2 to 3 teaspoons toasted
1 cup milk	sesame seed

❖ Preheat oven to 450 degrees.
❖ Combine flour, mayonnaise, milk and sugar in large bowl; mix well.
❖ Fill greased muffin cups ³/4 full. Sprinkle with sesame seed.
❖ Bake for 10 minutes. Cool in pan for 10 minutes.
❖ Yield: 12 rolls.

MULLED FRUIT SIPPER

2 quarts cranberry juice	2 cups apple juice
cocktail	1 cup orange juice
1 (46-ounce) can	4 (3-inch) cinnamon sticks
pineapple juice	3 whole nutmegs
1 (6-ounce) can frozen	1¹/2 teaspoons ground
lemonade concentrate,	ginger
thawed	

❖ Combine cranberry juice, pineapple juice, lemonade concentrate, apple juice and orange juice in large electric percolator. Place cinnamon sticks, nutmegs and ginger in percolator basket.
❖ Perk through complete cycle of percolator. Serve hot or cold.
❖ Yield: 1 gallon.

Roasted Rack of Pork, Cranberry and Hazelnut Stuffing, Chestnuts and Sugarplums, and Holiday Brussels Sprouts, pages 147 and 148

Menu

Afternoon Appetizers

Pesto Pie Stuffed Apricots
Pepper and Parmesan Wafers
Spinach Pinwheels
Baked Cranberry Brie
Appetizer Pizza
Creamy Mushroom Squares
Fruited Canapés

PESTO PIE

1 (2-pastry) package refrigerator pie pastries	¹/₂ cup prepared pesto
	Milk
	Paprika
1 cup shredded Monterey Jack cheese with jalapeño peppers	2 tablespoons pine nuts

❖ Preheat oven to 400 degrees.
❖ Let pastries stand at room temperature for 15 to 20 minutes. Place 1 pastry on lightly floured round 12-inch baking pan or baking sheet.
❖ Bake for 8 to 10 minutes or just until pastry begins to brown.
❖ Combine cheese and pesto in bowl; mix well. Spread over hot pastry to within ¹/₂ inch of edge. Place remaining pastry on top; seal edges and cut vents. Brush with milk; sprinkle with paprika and pine nuts, pressing pine nuts gently into crust.
❖ Bake for 15 to 18 minutes or until golden brown. Let stand for 10 minutes. Cut into 12 wedges; cut wedges into halves.
❖ Yield: 24 servings.

STUFFED APRICOTS

8 ounces cream cheese, softened	1 (6-ounce) package dried apricots
¹/₄ cup fruit chutney	¹/₂ cup water
2 tablespoons chopped green onions	¹/₂ cup finely chopped pecans

❖ Combine cream cheese, chutney and green onions in bowl; mix well. Chill, covered, for 1 hour.
❖ Bring apricots and water to a boil in medium saucepan, stirring occasionally. Reduce heat to low.
❖ Simmer, covered, for 4 minutes or until apricots are plump.

❖ Drain on paper towels. Let stand until cool.
❖ Spoon cream cheese mixture into apricots; top with pecans. Arrange on serving platter. Chill, covered, until firm.
❖ Yield: 40 appetizers.

PEPPER AND PARMESAN WAFERS

³/₄ cup all-purpose flour	³/₄ to 1 teaspoon cracked black pepper
1¹/₂ cups grated Parmesan cheese	¹/₄ cup unsalted butter
¹/₄ teaspoon salt	2 tablespoons water

❖ Mix flour, cheese, salt and pepper in medium bowl. Cut in butter until crumbly.
❖ Sprinkle with water 1 tablespoon at a time, tossing with fork to form dough.
❖ Shape into log 1¹/₂ inches in diameter. Chill for 1 hour or longer or freeze until needed.
❖ Preheat oven to 375 degrees.
❖ Cut log into ¹/₄-inch slices; place on ungreased baking sheet.
❖ Bake for 12 minutes or until golden brown. Remove to wire rack to cool.
❖ Yield: 38 wafers.

SPINACH PINWHEELS

2 (10-ounce) packages frozen chopped spinach, thawed, drained	1 cup sour cream
	1 cup mayonnaise
6 green onions with tops, chopped	1 envelope ranch salad dressing mix
3 slices bacon, crisp-fried, crumbled	1 (10-count) package large flour tortillas

❖ Combine first 6 ingredients in bowl; mix well.
❖ Spread mixture thinly on tortillas. Roll tortillas to enclose filling. Chill, covered, until firm. Cut rolls into ¹/₂-inch slices. Arrange on serving plate.
❖ Yield: 40 appetizers.

BAKED CRANBERRY BRIE

¹/₃ cup cranberry sauce	¹/₈ teaspoon nutmeg
2 tablespoons light brown sugar	1 (8-ounce) Brie
¹/₄ teaspoon orange extract	2 tablespoons chopped pecans

❖ Preheat oven to 500 degrees.
❖ Combine cranberry sauce, brown sugar, orange extract and nutmeg in bowl; mix well.
❖ Remove top rind of cheese, leaving ¹/₄-inch edge. Spoon cranberry mixture onto cheese; sprinkle with pecans.
❖ Bake for 4 to 5 minutes or just until heated.
❖ Serve with assorted crackers.
❖ Yield: 12 servings.

APPETIZER PIZZA

4 ounces whipped cream cheese with chives
1 (12-inch) prepared Boboli bread shell
1 (6-ounce) jar marinated artichoke hearts
1 cup chopped red and green bell peppers
1/2 cup sliced green olives
1/2 cup sliced black olives
1/2 cup cherry tomato quarters, drained
2 tablespoons sliced green onions
1/4 cup sliced fresh mushrooms
2 slices bacon, crisp-fried, crumbled

❖ Spread cream cheese over bread shell.
❖ Drain artichokes, reserving 2 tablespoons marinade; cut artichokes into halves. Mix with reserved marinade and next 6 ingredients in bowl.
❖ Spread over top; sprinkle with bacon.
❖ Yield: 12 servings.

CREAMY MUSHROOM SQUARES

1 (8-count) can crescent rolls
3 ounces cream cheese, softened
12 ounces fresh mushrooms, sliced
2 tablespoons margarine
1 tablespoon lemon juice
2 tablespoons finely chopped onion
1 tablespoon Worcestershire sauce
1/2 teaspoon garlic powder
Salt and pepper to taste
1/4 cup grated Parmesan cheese

❖ Preheat oven to 350 degrees.
❖ Press roll dough in greased 9-by-13-inch baking pan. Spread with cream cheese.
❖ Sauté mushrooms in margarine in medium skillet. Add next 6 ingredients; mix well. Cook until thickened, stirring frequently. Spread over cream cheese layer; sprinkle with Parmesan cheese.
❖ Bake for 30 minutes or until golden brown.
❖ Yield: 50 squares.

FRUITED CANAPÉS

8 ounces whipped cream cheese with pineapple
1/4 cup chutney
8 rectangles rye or wheat crisp bread
1 1/2 cups assorted fruit such as blueberries, sliced strawberries, mandarin oranges or kiwifruit
Confectioners' sugar

❖ Mix cream cheese and chutney in small bowl.
❖ Cut each crisp bread into halves with sharp knife. Spread with cream cheese mixture.
❖ Arrange drained fruit over cream cheese. Sift confectioners' sugar over tops. Serve immediately or chill, covered, for up to 1 hour.
❖ Yield: 16 servings.

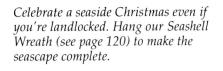

Celebrate a seaside Christmas even if you're landlocked. Hang our Seashell Wreath (see page 120) to make the seascape complete.

Menu

Sunset Soirée

Orange and Carrot Soup
Spinach and Tomato Salad
Penne with Sausage and Eggplant or
Upside-Down Pizza
Marinated Vegetables
Wine and Cheese Bread
Strawberry Cheesecake Dip

ORANGE AND CARROT SOUP

1 pound carrots, peeled, coarsely chopped	1/3 cup all-purpose flour
3 onions, coarsely chopped	6 cups chicken stock
2 cloves of garlic, minced	1 teaspoon sugar
2 tablespoons butter or margarine	Juice of 1 orange
	1 cup whipping cream
	Salt and pepper to taste

❖ Sauté carrots, onions and garlic in butter in heavy saucepan for 5 minutes. Stir in flour. Add chicken stock gradually, stirring constantly.
❖ Cook until thickened, stirring constantly. Simmer, covered, for 20 minutes. Add sugar. Simmer for 10 minutes longer.
❖ Process in blender until smooth. Return to saucepan. Fold in orange juice, whipping cream, salt and pepper.
❖ Cook over low heat just until heated through; do not boil.
❖ Serve immediately or chill to serve cold.
❖ Yield: 6 servings.

SPINACH AND TOMATO SALAD

3 tablespoons olive oil	1 1/2 pounds fresh spinach
3 tablespoons cider or wine vinegar	Chopped whites of 2 hard-cooked eggs
2 tablespoons water	12 cherry tomatoes, cut into quarters
1 to 2 teaspoons stone-ground mustard	1 small red onion, sliced into thin rings
1 tablespoon finely chopped mixed fresh herbs or 1/2 teaspoon dried Herbs de Provence	1/2 teaspoon lemon pepper
	2 hard-cooked egg yolks

❖ Combine olive oil, vinegar, water, mustard and herbs in small bowl; mix well. Chill in refrigerator.

❖ Tear spinach into bite-sized pieces, discarding stems. Combine with egg whites, tomatoes and onion in salad bowl.
❖ Add dressing and lemon pepper; toss lightly. Grate egg yolks over top. Serve immediately.
❖ May use parsley, basil, oregano, tarragon, chives or other herbs of choice in dressing.
❖ Yield: 6 to 8 servings.

PENNE WITH SAUSAGE AND EGGPLANT

1 (5-ounce) eggplant	2 tablespoons finely chopped cilantro or parsley
8 ounces sweet Italian sausage	
3/4 cup chopped tomato	8 ounces penne, cooked, drained
1/2 cup (or more) Wish-Bone olive oil vinaigrette salad dressing	Freshly ground pepper to taste

❖ Slice eggplant lengthwise into quarters; slice quarters 1/2 inch thick.
❖ Slice sausage 1/2 inch thick; place in 3-quart glass dish.
❖ Microwave on High for 4 minutes, stirring once. Add eggplant, tomato and salad dressing.
❖ Microwave, uncovered, for 5 minutes or until eggplant is tender, stirring once. Stir in cilantro.
❖ Toss with hot pasta in serving bowl; sprinkle with pepper.
❖ Yield: 6 servings.

UPSIDE-DOWN PIZZA

1 pound ground beef or ground turkey	1 tablespoon vegetable oil
1/3 cup chopped onion	1 cup baking mix
1 (15-ounce) can spaghetti sauce	1/4 teaspoon salt
	Shredded mozzarella cheese
1 egg	1/3 cup grated Parmesan cheese
1 cup milk	

❖ Preheat oven to 350 degrees.
❖ Brown ground beef with onion in skillet, stirring until ground beef is crumbly; drain. Stir in spaghetti sauce. Simmer for several minutes.
❖ Combine egg, milk and oil in bowl. Add baking mix and salt; mix well.
❖ Layer ground beef mixture, mozzarella cheese and batter in greased 9-by-13-inch baking dish. Sprinkle with Parmesan cheese.
❖ Bake for 15 to 30 minutes or until top is golden brown.
❖ Yield: 6 to 8 servings.

Penne with Sausage and Eggplant, page 152

Strawberries Romanoff, Vanilla-Mint Cream Puffs, and Citrus-Filled Meringues, page 155

MARINATED VEGETABLES

1 cup pearl onions
3 large carrots, sliced
1½ cups broccoli florets
1 small cucumber, sliced
1 red bell pepper, cut
   into rings
1 yellow bell pepper, cut
   into rings

1 cup cherry tomato
   halves, drained
1 cup loosely packed
   fresh basil leaves
1 clove of garlic, crushed
¾ cup olive oil
¼ cup red wine vinegar
Salt and pepper to taste

❖ Combine vegetables in large bowl. Add mixture of remaining ingredients to vegetables; toss gently.
❖ Marinate in refrigerator for 24 hours or longer.
❖ Yield: 6 servings.

WINE AND CHEESE BREAD

1⅛ cups all-purpose flour
½ teaspoon baking
   powder
¼ teaspoon cream of
   tartar
½ teaspoon salt
⅛ teaspoon baking soda
¼ cup instant nonfat dry
   milk
⅓ cup shortening

1 tablespoon sugar
1 tablespoon minced
   onion
1 egg, beaten
¼ cup milk
¼ cup white wine or
   water
½ teaspoon oregano
¼ cup grated Parmesan
   cheese

❖ Preheat oven to 425 degrees.
❖ Sift flour, baking powder, cream of tartar, salt, baking soda and dry milk powder into large bowl. Cut in shortening until crumbly.
❖ Add sugar, onion, egg, milk, wine and oregano; mix well.
❖ Spoon into greased 9-inch round baking pan. Sprinkle with Parmesan cheese.
❖ Bake for 15 to 20 minutes or until bread tests done.
❖ Invert onto wire rack to cool.
❖ Yield: 8 servings.

STRAWBERRY CHEESECAKE DIP

16 ounces light cream
   cheese, softened
½ cup strawberries
¼ cup sugar
¼ cup light sour cream
1 tablespoon orange juice

1 teaspoon vanilla extract
Fresh strawberries or
   pineapple cubes
Angel food cake cubes
Chocolate wafers or
   pirouette cookies

❖ Process cream cheese, ½ cup strawberries, sugar, sour cream, orange juice and vanilla in food processor until smooth.
❖ Spoon into serving bowl. Chill in refrigerator until serving time.
❖ Serve with fresh strawberries or pineapple cubes, cake cubes or cookies.
❖ Yield: 12 servings.

Menu

Midnight Merriment

Strawberries Romanoff
Vanilla-Mint Cream Puffs
Citrus-Filled Meringues
Christmas Trifle
Lemon-Filled Gingerbread Roll
Cinnamon Coffee

STRAWBERRIES ROMANOFF

1 (14-ounce) can Eagle® Brand sweetened condensed milk	1 (4-ounce) package vanilla instant pudding mix
3/4 cup cold water	2 cups Borden® whipping cream, whipped
3 to 4 tablespoons orange or cherry liqueur	1 quart fresh strawberries
Yellow food coloring (optional)	

❖ Blend condensed milk, water, liqueur and food coloring in large bowl. Add pudding mix; mix until smooth.
❖ Chill for 15 minutes. Fold in whipped cream. Chill until serving time.
❖ Reserve 1 cup strawberries; slice remaining strawberries. Fold sliced strawberries into pudding mixture.
❖ Garnish with reserved strawberries.
❖ Yield: 10 to 12 servings.

VANILLA-MINT CREAM PUFFS

1 (14-ounce) can Eagle® Brand sweetened condensed milk	1 cup Borden® whipping cream, whipped
2 tablespoons white Crème de Menthe	12 Cream Puffs Confectioners' sugar
2 tablespoons cold water	Chocolate ice cream topping (optional)
1 (4-ounce) package vanilla instant pudding mix	

❖ Combine first 3 ingredients in large bowl. Add pudding mix; beat until smooth.
❖ Chill for 5 minutes. Fold in whipped cream. Chill until serving time.
❖ Split Cream Puffs; remove any excess dough from centers.

❖ Spoon pudding mixture into Cream Puffs; sprinkle with confectioners' sugar.
❖ Serve with chocolate ice cream topping if desired. Store in refrigerator.
❖ Yield: 12 servings.

CREAM PUFFS

1 cup water	1 cup all-purpose flour
1/2 cup margarine	4 eggs

❖ Preheat oven to 400 degrees.
❖ Bring water and margarine to a rolling boil in medium saucepan. Stir in flour; reduce heat to low.
❖ Cook for 1 minute or until mixture forms a ball, stirring rapidly; remove from heat. Beat in eggs.
❖ Drop by scant 1/4 cupfuls 3 inches apart onto ungreased baking sheet.
❖ Bake for 35 to 40 minutes or until puffed and golden brown. Remove to wire rack to cool.
❖ Yield: 12 cream puffs.

CITRUS-FILLED MERINGUES

1 (14-ounce) can Eagle® Brand sweetened condensed milk	2 tablespoons bottled lemon juice
2 egg yolks	4 ounces whipped topping
1/2 cup frozen limeade concentrate, thawed	Green or yellow food coloring (optional)
	10 Meringue Shells

❖ Combine first 4 ingredients in medium saucepan; mix well.
❖ Cook mixture over medium heat until slightly thickened, stirring rapidly.
❖ Cool for 15 minutes. Chill for 30 minutes. Fold in whipped topping and food coloring. Spoon into Meringue Shells. Chill until serving time. Garnish as desired.
❖ Yield: 10 servings.

MERINGUE SHELLS

6 egg whites	1 teaspoon vanilla extract
1/4 teaspoon cream of tartar	1/4 teaspoon salt
	1 cup sugar

❖ Preheat oven to 225 degrees.
❖ Line baking sheet with brown paper; draw ten 3-inch circles 2 inches apart on brown paper.
❖ Beat first 4 ingredients at medium speed in large mixer bowl until soft peaks form. Add sugar gradually, beating at high speed until stiff but not dry. Spoon into pastry bag fitted with star tip.
❖ Pipe into circles on brown paper to form shells.
❖ Bake for 1 hour. Turn off oven. Let meringues stand in oven for 1 hour longer.
❖ Yield: 10 meringue shells.

CHRISTMAS TRIFLE

1 tablespoon unsalted butter	2 cups cranberries
1/2 cup sliced almonds	1/4 cup sugar
2 tablespoons sugar	1/2 cup water
Vanilla Custard	1 teaspoon grated lemon zest
1 (10-ounce) package frozen raspberries in light syrup, thawed, drained	1 teaspoon lemon juice
	1 round angel food cake
	Fresh raspberries
1 teaspoon raspberry liqueur	

❖ Melt 1 tablespoon butter in small skillet over medium-high heat. Stir in almonds and 1 tablespoon sugar. Cook for 5 minutes or until almonds are golden brown. Sprinkle with 1 tablespoon sugar. Cool on waxed paper. Store in airtight container.
❖ Combine 1 cup chilled Vanilla Custard with raspberries and liqueur in food processor container. Process until smooth. Cover surface directly with plastic wrap. Chill in refrigerator.
❖ Combine cranberries, 1/4 cup sugar, water, lemon zest and lemon juice in medium saucepan.
❖ Bring to a boil; reduce heat. Simmer for 10 minutes or until berries pop, stirring occasionally.
❖ Chill in refrigerator.
❖ Cut cake horizontally into 3 layers with serrated knife. Trim 2 layers to fit into straight-sided 2 1/2-quart glass dish.
❖ Place 1 cake layer in dish; fill center with pieces cut from third cake layer. Spread half the cranberry mixture and all the raspberry custard over cake layer. Add remaining cake layer, filling center with cake pieces as before. Spread with remaining cranberry mixture and remaining Vanilla Custard.
❖ Chill, covered, for 1 to 24 hours. Top with sugared almonds and fresh raspberries.
❖ Yield: 16 servings.

VANILLA CUSTARD

1 cup milk	1 tablespoon cornstarch
1 cup whipping cream	2 eggs
1/2 cup sugar	6 tablespoons unsalted butter, chopped
2 tablespoons all-purpose flour	1/2 teaspoon vanilla extract

❖ Bring milk and cream just to a simmer in medium saucepan; set aside.
❖ Mix 1/2 cup sugar, flour and cornstarch in bowl. Add eggs; mix well.
❖ Whisk 1/4 of the hot milk mixture into egg mixture; whisk egg mixture into hot milk mixture in saucepan.

❖ Bring to a boil over medium-high heat, whisking constantly. Cook for 8 minutes or until thickened, whisking constantly. Remove from heat.
❖ Stir in 6 tablespoons butter and vanilla. Cover surface directly with plastic wrap. Cool to room temperature. Chill, covered, for 30 minutes.
❖ Yield: 3 cups.

LEMON-FILLED GINGERBREAD ROLL

1 cup all-purpose flour	1/2 cup sugar
1 1/4 teaspoons baking powder	2 tablespoons butter or margarine
1 1/2 teaspoons cinnamon	1/4 cup milk
1 1/2 teaspoons ginger	1 (21-ounce) can lemon pie filling
3 eggs	Candied lemon peel
3 egg yolks	Strawberries
1/2 cup light molasses	

❖ Preheat oven to 400 degrees.
❖ Grease 10-by-15-inch jelly-roll pan. Line with waxed paper; grease waxed paper.
❖ Mix flour, baking powder, cinnamon and ginger together. Beat eggs, egg yolks, molasses and sugar at high speed in mixer bowl for 10 to 15 minutes or until thick and lemon-colored. Fold in flour mixture gently.
❖ Melt butter in milk in small saucepan over medium heat. Fold into cake batter. Spoon into prepared pan.
❖ Bake for 15 to 20 minutes or until top of cake springs back when lightly touched.
❖ Invert immediately onto kitchen towel; peel waxed paper carefully from cake. Roll up cake from long side in towel. Cool seam side down on wire rack.
❖ Unroll cooled cake. Spread with pie filling. Roll cake to enclose filling. Place on serving plate. Garnish with candied lemon peel and strawberries.
❖ Yield: 12 servings.

CINNAMON COFFEE

6 cups freshly brewed coffee	3 ounces cinnamon schnapps
3 ounces Kahlua	Whipped cream

❖ Pour coffee into serving cups.
❖ Stir 1/2 ounce Kahlua and 1/2 ounce cinnamon schnapps into each serving.
❖ Garnish with whipped cream.
❖ Yield: 6 servings.

Glazed Roasted Turkey, Green Onion and Corn Bread Stuffing, Mashed Potato Casserole, and Double-Layer Pumpkin Pie, pages 159, 160, and 161

A Nouveau Christmas Classic

*I*f the idea of just another turkey dinner is
uninspiring, take a look at the wonderful new
recipes featured in our *Nouveau Christmas Classic.*
Our recipes have a fun and delicious new flair,
yet are traditional enough to please Grandma . . .
stuffing made with croissants and a make-ahead
potato casserole. And for dessert, we have a
Double-Layer Pumpkin Pie that will knock the
Christmas stockings off your guests. Speaking of
guests, why not invite everyone to bring an
exciting new dish to dinner? With these recipes,
you may find our turkey dinner with a twist
becomes an instant classic at your house.

Menu

Endive Antipasto
Roquefort Diablotins
Butternut Bisque or Tomato Bouillon
Stuffed Apples Waldorf
Roast Beef Tenderloin with Horseradish
and Chive Sauce or
Glazed Roasted Turkey with
Choice of Stuffings
Restuffed Sweet Potatoes or
Mashed Potato Casserole
Caramelized Onions   Scalloped Corn
Brown Rice Sally Lunn Bread
Honeyed Fruit and Nut Tart or
Double-Layer Pumpkin Pie

ENDIVE ANTIPASTO

2 heads Belgian endive	1/3 cup chopped salami
1 (6-ounce) jar marinated artichokes, drained, chopped	1/4 cup chopped black olives
1/2 cup chopped zucchini	3 tablespoons creamy garlic salad dressing

❖ Separate endive leaves; wash leaves and pat dry. Chill in plastic bag in refrigerator.
❖ Combine artichokes, zucchini, salami, olives and salad dressing in bowl; mix well.
❖ Spoon artichoke mixture into endive leaves. Arrange in spoke design on serving plate.
❖ Yield: 32 appetizers.

ROQUEFORT DIABLOTINS

1 cup crumbled Roquefort cheese	1/2 cup chopped pecans
1/2 cup butter or margarine, softened	1 loaf French bread, sliced

❖ Combine cheese and butter in bowl; mix until smooth. Mix in pecans.
❖ Preheat broiler.
❖ Place bread on baking sheet. Broil until toasted on 1 side; turn. Spread with cheese mixture.
❖ Broil until bubbly. Serve hot.
❖ Yield: 24 appetizers.

BUTTERNUT BISQUE

1 cup chopped onion	4 cups chicken stock
1/4 cup butter or margarine	1 tablespoon molasses
4 cups chopped peeled butternut squash	2 tablespoons honey
	1/4 teaspoon nutmeg
2 cups chopped peeled apples	2 teaspoons salt
	1/4 teaspoon pepper
1 cup chopped celery	1 cup whipping cream
	1/2 cup chopped pecans

❖ Sauté onion in butter in heavy saucepan until tender. Add squash, apples, celery and stock.
❖ Simmer, covered, for 15 minutes or until tender. Cool. Purée in blender. Return to saucepan.
❖ Bring to a simmer. Stir in molasses, honey, nutmeg, salt, pepper and 1/2 cup cream. Heat just to serving temperature; do not boil.
❖ Whip remaining 1/2 cup cream in bowl until soft peaks form. Ladle soup into soup bowls. Top with whipped cream and pecans.
❖ Yield: 8 to 12 servings.

TOMATO BOUILLON

1 small onion, chopped	2 tablespoons fennel
3 cups tomato juice	2 whole cloves
1/4 cup chopped celery	1 tablespoon fresh basil
1/2 small bay leaf	Sour cream

❖ Sauté onion in nonstick saucepan sprayed with nonstick cooking spray until tender. Add tomato juice, celery and herbs; mix well.
❖ Simmer for 5 minutes. Skim and strain soup.
❖ Garnish servings with dollop of sour cream.
❖ Yield: 4 servings.

STUFFED APPLES WALDORF

6 large cooking apples	1/2 cup chopped celery
2 cups water	1/3 cup chopped toasted pecans
1 cup red-hot cinnamon candies	
	1/3 cup mayonnaise
1 cup raisins or currants	Lettuce leaves

❖ Cut peeled apples into halves crosswise; remove cores, leaving 1 inch holes.
❖ Bring water and candies to a boil in heavy saucepan, stirring to dissolve candies.
❖ Simmer apples 1/2 at a time for 3 to 4 minutes or until cooked through.
❖ Combine raisins, celery, pecans and mayonnaise in bowl; mix well. Spoon into centers of apples.
❖ Chill, covered, for 2 hours or longer. Serve on lettuce-lined serving plates.
❖ May use spiced apple rings if desired.
❖ Yield: 12 servings.

ROAST BEEF TENDERLOIN WITH HORSERADISH AND CHIVE SAUCE

2 (3-pound) beef tenderloin pieces	1½ cups sour cream or plain yogurt
2 tablespoons crumbled dried rosemary	⅓ cup chopped fresh chives
3 tablespoons cracked pepper	¼ cup prepared horseradish
¼ cup soy sauce	¼ cup drained capers
¼ cup butter or margarine, softened	Freshly ground pepper to taste
1½ cups mayonnaise	Ornamental kale

❖ Rub beef with rosemary and cracked pepper. Let stand at room temperature for 2 hours.
❖ Preheat oven to 500 degrees.
❖ Brush beef with soy sauce; rub with butter. Place on rack in roasting pan. Insert meat thermometer into thickest portion of beef.
❖ Reduce oven temperature to 400 degrees.
❖ Roast beef for 40 minutes or until meat thermometer registers 120 degrees for rare. Chill beef in refrigerator.
❖ Combine mayonnaise, sour cream, chives, horseradish, capers and ground pepper in medium bowl; mix well. Spoon into serving bowl.
❖ Cut beef tenderloin into thin slices. Arrange on kale-lined serving plate. Serve chilled or at room temperature with sauce.
❖ Yield: 12 servings.

GLAZED ROASTED TURKEY

1 (12-pound) turkey	½ cup peach preserves
Olive oil	2 tablespoons bourbon or orange juice
Green Onion and Corn Bread Stuffing or Herbed Croissant Stuffing	2 teaspoons Angostura bitters
Butter or margarine	Red grapes

❖ Preheat oven to 325 degrees.
❖ Rinse turkey inside and out; pat dry with paper towels. Reserve giblets for another use. Rub inside with olive oil.
❖ Spoon choice of stuffing into body and neck cavities of turkey. Place in shallow roasting pan.
❖ Rub turkey with butter. Insert meat thermometer into thickest part of turkey thigh. Cover loosely with foil.
❖ Roast for 4 hours.
❖ Combine preserves, bourbon and bitters in small saucepan; mix well.
❖ Cook over low heat until preserves melt, stirring to mix well.
❖ Brush turkey with preserve mixture.
❖ Roast, uncovered, for 30 minutes longer or to 170 degrees on meat thermometer.

❖ Remove turkey to serving platter. Tent with foil; let stand for 15 minutes before carving. Garnish with grapes.
❖ Yield: 12 servings.

GREEN ONION AND CORN BREAD STUFFING

1 (10-ounce) can French onion soup	1 cup chopped celery
1 soup can water	1½ teaspoons poultry seasoning
¼ cup margarine	2 (8-ounce) packages corn bread stuffing mix
1 cup thinly sliced green onions	

❖ Combine soup, water, margarine, green onions, celery and poultry seasoning in 5-quart saucepan; mix well.
❖ Bring to a boil, stirring constantly; remove from heat.
❖ Stir in corn bread stuffing mix. Stuff 12-pound turkey or spoon into 1½-quart baking dish sprayed with nonstick cooking spray.
❖ Roast using turkey directions or bake, covered, in preheated 325-degree oven for 45 minutes or until browned.
❖ Yield: 12 servings.

HERBED CROISSANT STUFFING

8 ounces bacon, chopped	1 tablespoon each chopped fresh thyme, marjoram, sage and rosemary
2 medium onions, chopped	
2 bunches scallions, chopped	Salt and pepper to taste
6 croissants, torn into small pieces	2 to 4 tablespoons chicken broth or brandy (optional)

❖ Cook bacon in large skillet until crisp. Remove with slotted spoon and drain, reserving ½ cup drippings in skillet.
❖ Sauté onions and scallions in reserved drippings until tender.
❖ Add croissants, bacon, thyme, marjoram, sage, rosemary, salt and pepper; toss to mix well. Add chicken broth or brandy for moister stuffing.
❖ Stuff 12-pound turkey or spoon into 1½-quart baking dish.
❖ Roast using turkey directions or bake, covered, in preheated 325-degree oven for 30 minutes or until browned.
❖ Use day-old croissants. May substitute 1 teaspoon dried herbs for fresh herbs.
❖ Yield: 12 servings.

RESTUFFED SWEET POTATOES

12 small sweet potatoes	1/4 cup butter or margarine
Vegetable oil	1 to 2 tablespoons sherry
8 ounces Neufchâtel cheese or cream cheese, softened	1 1/4 teaspoons salt
	1/2 teaspoon pepper
1/4 cup packed light brown sugar	1/3 cup coarsely chopped pecans

❖ Preheat oven to 375 degrees.
❖ Prick sweet potatoes all over with fork. Rub lightly with oil. Place on baking sheet.
❖ Bake for 1 hour or until tender. Cool slightly. Cut 1/2-inch strip from long side of each sweet potato. Scoop out pulp with spoon, reserving 1/4-inch thick shells.
❖ Beat sweet potato pulp in mixer bowl until smooth. Add Neufchâtel cheese, brown sugar, butter, sherry, salt and pepper; mix well. Spoon into pastry bag fitted with large star tip. Pipe into reserved shells.
❖ Place on baking sheet. Sprinkle with pecans.
❖ Reduce oven temperature to 350 degrees. Bake potatoes for 30 minutes or until heated through.
❖ May prepare and refrigerate for up to 2 days before reheating. Do not eat sweet potato shells.
❖ Yield: 12 servings.

MASHED POTATO CASSEROLE

12 cups mashed cooked potatoes	1/4 cup finely chopped green onions
8 ounces whipped cream cheese	2 tablespoons finely chopped parsley
2 eggs, beaten	Butter or margarine

❖ Preheat oven to 400 degrees.
❖ Beat potatoes and cream cheese in mixer bowl until smooth. Add egg, green onions and parsley; mix well.
❖ Spoon into greased 1 1/2- to 2-quart baking dish; dot with butter.
❖ Bake for 30 minutes.
❖ Yield: 12 servings.

CARAMELIZED ONIONS

12 medium onions, peeled	1/4 cup dark brown sugar
1/2 cup corn oil	Salt to taste
1/2 cup red wine vinegar	

❖ Preheat oven to 350 degrees.
❖ Cut off root ends of onions; cut out centers of tops. Combine oil and vinegar in bowl; mix well.
❖ Place 1 teaspoon brown sugar in center of each onion. Add 1/2 teaspoon oil and vinegar mixture to each onion. Sprinkle with salt.
❖ Place on baking sheet. Brush onions with remaining oil and vinegar mixture.
❖ Bake, covered, for 30 minutes or until tender, basting 2 times with oil and vinegar mixture.
❖ Yield: 12 servings.

SCALLOPED CORN

1 onion, chopped	1 (17-ounce) can whole kernel corn, drained
1 cup chopped green bell pepper	1 (8-ounce) package corn bread mix
1/2 cup butter or margarine	1 cup sour cream
3 eggs, beaten	1 cup shredded Cheddar cheese
1 (17-ounce) can cream-style corn	

❖ Preheat oven to 350 degrees.
❖ Sauté onion and green pepper in butter in skillet until tender.
❖ Combine eggs, cream-style corn, whole kernel corn and corn bread mix in bowl; mix well. Add sautéed vegetables; mix well.
❖ Spoon into 6-cup baking dish. Spread with sour cream; sprinkle with cheese.
❖ Bake for 40 minutes or until bubbly.
❖ Yield: 12 servings.

BROWN RICE SALLY LUNN BREAD

4 cups (about) all-purpose flour	1/2 cup butter or margarine, chopped
1/4 cup sugar	3 eggs, at room temperature
1 envelope dry yeast	
1 teaspoon salt	1 1/2 cups cooked brown rice
2/3 cup milk	
1/3 cup water	

❖ Mix 1 1/4 cups flour, sugar, yeast and salt in large bowl.
❖ Heat milk, water and butter to 120 to 130 degrees in small saucepan.
❖ Add to flour mixture gradually, beating constantly for 2 minutes.
❖ Beat in eggs. Add remaining flour gradually, beating constantly. Add rice; mix well.
❖ Let rise, covered, in warm place for 1 hour or until doubled in bulk. Stir dough down.
❖ Spoon into greased 10-inch bundt pan.
❖ Let rise, covered, for 30 to 40 minutes or until doubled in bulk.
❖ Preheat oven to 375 degrees.
❖ Bake bread for 30 to 40 minutes or until golden brown. Cool in pan for 5 minutes. Remove to wire rack to cool completely.
❖ Yield: 12 servings.

HONEYED FRUIT AND NUT TART

1/4 cup honey	2 tablespoons margarine
1/2 cup sugar	2/3 cup margarine,
1/4 cup water	chopped
11/2 cups chopped toasted	2 cups all-purpose flour
pistachio nuts	1 egg
1/2 cup raisins or mixed	1/4 cup cold water
dried fruit bits	1 egg yolk, beaten
1/2 cup milk	Whipped cream

❖ Bring first 3 ingredients to a boil in saucepan over medium heat, stirring to mix well. Reduce heat to medium-low. Cook for 15 minutes or until mixture turns a light caramel color, stirring frequently. Stir in pistachio nuts, raisins, milk and 2 tablespoons margarine. Cook for 5 minutes or until slightly thickened, stirring occasionally. Cool.
❖ Cut 2/3 cup margarine into flour in bowl. Add mixture of egg and cold water; mix with fork to form dough. Divide into 2 portions. Chill while filling cools.
❖ Preheat oven to 375 degrees.
❖ Roll dough into one 11-inch circle and one 10-inch circle on floured surface. Fit 11-inch circle into straight-sided 9-inch tart pan. Spoon in filling.
❖ Top with remaining pastry. Fold lower pastry toward center over upper pastry; trim and seal edges. Prick lightly with fork. Brush with egg yolk.
❖ Bake for 40 to 50 minutes or until golden brown.
❖ Cool on wire rack. Serve with whipped cream.
❖ Yield: 8 to 12 servings.

DOUBLE-LAYER PUMPKIN PIE

3 ounces cream cheese,	2 (4-ounce) packages
softened	vanilla instant
1 tablespoon cold milk	pudding mix
1 tablespoon sugar	1 (16-ounce) can pumpkin
11/2 cups whipped	1 teaspoon cinnamon
topping	1/2 teaspoon ginger
1 baked (9-inch) pie shell	1/4 teaspoon ground cloves
1 cup milk	Whipped topping

Corral your guests with a western theme: bandanas, badges, and boots make a great table setting and good favors.

❖ Combine cream cheese, 1 tablespoon milk and sugar in bowl; whisk until smooth.
❖ Fold in 11/2 cups whipped topping. Spread in baked pie shell.
❖ Combine 1 cup milk and pudding mix in bowl; whisk for 2 minutes or until well blended. Let stand for 3 minutes.
❖ Add pumpkin, cinnamon, ginger and cloves; mix well.
❖ Spread over cream cheese layer.
❖ Chill for 2 hours or longer. Pipe additional whipped topping around edge of pie.
❖ Yield: 8 servings.

Play It Again, Santa

Re-use and recycle are the buzz-words of the 1990s, and they apply to the kitchen too. With a little creative planning, you can turn leftovers into makeovers and a wide variety of tantalizing new dishes. *Play it Again, Santa* includes soups, sandwiches, salads, casseroles, and more—all made over from the holiday turkey or ham. Side dish makeovers will give new life to leftover mashed potatoes, relishes, and vegetables. Would you believe a salad with popcorn? Try it! And wait till you taste our desserts! With these delicious planned makeovers, you'll even look forward to leftovers!

Makeover Specialties

Baked Tortellini and Ham
Ham and Sweet Potato Hash
Ham-Filled Sweet Potato Biscuits
Curried Turkey Spread
Turkey Tortilla Soup
Quick Turkey Cassoulet
Mexican Turkey and Dressing Casserole
Turkey Reuben Casserole
Fruited Turkey and Rice Salad
Sweet Potato Salad
Popcorn Salad
Spicy Cranberry Dip
Cranberry-Marbled Pumpkin Pie
Nutmeg Coffee Nog

BAKED TORTELLINI AND HAM

A good makeover for ham and broccoli

1/2 cup butter or margarine, softened	1 cup grated Parmesan cheese
2 tablespoons mayonnaise	8 ounces cheese tortellini, cooked
4 ounces cream cheese, softened	1 1/2 cups chopped cooked ham
1/2 cup half and half	1 cup chopped cooked broccoli
1 teaspoon basil	1 tomato, chopped
1/2 teaspoon garlic powder	
1/4 teaspoon pepper	

❖ Preheat oven to 350 degrees.
❖ Combine butter, mayonnaise, cream cheese, half and half, basil, garlic powder and pepper in bowl; mix well.
❖ Fold in Parmesan cheese, tortellini, ham and broccoli. Spoon into 9-by-9-inch baking dish.
❖ Bake for 25 minutes. Top with tomato. Bake for 5 minutes longer.
❖ Yield: 6 servings.

HAM AND SWEET POTATO HASH

Delectable brunch dish with ham and sweet potatoes

1 pound cooked ham, chopped	1 tablespoon chopped fresh basil
1 1/2 cups chopped cooked sweet potatoes	Salt and freshly ground pepper to taste
2 medium onions, minced	3 tablespoons butter or margarine
1/2 large green bell pepper, chopped	4 to 6 poached eggs
3/4 cup whipping cream	Chopped parsley

❖ Combine ham, sweet potatoes, onions, green pepper, cream, basil, salt and pepper in bowl; mix well.
❖ Melt butter in large heavy skillet over medium heat. Spread ham mixture evenly in skillet.
❖ Cook over medium-high heat for 15 minutes or until brown and crusty. Transfer brown side up to platter.
❖ Top with poached eggs and parsley.
❖ Yield: 4 to 6 servings.

HAM-FILLED SWEET POTATO BISCUITS

An innovative use of cooked sweet potatoes and ham for a holiday appetizer favorite

3 cups all-purpose flour	3/4 cup mashed cooked sweet potatoes
2 tablespoons sugar	1 cup buttermilk
2 teaspoons baking powder	14 ounces very thin slices baked ham
1/2 teaspoon baking soda	
Salt to taste	
1/4 cup butter-flavored shortening	

❖ Preheat oven to 450 degrees.
❖ Mix flour, sugar, baking powder, baking soda and salt in large bowl.
❖ Cut in shortening until crumbly. Add sweet potatoes and buttermilk; mix until moistened.
❖ Knead 4 or 5 times on floured surface. Roll 1/2 inch thick; cut with 2-inch biscuit cutter. Place on lightly greased baking sheet.
❖ Bake for 8 to 10 minutes or until light brown.
❖ Split biscuits; fill with ham. Serve hot or at room temperature.
❖ Yield: 14 servings.

Turkey Tortilla Soup, page 164

CURRIED TURKEY SPREAD

Transforms leftover turkey into a delicious appetizer

16 ounces cream cheese, softened
2 cups cottage cheese
1/2 cup sour cream
4 teaspoons curry powder
1 (10-ounce) jar chutney
2/3 cup chopped green onions
2/3 cup raisins
2/3 cup coconut
2 cups chopped cooked turkey
1 cup chopped salted peanuts
1/4 cup chopped green onions
Assorted crackers

❖ Combine cream cheese, cottage cheese, sour cream and curry powder in bowl; beat until smooth. Spread in 9-by-13-inch dish.
❖ Spoon chutney over top; sprinkle with mixture of 2/3 cup green onions, raisins and coconut; top with turkey.
❖ Garnish with peanuts and 1/4 cup chopped green onions.
❖ Serve with crackers.
❖ Yield: 20 servings.

TURKEY TORTILLA SOUP

So to become such a family favorite, you might have to buy the leftovers!

1 cup chopped onion
1 teaspoon olive oil
1 (4-ounce) can chopped green chilies
1 envelope taco seasoning mix
1 (16-ounce) can tomatoes
6 cups turkey broth or reduced-sodium chicken bouillon
1 (10-ounce) package frozen corn
2 cups chopped cooked turkey
1/3 cup chopped fresh cilantro
8 ounces unsalted tortilla chips, broken
1 cup shredded Monterey Jack cheese

❖ Sauté onion in olive oil in 5-quart saucepan for 3 to 4 minutes or until tender. Stir in green chilies and taco seasoning mix.
❖ Cook for 1 minute. Add tomatoes; crush with spoon. Stir in turkey broth.
❖ Bring to a boil. Add corn and turkey. Reduce heat to low.
❖ Simmer for 5 minutes. Stir in cilantro.
❖ Ladle into soup bowls. Top with tortilla chips and shredded cheese.
❖ Yield: 8 servings.

QUICK TURKEY CASSOULET

A hearty stew to warm up a cold holiday night

1 pound kielbasa
1 pound carrots
1 tablespoon vegetable oil
2 large onions, sliced
2 stalks celery, sliced
2 cups chopped cooked turkey
1 (16-ounce) can tomatoes
3 (16-ounce) cans cannellini or pinto beans, drained
1 beef bouillon cube
1 bay leaf
1 3/4 cups water
1/2 cup fresh bread crumbs
Chopped parsley
Salt to taste

❖ Cut kielbasa and carrots into 1/2-inch pieces.
❖ Parboil carrots in saucepan; set aside. Cook kielbasa in heavy 5-quart saucepan over medium heat until brown; remove to plate.
❖ Add oil, carrots, onions and celery to drippings in saucepan. Cook until vegetables are tender.
❖ Add kielbasa, turkey, tomatoes, beans, bouillon cube, bay leaf and water; mix well. Sprinkle with bread crumbs.
❖ Simmer for 30 minutes; discard bay leaf. Sprinkle servings with parsley and salt.
❖ Yield: 8 servings.

MEXICAN TURKEY AND DRESSING CASSEROLE

Turkey and dressing leftovers—the new way

1 (8-ounce) package Mexican corn bread mix
1/2 cup melted butter or margarine
1 cup water
4 1/2 cups chopped cooked turkey
1/2 cup chopped onion
Chopped fresh garlic to taste
1/2 cup chopped celery
1/2 cup mayonnaise
2 eggs
1 1/2 cups milk
2 (10-ounce) cans cream of mushroom soup

❖ Preheat oven to 350 degrees.
❖ Combine corn bread mix, butter and water in large bowl; mix well. Spread half the mixture into greased 11-by-14-inch baking dish.
❖ Combine turkey, onion, garlic, celery and mayonnaise in medium bowl; mix well. Spread in prepared baking dish.
❖ Beat eggs and milk in small bowl. Spoon over turkey mixture. Top with remaining corn bread batter. Top with soup.
❖ Bake for 1 hour or until bubbly in center.
❖ Yield: 8 to 10 servings.

Cranberry-Marbled Pumpkin Pie, page 167

TURKEY REUBEN CASSEROLE

An easy and hearty one-dish meal

1 (11-ounce) can
  sauerkraut, drained
2 tablespoons butter or
  margarine
1/2 to 1 cup Thousand
  Island salad dressing
1 pound cooked turkey,
  thinly sliced

8 ounces shredded Swiss
  cheese
1 (10-count) can flaky
  biscuits
2 crisp rye crackers,
  crushed
1/4 teaspoon caraway seed
  (optional)

❖ Preheat oven to 350 degrees.
❖ Spread sauerkraut into 8-by-12-inch baking
dish. Dot with butter and salad dressing.
❖ Arrange turkey over top; sprinkle with cheese.
❖ Bake, covered, for 15 minutes. Separate each
biscuit into 3 layers. Arrange over casserole in 3
overlapping rows. Sprinkle with cracker crumbs
and caraway seed.
❖ Increase oven temperature to 400 degrees.
❖ Bake for 15 to 20 minutes longer or until
biscuits are golden brown.
❖ Yield: 6 servings.

FRUITED TURKEY AND RICE SALAD

Worth making—even without leftovers

1/2 cup slivered almonds
1/2 tablespoon butter or
  margarine
2 pounds cooked turkey,
  chopped
2 cups cooked rice
2 tablespoons chopped
  onion

2 cups chopped celery
2 cups green grape halves
2 (11-ounce) cans
  mandarin oranges,
  drained
2 cups mayonnaise
2 cups ranch salad
  dressing

❖ Sauté almonds in butter in small skillet until
golden brown.
❖ Combine turkey, rice, onion, celery, grapes,
oranges, mayonnaise and salad dressing in large
bowl; mix well. Spoon into large serving bowl.
❖ Sprinkle with almonds. Chill until serving time.
❖ Yield: 15 servings.

*Warm up your table with wooly scarf runners,
mitten napkin and tableware holders, and an entire
family of snow people.*

SWEET POTATO SALAD

Bound to become a year-round favorite

2 cups cubed cooked
  sweet potatoes
1 apple, chopped
1 cup chopped celery
1 (11-ounce) can
  mandarin oranges,
  drained
1/2 cup chopped walnuts

1 (8-ounce) can pineapple
  tidbits, drained
1/4 cup sour cream
1/4 cup mayonnaise
2 tablespoons milk
1/2 teaspoon salt
Lettuce leaves

❖ Combine sweet potatoes, apple, celery, oranges, walnuts and pineapple in large bowl.
❖ Combine sour cream, mayonnaise, milk and salt in small bowl; mix well. Add to sweet potato mixture; mix gently. Chill until serving time.
❖ Serve on lettuce-lined serving plates.
❖ Yield: 8 servings.

POPCORN SALAD

Make extra popcorn when decorating the tree

12 cups popped popcorn
1 1/2 cups chopped green
  onions
1 1/2 cups shredded
  longhorn cheese

1 1/2 cups chopped celery
1 red bell pepper, chopped
1 pound bacon, crisp-
  fried, crumbled
1/2 cup mayonnaise

❖ Combine all ingredients in bowl; mix well. Spoon into serving bowl. Serve immediately.
❖ Yield: 12 servings.

SPICY CRANBERRY DIP

Uses leftover cranberry sauce as well as turkey and ham for a tasty appetizer

2 cups jellied cranberry
  sauce
3 tablespoons prepared
  horseradish
2 tablespoons honey
1 tablespoon
  Worcestershire sauce
1 tablespoon lemon juice

1 clove of garlic, minced
1/2 teaspoon ground red
  pepper
Orange slices
Pineapple chunks
Cooked turkey, cubed
Cooked ham, cubed

❖ Combine cranberry sauce, horseradish, honey, Worcestershire sauce, lemon juice, garlic and red pepper in medium saucepan.
❖ Bring to a boil over medium heat; reduce heat to low. Simmer, covered, for 5 minutes.
❖ Serve warm with fruit, turkey and ham.
❖ Yield: 24 servings.

CRANBERRY-MARBLED PUMPKIN PIE

Dresses up pumpkin pie and uses leftover cranberry sauce at the same time

1 cup vanilla wafer
  crumbs
1/8 teaspoon each ground
  cloves, cinnamon and
  nutmeg
1 tablespoon melted
  butter or margarine
1 cup jellied cranberry
  sauce
1 tablespoon water

2 envelopes Knox
  unflavored gelatin
1/2 cup cold skim milk
3/4 cup skim milk
2 cups canned pumpkin
3/4 cup packed light
  brown sugar
1 teaspoon vanilla extract
1/2 teaspoon salt
1/2 teaspoon cinnamon

❖ Preheat oven to 350 degrees.
❖ Mix cookie crumbs, cloves, 1/8 teaspoon cinnamon, nutmeg and butter in small bowl.
❖ Press over bottom and side of 9-inch pie plate, forming high rim.
❖ Bake for 5 minutes. Let stand until cool.
❖ Combine cranberry sauce and water in small saucepan; mix until smooth. Sprinkle 1/2 teaspoon gelatin over mixture. Let stand for 3 minutes.
❖ Cook over low heat for 5 minutes or until gelatin dissolves, stirring to mix well; set aside.
❖ Sprinkle remaining gelatin over 1/2 cup cold milk in blender container; let stand for 3 minutes.
❖ Bring 3/4 cup milk to a boil in small saucepan. Add to blender container; process at low speed for 2 minutes or until gelatin dissolves.
❖ Add pumpkin, brown sugar, vanilla, salt and 1/2 teaspoon cinnamon; process for 2 minutes or until blended, scraping container side twice. Spoon into pie shell.
❖ Spoon cranberry mixture over pumpkin mixture; swirl with knife to marbleize. Chill for 3 hours or until firm.
❖ Yield: 8 servings.

NUTMEG COFFEE NOG

Perfect for recycling breakfast coffee at dinner time

1 cup milk
1 cup light cream
2 egg yolks, beaten
2 tablespoons sugar

Nutmeg to taste
2 cups double-strength
  coffee
Whipped cream

❖ Combine milk and cream in heavy medium saucepan. Beat egg yolks with sugar and nutmeg in bowl. Add to milk mixture.
❖ Cook over medium heat until mixture coats metal spoon, stirring constantly.
❖ Whisk in coffee. Pour into mugs. Top with whipped cream and additional nutmeg.
❖ Yield: 6 to 8 servings.

And to All a Sweet Night

There's an old French tradition that dates back to antiquity. On Christmas Eve, before going to church services, families and friends gather together for a luscious buffet of thirteen desserts symbolizes Christ and His apostles. We think this is a tradition worth keeping even with fewer desserts. This year, invite your family and friends for a late night Christmas Eve buffet offering a tempting array of new and old dessert treats. Everyone has a sweet tooth at Christmas! And these picture-perfect desserts satisfy more than treat-cravings. Ideal centerpiece dishes include Classic Holiday Pecan Cake, an elaborate Chocolate Peppermint Log, Easy Lemon Crumb Bars, a Pistachio Cookie Tree and more—sweet treats to please all, *and to all a Sweet Night!*

CHOCOLATE-PECAN CHEESECAKE

3/4 cup graham cracker crumbs	4 eggs
3/4 cup chopped pecans, toasted	1 (14-ounce) can Eagle® Brand sweetened condensed milk
1/4 cup packed light brown sugar	1 tablespoon vanilla extract
1/4 cup melted butter or margarine	1 (10-ounce) package frozen red raspberries in syrup, thawed
1/3 cup Hershey's baking cocoa	1/4 cup red currant jelly or red raspberry jam
1/4 cup melted butter or margarine	1 tablespoon cornstarch
24 ounces cream cheese, softened	1 cup whipping cream Pecan halves

❖ Preheat oven to 300 degrees.
❖ Combine cracker crumbs, chopped pecans, brown sugar and 1/4 cup butter in bowl; mix well. Press over bottom of 9-inch springform pan.
❖ Combine baking cocoa and 1/4 cup butter in bowl; mix until smooth.
❖ Beat cream cheese in large mixer bowl until light. Add cocoa mixture; mix well. Beat in eggs, condensed milk and vanilla. Spoon into prepared pan.
❖ Bake for 1 hour or until set. Cool to room temperature. Chill in refrigerator. Remove side of pan.

❖ Combine undrained raspberries with jelly and cornstarch in small saucepan.
❖ Cook until thickened, stirring constantly. Cool to room temperature. Chill in refrigerator.
❖ Beat whipping cream in mixer bowl until soft peaks form.
❖ Top cheesecake with whipped cream; garnish with pecan halves.
❖ Serve in raspberry sauce on serving plates.
❖ Yield: 12 servings.

CHOCOLATE AND CHERRIES TRIFLE

1 (14-ounce) can Eagle® Brand sweetened condensed milk	1 1/2 cups whipped topping
1/2 cup Hershey's baking cocoa	1 (10-ounce) loaf pound cake
2 tablespoons butter or margarine	1 (21-ounce) can cherry pie filling, chilled
2 tablespoons water	2 cups whipped topping
1 1/2 teaspoons vanilla extract	1 cup chopped pecans
6 ounces cream cheese, softened	Whipped topping
	Pecan halves

❖ Combine condensed milk, baking cocoa, butter and water in medium saucepan; mix well.
❖ Cook over low heat until butter melts; remove from heat. Stir in vanilla. Cool to room temperature.
❖ Beat cream cheese in large mixer bowl until fluffy. Beat in chocolate mixture gradually.
❖ Chill for 10 minutes. Fold in 1 1/2 cups whipped topping.
❖ Cut cake vertically into thirds; slice into strips.
❖ Layer half the cake strips and half the chocolate mixture in 3- to 3 1/2-quart glass bowl. Spread with cherry pie filling and 2 cups whipped topping; sprinkle with 1 cup pecans. Add layers of remaining cake and chocolate mixture.
❖ Chill for 5 hours or longer.
❖ Garnish with additional whipped topping and pecan halves.
❖ Yield: 10 to 12 servings.

CLASSIC HOLIDAY PECAN CAKE

1/2 cup chopped pecans
8 ounces cream cheese, softened
1 cup butter or margarine, softened
1 1/2 cups sugar
1 1/2 teaspoons vanilla extract
1 1/2 teaspoons cinnamon
1/4 teaspoon nutmeg
4 eggs

2 cups all-purpose flour
1 1/2 teaspoons baking powder
1 (8-ounce) jar maraschino cherries, drained, coarsely chopped
1 cup coarsely chopped pecans
1 1/2 cups confectioners' sugar
2 tablespoons milk

❖ Preheat oven to 325 degrees. Grease fluted or straight tube pan; sprinkle with 1/2 cup pecans.
❖ Combine next 6 ingredients in large mixer bowl; beat until fluffy. Beat in eggs 1 at a time.

Chocolate-Pecan Cheesecake, Chocolate and Cherries Trifle, Classic Holiday Pecan Cake, Fudgy Chocolate Pecan Bars, Chocolate Peppermint Log, and Easy Lemon Crumb Bars, pages 168, 169, and 170

❖ Add mixture of flour and baking powder; mix well. Stir in cherries and 1 cup pecans. Spoon into prepared tube pan.
❖ Bake for 1 hour and 5 minutes or until wooden pick inserted near center comes out clean. Cool in pan for 5 minutes. Remove to wire rack to cool completely.
❖ Blend confectioners' sugar and milk in small bowl. Drizzle over cake. Garnish as desired. Store in airtight container at room temperature.
❖ Yield: 16 servings.

FUDGY CHOCOLATE PECAN BARS

1 cup all-purpose flour
1/2 cup Hershey's baking cocoa
2/3 cup sugar
1/2 teaspoon salt
3/4 cup butter or margarine, chilled
2 eggs

1 (14-ounce) can Eagle® Brand sweetened condensed milk
11/2 teaspoons maple flavoring
2 cups pecan halves or pieces

❖ Preheat oven to 350 degrees.
❖ Mix flour, baking cocoa, sugar and salt in bowl.
❖ Cut in butter until crumbly. Stir in 1 egg. Press into greased foil-lined 9-by-13-inch baking dish.
❖ Bake for 12 minutes.
❖ Combine 1 egg, condensed milk and maple flavoring in medium bowl; beat until smooth. Stir in pecans. Pour over baked layer, distributing pecans evenly.
❖ Bake for 16 minutes longer or until set. Cool to room temperature.
❖ Cut into bars. Store in airtight container at room temperature.
❖ Yield: 2 to 3 dozen.

CHOCOLATE PEPPERMINT LOG

4 egg whites
1/2 cup sugar
4 egg yolks
1 teaspoon vanilla extract
1/3 cup sugar
1/2 cup all-purpose flour
1/3 cup Hershey's baking cocoa
1/4 teaspoon baking powder
1/4 teaspoon baking soda
1/8 teaspoon salt
1/3 cup water
1 cup whipping cream
1/4 cup confectioners' sugar

1/4 cup crushed peppermint candies or 1/2 teaspoon peppermint extract
Red food coloring (optional)
2 tablespoons butter or margarine
2 tablespoons Hershey's baking cocoa
2 tablespoons water
1 cup confectioners' sugar
1/2 teaspoon vanilla extract

❖ Preheat oven to 375 degrees.
❖ Line 10-by-15-inch cake pan with foil, extending foil 1 inch over edges; grease foil.
❖ Beat egg whites at high speed in mixer bowl until soft peaks form. Beat in 1/2 cup sugar gradually, beating until stiff but not dry; set aside.
❖ Beat egg yolks and 1 teaspoon vanilla at medium speed in small mixer bowl for 3 minutes.
❖ Beat in 1/3 cup sugar gradually; beat for 2 minutes longer.
❖ Mix flour, baking cocoa, baking powder, baking soda and salt together.

❖ Add to egg yolk mixture alternately with 1/3 cup water, mixing just until smooth after each addition.
❖ Fold into stiffly beaten egg whites gently. Spread evenly in prepared cake pan.
❖ Bake for 12 minutes or until top springs back when lightly touched. Invert immediately onto towel sprinkled with confectioners' sugar; remove foil.
❖ Roll up in towel from narrow side. Let stand until cool.
❖ Beat whipping cream in mixer bowl until soft peaks form. Beat in 1/4 cup confectioners' sugar, peppermint candies and food coloring.
❖ Unroll cake. Spread with peppermint filling. Roll as for jelly roll to enclose filling. Place seam side down on serving plate.
❖ Melt butter in small saucepan. Add 2 tablespoons baking cocoa and 2 tablespoons water.
❖ Cook until smooth, stirring constantly; do not boil. Remove from heat. Beat in remaining 1 cup confectioners' sugar and 1/2 teaspoon vanilla. Cool slightly. Spread over log.
❖ Chill, covered, in refrigerator.
❖ Garnish as desired.
❖ Yield: 10 to 12 servings.

EASY LEMON CRUMB BARS

1 (2-layer) package lemon cake mix
1/4 cup vegetable oil
1 egg
1 (14-ounce) can Eagle® Brand sweetened condensed milk
1 (4-ounce) package lemon pudding and pie filling mix

11/2 teaspoons grated lemon rind
1 cup confectioners' sugar, sifted
4 to 5 teaspoons water
1/2 teaspoon grated lemon rind

❖ Preheat oven to 350 degrees.
❖ Combine cake mix, oil and egg in large mixer bowl; beat at medium speed until crumbly.
❖ Reserve 11/2 cups crumb mixture. Press remaining crumbs over bottom of 9-by-13-inch baking pan.
❖ Combine condensed milk and pudding mix in small mixer bowl; beat until smooth. Stir in 11/2 teaspoons lemon rind. Spread in prepared pan. Top with reserved crumbs.
❖ Bake for 20 to 25 minutes or until set. Cool on wire rack.
❖ Combine confectioners' sugar, water and 1/2 teaspoon lemon rind in small bowl; mix well. Drizzle over baked layer. Cut into bars.
❖ Store, covered, at room temperature.
❖ Yield: 2 to 3 dozen.

Pistachio Cookie Tree

PISTACHIO COOKIE TREE

3 cups butter or
  margarine, softened
2¼ cups sugar
3 egg yolks
4 teaspoons pistachio or
  almond extract
7 cups flour
3 cups finely chopped
  natural California
  pistachios
2 (4¼-ounce) tubes
  white decorator icing
1 cup finely chopped
  natural California
  pistachios
Craft glue
1 (¼-by-10-inch) dowel
1 (8-inch) base with
  (¼-inch) hole in center
1 cardboard star
Natural California
  pistachios in the shell

❖ Preheat oven to 350
degrees.
❖ Cream butter in
large mixer bowl until
light. Add sugar, egg
yolks and pistachio extract; beat until fluffy.
❖ Add flour and 3 cups pistachios gradually,
mixing well after each addition.
❖ Roll a small portion at a time ⅛ inch thick on
floured surface. Cut into oval shapes measuring
6½ inches, 5½ inches and 4 inches across and
making equal numbers of each size. Make hole
slightly off-center in each oval with straw or
chopstick. Place on cookie sheet.
❖ Bake for 10 minutes. Cover loosely with foil.
Bake for 12 to 14 minutes longer or until crisp.
Cool on cookie sheet until firm; remove to wire
rack to cool completely.
❖ Pipe icing onto outer edge of each oval; sprinkle
with 1 cup pistachios. Let stand until firm.
❖ Glue dowel in hole in base. Let stand until dry.
Place cookies on dowel using photograph
illustration. Top with cardboard star decorated
with unshelled pistachios.
❖ Yield: 1 cookie tree.

HEAVENLY PECAN CHIFFON PIE

1 envelope unflavored
  gelatin
½ cup cold water
1 cup dark corn syrup
⅔ cup packed light
  brown sugar
3 egg yolks, beaten
½ to ¾ cup chopped
  pecans
3 egg whites, stiffly
  beaten
1 cup whipping cream,
  whipped
1 baked (9-inch) pie shell

❖ Soften gelatin in cold water in small bowl.
❖ Combine corn syrup, brown sugar and egg
yolks in saucepan; mix well.
❖ Cook over low heat until thickened, stirring
constantly. Stir in gelatin until dissolved. Cool to
room temperature.
❖ Fold pecans, egg whites and whipped cream
gently into cooled mixture. Spoon into pie shell.
❖ Chill until serving time.
❖ Yield: 8 servings.

Craft and Project Index

Recipe Index

Photograph Index